THE POLISH UNDERGROUND STATE
A GUIDE TO THE UNDERGROUND,
1939-1945

BY STEFAN KORBONSKI

Translated from the Polish original by
MARTA ERDMAN

EAST EUROPEAN QUARTERLY, BOULDER
DISTRIBUTED BY COLUMBIA UNIVERSITY PRESS
NEW YORK

1978

EAST EUROPEAN MONOGRAPH SERIES, NO. XXXIX 1 0

The publication of this book was made possible through a grant from the Joseph B. Slotkowski Publication Fund of the Kosciuszko Foundation and the Polish Institute of Arts and Sciences in America, Inc.

STEFAN KORBONSKI was born at Praszka, in Poland in the year 1903. Educated at a school in Czestochowa, he left in December 1918, volunteered for the Polish army, took part in the defense of Lwow against the Ukrainians, and then went back to school. In 1920, during the Polish-Russian war, he enlisted again and in 1921 fought against the Germans in the Silesian uprising. On leaving the army he studied law at Poznan University, entered the ranks of the Polish Peasant Party in 1925, and in 1929 set up in practice as a lawyer in Warsaw. Continuing his political activities, he was elected in 1936 chairman of the Peasant Party in the Bialystok province, and member of the party court.

In 1939 Mr. Korbonski served as lieutenant in the Polish Army. He was taken a prisoner by the Russian troops but escaped and returned to Warsaw where he helped to organize the Polish Underground Movement. He became a member of the Political Coordinating Committee which directed the entire Polish underground fight against the Germans.

In 1941 he retired from this Committee and was appointed Chief of the Civil Resistance. In this capacity he organized underground courts which condemned about two hundred traitors, Gestapo agents, etc., to death and these sentences were also carried out. He established underground radio communication with the Polish Government in Exile in London, organized the sabotage in production, transport, agriculture and the action of the general resistance of the Polish nation.

During the Warsaw Uprising in 1944 he was also appointed Secretary of the Interior in the underground government and in March 1945 acting underground Deputy Prime Minister and Delegate in Poland of the London Polish government. Mr. Stefan Korbonski carried out the duties of Chief of the Polish Underground State until his own arrest by the Soviet NKVD on June 28, 1945.

After the formation of the Polish so-called Government of National Unity, he was released from prison on the ground of the so-called "amnesty law." He was then elected chairman of the Warsaw District of the Polish Peasant Party and after the general elections held on January 19, 1947, he became a member of parliament for the city of Warsaw. He then joined the Executive Committee of the Polish Peasant Party.

In October 1947, when it became apparent that he would be arrested for a second time because of his anti-communist activity, he and his wife, Zofia, fled from Warsaw and found a hiding place on the shore of the Baltic Sea. On the 5th of November 1947 they managed to escape to Sweden by boat and due to the favorable attitude of the U. S. Government reached the United States on November 26, 1947.

At present Mr. Korbonski is Chairman of the Polish Council of Unity in the United States, and Chairman of the Polish Delegation to the Assembly of Captive European Nations [ACEN]. He was elected Chairman of the ACEN for the years: 1958/59, 1966/67, 1971/71, 1972/73, 1973/74, 1974/75, 1975/76, and 1976/77.

Mr. Korbonski, who is a member of the Polish Institute for Arts and Sciences and of the International Pen Club in Exile, is the author of the following books:

Fighting Warsaw, first edition, Macmillan Company, New York, 1956 and George Allen & Unwin, London, 1956. Second edition, Funk & Wagnalls, New York, 1968 [hardcover and paperback].

Warsaw in Chains, Macmillan Company, New York, 1959 and George Allen & Unwin, London, 1959.

Warsaw in Exile, Frederic A. Praeger Publishers, New York, 1966 and George Allen & Unwin, London, 1966.

Between the Hammer and the Anvil, [in Polish], Gryf Publications, Ltd., London, 1969.

Polish Underground State—a guide to the Underground, 1939-1945 [in Polish], Institut Litteraire, Paris, 1975.

In 1973 Mr. Korbonski received the Alfred Jurzykowski Foundation Award in Literature.

Mr. Korbonski has the following Polish military decorations: 1. Virtuti Military Cross, 2. Medal for the War of 1920 against Soviet Russia, 3. Silesia Uprising Cross of Valor, 4. Underground Home Army Cross, 5. Medal for the War of 1939-1944, 6. Golden Cross of Merit.

CONTENTS

Foreword   viii

I. SETTING FOR THE BIRTH AND DEVELOPMENT OF
THE POLISH UNDERGROUND STATE   1

  1. Territories Incorporated into the Reich   1
  2. Territories Incorporated into the USSR   4
  3. The *General Gouvernement*   7
  4. The Pattern of Struggle   11

II. THE SERVICE FOR POLAND'S VICTORY (SPV)   14

III. THE UNION FOR ARMED STRUGGLE (UAS)   22

IV. THE COLLECTIVE DELEGACY   34

V. THE GOVERNMENT DELEGATES   36

VI. THE POLITICAL BUREAU AND THE CCOF   40

VII. THE GOVERNMENT DELEGACY   43

  1. The Scope of the Government Delegate's Activities   43
  2. The Presidium Office   43
  3. Department of Internal Affairs   45
  4. Department of Information and Press   47
  5. Department of Education and Culture   49
  6. Department of Labor and Social Welfare   51
  7. Department of Industry and Commerce   52
  8. Department of Agriculture   52
  9. Department of Justice   52
  10. Department of Liquidating the Effects of War   53
  11. Department of Public Works and Reconstruction   53
  12. Department of National Defense   53
  13. Other Departments   54

VIII. DECREES, PRONOUNCEMENTS AND PROCLAM-
ATIONS OF THE GOVERNMENT DELEGATES   56

IX. THE HOME ARMY   57

  1. The Organization   57
  2. Consolidating the Underground   58
  3. Liaison   59
  4. Training   60
  5. Intelligence   61
  6. Arms and Equipment   63
  7. Finances   65
  8. Information and Propaganda   66
  9. Military Bureaus Administration ("Briefcase")   69

X. CIVIL RESISTANCE   71

  1. Code of Rights and Obligations
of a Pole Under Occupation   71
  2. Directorate of Civil Resistance   72
  3. Underground Courts of Justice   74

4. SWIT Radio Station ("Anusia")   76

5. Actions Taken by the Directorate of Civil Resistance
Against Forced Labor, Agricultural Quotas, Cinema
and Lottery   78

6. Demonstrations Organized by Civil Resistance   81

XI.DIRECTORATE OF UNDERGROUND STRUGGLE   83

1. Sabotage and Diversion   83
2. Partisan Warfare   89
3. Diversionary Propaganda (Action "N")   92

XII.NATIONAL POLITICAL REPRESENTATION   96

XIII.THE COUNCIL OF NATIONAL UNITY   98

XIV.UNDERGROUND ORGANIZATIONS OF THE
BBWR AND THE *OZON*   101

1. The Assembly of Organizations for Independence   101
2. The Camp of Fighting Poland   102

XV.UNDERGROUND ORGANIZATIONS OF THE *ONR*   104

1. National Armed Forces (*NSZ*)   104
2. The National Confederation   108

XVI.THE COMMUNIST AND PRO-COMMUNIST
UNDERGROUND AND THE CIVIC ANTI-
COMMUNIST COMMITTEE   110

1. The Polish Workers Party   110
2. Centralization of the Democratic, Socialist
and Syndicalist Parties   113
3. Civic Anticommunist Committee   115

XVII.UNDERGROUND PRESS AND PUBLICATIONS   117

XVIII.JEWS UNDER OCCUPATION   120

1. Organizing a Holocaust   120
2. Liaison with the Ghetto   122
3. The Jewish Underground   123
4. The Council of Assistance to the Jews   124
5. Mission of Emissary Jan Karski   128
6. Demands for Retaliation   129
7. Uprising in the Warsaw Ghetto   130
8. Jewish Partisan Units   135
9. Polish Losses Due to Helping Jews   136
10. Why was Poland Chosen the Site of Extermination?   138

XIX.COLLABORATION   140

XX. KATYN   144

1. The Shocking Discovery   144
2. Katyn at the Nuremberg Trials   148

XXI.BEFORE "TEMPEST"   150

XXII."TEMPEST"   155

1. "Tempest" in the Wolyn Province   155
2. "Tempest" in the Wilno District   157
3. "Tempest in Southeastern Poland   158

4. "Tempest" in the Lublin District 160
5. "Tempest" in the Bialystok District 161
6. "Tempest" in the Polesie Province 161
7. "Tempest" in the Capital Region 162
8. "Tempest" in the Lodz District 162
9. "Tempest" in the Radom District 162
10. "Tempest" in the Krakow District 163
11. Operation "Jula" 165
12. A Balance Sheet for "Tempest" 165

XXIII. THE WARSAW RISING 168

1. Making the Decision 168
2. The Course of the Struggle 181
3. The Soviet "Help" 187
4. Civil Authorities During the Warsaw Rising 192
5. Life in Embattled Warsaw 198

XXIV. UNDERGROUND AUTHORITIES AFTER
THE WARSAW RISING 204

1. Civil Authorities 204
2. Military Authorities 299

XXV. THE BEGINNING OF SOVIET OCCUPATION 213

1. The Yalta Conference 213
2. The Arrest of the Fifteen 216

XXVI. FINAL MONTHS OF THE POLISH
UNDERGROUND STATE 220

1. Situation Within Poland 220
2. Reorganization of the Government Delegacy 223
3. Delegate for the Armed Forces in Poland 226
4. The Council for National Unity 227
5. Deliberations in Moscow on the Formation
of the Provisional Government of National
Unity 233
6. The Trial of 16 Leaders of Underground
Poland 235
7. The End of the Polish Underground State 236

XXVII. EPILOGUE 238

SOURCES 245

APPENDIX
LIST OF THE "RIGHTEOUS AMONG THE NATIONS" 253

INDEX OF NAMES 257

LIST OF UNDERGROUND ORGANIZATIONS 266

FOREWORD

Many books have been written about the underground movement in Poland during World War II, but in none of them can one find a comprehensive, overall account of the movement. The most authoritative among these books, *Polish Armed Forces in World War II* (vol. 3, "The Home Army"), often cited as a source in the present work, gives a detailed picture of the organization and the combat actions of the military underground, but devotes only marginal attention to the civil underground. This is understandable, since this impressive work is devoted primarily to the Home Army. On the other hand, books dealing with the Home Army focus for the most part on the Warsaw Rising, passing over or neglecting other, less renowned military engagements. This, too, is understandable. The Warsaw Rising was the high point of the Home Army's struggles, and all other actions pale by comparison. But this creates a certain imbalance and gaps in presentation; there is a lack of works devoted to the civil underground which comprised the political life in occupied Poland, administration of justice, clandestine education, actions of civil struggle and self-defense, and others. Fragmentary accounts and reminiscences, both political and military, do not quite fill the gap. And yet, it was the merging of the activities of the civil and the military underground that had produced that phenomenon, unique in the history of Poland and of World War II—the Polish Underground State, which had all the attributes of statehood: government, parliament, courts, and military forces known as the Home Army.

It is, therefore, the task of the present work to give a brief, almost encyclopedic, but well balanced account of the sum total of efforts leading to the creation of the underground state. This book is intended to serve as a guide to the underground, which accounts for the somewhat burdensome accumulation of facts and events, statistical data, names and dates cited here. They should, however, be salvaged before they sink into oblivion with the passing of time. And since every one of the 27 chapters of this book deals with a subject that legitimately deserves a book of its own, let us hope that in those 27 volumes that perhaps one day will be written by future historians any excess of information will dissolve without a trace. Those future 27 volumes will seem paltry in comparison with some 40 thousand books about the Civil War that have already been published in the

United States; their list grows longer with each year, with each new discovery that some event has been omitted or insufficiently researched.

In many of the events described here, the author took part himself. This is both good and bad. Good, because of the authenticity of the account. Bad, because it hampers the achievement of a perfect objectivity, if such a thing exists at all. Wherever it was possible, the author's own recollections were bolstered by the proper documentation. Among those sources are not only such Polish emigre publications as "The Home Army" (vol. 3 of the above mentioned *Polish Armed Forces in World War II Historical Notebooks* and *The Home Army in Documents,* but also works published in Poland after the war, i.e., those among them which, according to the author's best judgment did not falsify facts, dates, and names, but merely provided them with the required "marxist interpretation," which—it goes without saying—was eliminated from this account.

Stefan Korbonski

I

SETTING FOR THE BIRTH AND DEVELOPMENT OF THE POLISH UNDERGROUND STATE

1. Territories Incorporated into the Reich

Those who set about organizing the Polish underground had to face different conditions in each of the three zones into which Poland had been divided by the two invaders. In the western territories, incorporated into the Reich by Adolf Hitler's decree of October 8, 1939 (the districts of Poznan, Pomerania, Silesia, most of the Lodz district, the northern part of the Warsaw district, and smaller parts of the Krakow and Kielce districts), the Poles were stripped of all rights and subject, together with the Jews, to special legislation. To accommodate the influx of the new German population, arriving either from the Reich or from the USSR (through population exchange), Polish farms, workshops, medical and dental offices, business places and houses were confiscated and turned over to the new settlers. Polish inhabitants of the territories incorporated into the Reich were transformed into serfs and forbidden under harsh penalties, like the serfs in olden days, to leave their places of work. In 1942, all Polish men born between 1910 and 1924 were registered on a *Volksliste* and forcibly drafted into the German army. A system of rationing that provided only bare sustenance (and of the worst quality), coupled with starvation wages, brought extreme hardships to the Polish population of these territories, particularly since all payments such as pensions or health insurance were stopped.

In addition, all secondary schools and institutions of higher learning were closed, while in the primary schools only the German language and arithmetic could be taught. The use of the Polish language outside of homes were forbidden; the Polish-language press was liquidated; libraries and bookshops were burned; archives and museums were either transferred to the Reich or destroyed; wayside chapels or crosses, tombstones in the cemeteries were demolished, and the cemeteries themselves often plowed over; all Polish markers, inscriptions and signboards were removed, and the names of towns and villages changed to new German names—in one word, all traces of anything Polish were ruthlessly erased. One church only was left in each county—all others were either burned down or closed; sermons, prayers and church hymns in Polish were forbidden; most of the priests were arrested and sent to concentration camps.

Gradually, there began a forced transfer of population—particularly, of the remnants of the intelligentsia—to the second German-occupied zone, the so-called *General Gouvernement*. This action affected two million people. They were permitted to take along only their personal effects; loaded like cattle, they were transported in sealed cars to *General Gouvernement*, where they were dumped out, frequently at night, at a small railroad station or even in an open field.

Worst of all was the universal reign of terror and the stringent restrictions placed on individual freedom. Already in the very first days of the occupation, leaders in each community—particularly, political leaders, mayors, landowners, local officials, priests, teachers, lawyers and doctors—were seized and shot, executed publicly and ostentatiously in the market squares of their respective towns and villages. Those who escaped those early executions, were to meet their end later in concentration camps or the prison at Mlynska Street in Poznan, where a guillotine had been installed and kept busy day and night. The town of Bydgoszcz was the most cruelly afflicted: in reprisal for the liquidation there of a German diversionary band by Polish military units at the very outset of the war (September 3-4, 1939), over 20,000 inhabitants were murdered on the so-called "bloody Sunday."

A system evolved whereby every German, whether civilian or wearing the uniform of one of the innumerable military, party, auxiliary or police organizations, became an absolute master over the life and death of any Pole. In practice this meant that any German could kill any Pole with impunity. There were many documented instances of murders because of some personal grudges dating back to prewar days, or because the victims were veterans of anti-German uprisings in Silesia or the Poznan district in 1918-21. In addition, there were also sporadic killings. For instance, a Pole could, and often did, get shot for not getting off the sidewalk to make room for a German approaching from the opposite direction, or for failing to take off his hat before a German. People were also killed for illicit fishing, for slaughtering a pig for their own use, for stealing fruit from the orchards, for riding a train without a ticket, etc. German courts pronounced wholesale death sentences, primarily for the so-called "economic sabotage" and for infractions against even the least important regulations imposed by the invaders, which ordinarily, and under normal conditions, would bring no more than an arrest and a fine.

One particularly shocking case was that of Zofia Czechon, a Polish woman sentenced by the court in Plock to a fine of 1000 German marks or three months in jail, because her dog, although muzzled, had the effrontery to "bark hostilely and snarl" at the dog of the German *Oberinspektor* Richard Kunat.

As far as restrictions on individual freedom were concerned, the ban on free movement, particularly on travel by railroad, was the most keenly felt. In order to travel anywhere, one had to obtain a pass, stating in detail the route to be taken and the duration of the trip. All bicycles owned by Poles were confiscated. The only exception was made for those who worked far away from their homes, but in those instances, their passes prescribed precisely the route they were to take to their places of work. To veer from this route meant to incur severe punishment, in addition to beating, kicking and face slapping.

All Germans—both those who had lived on those territories before the war and those who later swarmed over the territories incorporated into the Reich—were expected to spy on their Polish neighbors, not only at their places of work, but also generally elsewhere, and had to report everything they observed to the authorities. In one word, the territories incorporated into the Reich were turned into one big prison, ruled by the dreaded Gestapo.[1]

Everything was done with one goal in mind: to change those lands over into truly German lands, and to get rid of those Poles who could not be exterminated by transferring them to the *General Gouvernement*.

Despite this reign of terror and the strict restrictions placed on individual freedom, the underground movement in the western territories sprang into existence spontaneously, as it did in all Poland. The cities of Poznan and Lodz were the leaders. In order to appreciate what was involved, one has to understand the "facts of life" of the conspiracy. A conspiracy is impossible without a regular contact between its members, either in one locality or in several places, often far apart. Thus it was necessary to travel a great deal and to stay overnight or meet people in various places without registering with the police (as required) and without attracting the attention of German neighbors. It was also necessary to transport letters, underground publications, and arms. Finally, conspiratorial activities required a certain mobility within the immediate neighborhood. All this was out of the question in the incorporated territories, and yet the underground network came into being because the brave people of Silesia, Pomerania, and the district of Poznan knew how to circumvent innumerable orders and prohibitions and how to overcome all obstacles at the risk of life and freedom. Though the underground network in the western territories was handicapped, as compared with the organization built under considerably easier conditions prevailing in the *General Gouvernement*, still it managed to extend its operations even over the prewar frontier of the Reich, as far as the Opole Silesia.

2. Territories incorporated into the USSR

Under the Soviet occupation—which included the districts of Wilno, Polesie, Bialystok, Wolyn, Tarnopol, Lwow, and Stanislawow—conditions were much the same. Although these districts were also incorporated, the procedure which made them a part of the USSR was far more refined than that adopted by the Germans. Instead of the brutal Nazi decree of incorporation, elections were ordered to be held on October 22, 1939. On that day, the inhabitants of those territories, terrorized by the NKVD, "elected" 2,410 delegates, hand-picked by the NKVD and drawn for the most part from among the newly arrived Russians, totally unknown to the local people; thus elected, the delegates then applied to the Supreme Council in Moscow for the admission of the "liberated" eastern Polish territories into the Soviet Union. The Supreme Soviet graciously granted their request and by the decrees of November 1 and November 2, 1939, the northern districts were incorporated into the Byelorussian SSR and the southern districts into the Ukrainian SSR. The final result was the same as in the west, but the method of incorporation permitted the Soviets to parry all accusations of force and violence by claiming the "spontaneous will of the people." A crowning touch was added to this lawless procedure with the decree of November 29, 1939, which conferred Soviet citizenship on all inhabitants of the occupied territories; in consequence, all young men were made subject to military service in the Soviet army.

A succession of "economic refoms" accomplished results that were identical with those achieved by the Nazi policies in the west—the Polish population were reduced to utter destitution. The Soviets took over not only all prewar Polish state property, but also all private estates, factories, sugar refineries, distilleries, saw mills and all other industrial enterprises, banks and savings institutions. They then proceeded to loot this wealth by carrying it away to the USSR. Many factories were closed, creating unemployment. The Polish currency (*zloty*) was taken out of circulation and all bank and savings accounts were blocked. Ruthless requisitions by the Soviet army of both food and feed, as well as frantic buying out of store inventories by the imported Soviet military and civilian employees, created such shortages that even salt and matches became unavailable and poverty reigned supreme.

In the eastern territories, too, all traces of a Polish past were doomed to obliteration. Instead of the Polish language, the Ukrainian and the Byelorussian were introduced as official languages; this was on paper only, for in practice this meant the Russian language. A few thousands of churches, monasteries and convents were closed, and their buildings put to other uses. Roadside chapels were torn down, here as in the west, and roadside crosses hacked down and burned.

The greatest similarities between the two oppressors, however, could be found in their deportation policies. From the western territories, the Germans forcibly deported about two million people to the *General Gouvernement*; from the eastern territories, the Russians— in four massive operations—deported into the depths of the Soviet Union, mostly to Asia, about 1,700,000 people. Both the German and the Soviet operations were carried out with one goal in mind: to strip the occupied territories of all Polish elements, and both were conducted with the same utter ruthlessness. Men, women, and children were snatched from their homes without any warning and permitted to take with them only the barest personal necessities.

Only in the field of education did the two invaders' policies show any marked variations. The Germans closed all secondary schools and all institutions of higher learning, while in the primary schools only German and arithmetic were permitted to be taught. The Russians, on the other hand, retained the prewar structure of the educational system, but converted all programs along Soviet patterns and introduced variations based on nationality; Russian language was compulsory, as was history (Soviet brand) and subjects required in Soviet schools, such as political-ideological indoctrination. All schools were divided into Ukrainian, Byelorussian, Jewish and Polish. In this last group, Polish language was tolerated. The aim of such a system of education, reinforced by a flood of propaganda through radio and films, was to indoctrinate according to communist lights the youth of all four national groups.

The policy of terror was instituted immediately after Poland's eastern territories were occupied by the Soviet armies. Hundreds of priests and monks, judges, prosecutors, police officers, political and social leaders, deputies and senators, government functionaries and officials of local governments were murdered outright. The slaughter reached its peak after the outbreak of the Nazi-Soviet war on June 21, 1941, when all political prisoners were murdered. Total Polish losses due to this policy of murder are estimated at close to 100,000 people; included in this number are 15,000 army officers (mostly from the reserves, i.e., men who in civilian life formed the backbone of the educated and professional classes in Poland) who were interned in the USSR after September 17, 1939, and murdered in the spring of 1940. The mass grave of some of these officers was found by the Germans in 1941 in the Katyn Forest near Smolensk. It contained 4,253 bodies.

Although the two occupiers used different methods of control in many respects, the final result was always the same. The Germans exercised a highly visible, almost physical control over nearly every move of every Pole. The Soviets tolerated free moving about while exercising equally strict control in a less obvious way, mostly with the help of the local Communists, familiar with the local scene, as well as large numbers of recruited local informers. In the western territories, national differences formed an abyss between the oppressors and the oppressed, and made it more difficult for the Germans to establish control; in the eastern territories, however, the surveillance was facilitated by the fact that, with the exception of the NKVD, both those who exercised control and those who were controlled belonged to one of the four national groups—Polish, Ukrainian, Byelorussian, or Jewish. Finally, in building up a network of surveillance, the NKVD cunningly took advantage of various national antagonisms, playing up the so-called national minorities against the Poles. This scheme created a double, criss-crossing, and therefore more efficient network of control.

Even so, the rise of the underground movement could not be stemmed. In the eastern territories, as in all Poland, it came into being spontaneously, particularly in the cities and towns where the Polish population was in a majority, even in those areas where the villages in the surrounding countryside were predominantly Byelorussian or Ukrainian. The cities of Lwow and Wilno were the leaders. Even though the conditions under which the underground movement in Soviet-occupied Poland was born were somewhat easier than in the territories incorporated into the Reich, still they made it impossible for the movement to develop as well as in the *General Gouvernement*. The situation changed radically, and for the better, only after the outbreak of the Nazi-Soviet war on June 21, 1941, and after the lightning takeover of these territories by the Germans. Although the line of demarcation between the *General Gouvernement* and the former Soviet-occupied zone was maintained, which made all communication difficult, still the underground in the eastern territories from that time on became very similar to the underground in the *General Gouvernement*, if for no other reason, than because of the selfsame identity and methods of the oppressor.

3. The General Gouvernement (GG)

Hitler's decree of October 12, 1939, created the so-called *General Gouvernement*, with a population of about 12 million people; it was carved out of the Lublin district, part of the Lwow district, and most of the Warsaw, Krakow and Kielce districts. The *General Gouvernement* was designated, in the first stage of the German master plan, as a gathering place for all Poles; they were to become a nation of serfs, a reservoir of labor, doomed to extinction during the later stages of the plan, either through a massive German colonization or through various measures aimed at biological destruction (e.g., a ban on marriages, hunger, overwork), or finally—and assuming, of course, Germany's ultimate victory over the Soviet Union—through deportation of all the surviving Poles to Siberia (General Eastern Plan). Only the Jews were to fare worse than the Poles, according to the plan: they were to be confined in ghettos within the *General Gouvernement* and killed off in concentration camps already during the first stage of the plan.

The initial attack—both in the territories incorporated into the Reich and those incorporated into the USSR—was directed against the intelligentsia, the so-called leading class, marked for destruction. Individual arrests were conducted on a massive scale. Political and social leaders, deputies and senators, professors and scholars, judges, attorneys, doctors, industrialists, government officials, reserve officers, etc., were swept into the net. Those taken in Warsaw were first placed in the Pawiak prison and later taken to concentration camps in Germany. When the Auschwitz concentration camp was opened on June 14, 1940, most of them were sent there. Large-scale operations against the intelligentsia began with the arrest of 115 professors of the Krakow University on November 6, 1939; they were taken to the Sachsenhausen concentration camp, where many of them perished. The first mass execution took place in Wawer near Warsaw on December 27, 1939; on that day, 107 men were snatched from their homes in the middle of the night and shot summarily in reprisal for the wounding of two German soldiers by a Polish criminal. Beginning with June 20, 1940, mass executions were carried out in the Palmiry Woods, which became a sort of handy execution place where the people of Warsaw were taken to be shot. The first street roundup took place in Warsaw on May 8, 1940; over a thousand people were seized on that day and carried off to concentration camps in Germany, many of them never to return. Similar street roundups were also staged in other cities of the *General Gouvernement*. Finally, on November 25, 1940, the Warsaw ghetto was sealed off from the world, shutting within its walls over half a million Jews condemned to a death of starvation or—those who managed to survive—in gas chambers of the concentration camps in Treblinka, Chelm, Auschwitz and others. Successive waves of terror rolled on one after another, designed to gradually destroy the population of the recalcitrant cities, particularly the intelligentsia, and to terrorize all Poles into docile subservience to the will of the oppressor.

The high point of terror—aside from the unprecedented in the history of mankind extermination of some 6 million Jews, both Polish and those brought to Poland from other countries—were the mass executions staged on the streets of cities, towns and villages of the *General Gouvernement*. The slaughter was conducted ostensibly in order to carry out a decree issued by Governor Hans Frank on October 2, 1943, aimed at the suppression of all attempts to thwart the German work of reconstruction in the *General Gouvernement*. This decree prescribed the death penalty for infractions of even the most insignificant German regulations, let alone decrees and orders. The death penalty could be meted out, for instance, for illegal slaughter or sale of meat, for raising prices, and other similar offenses. Under the guise of this decree, in Warsaw alone, between October 15, 1943 and August 1, 1944, when the Warsaw Rising broke out, about 9,500 people were caught in the streets and shot, often in the very heart of the city (3,213 according to the official German statistics).[2] After the prisoners' work details removed the bodies from the place of execution, people of Warsaw would cover the site with flowers, light candles, and kneel down in prayer. Not infrequently, the kneeling mourners were shot, too. As for the rest of the country, detailed statistics are not available, but the losses are estimated at several thousand. The goal of these executions, amounting to simple murder of individuals picked at random, was always the same: to terrorize the rebellious Poles and to cow them into total submission.

Simultaneously, there began a wholesale exploitation of the country, which was to provide labor and food for the Reich. Huge delivery quotas of grain, cattle, butter, milk and eggs were imposed, stripping the countryside of all food. Only the universally practiced sabotage (punishable by death), made it possible for the people in the countryside to survive and even to smuggle some food to the cities, whose inhabitants received only subsistence rations, too small to live on, but too large to die of starvation. Everybody was compelled to work: throughout the occupation years, some 2 million people were shipped off to the Reich for forced labor.

All secondary and higher educational institutions in *GG* were closed; the teaching of history and geography in primary and trade schools was prohibited. All museums, archives and libraries were liquidated, and their contents either destroyed or taken to Germany. Historical monuments and markers were destroyed, as was everything that could remind people of Poland's history. Finally, all state industries became the property of the Reich, while private enterprises, larger farms and estates were turned over to German trustees, which was tantamount to expropriation.

Still, there were considerable differences between conditions prevailing in the territories incorporated into the Reich or into the Soviet Union and those in the *General Gouvernement*. The most important of these was that the population of the *General Gouvernement* was not subject to forced resettlement, while in other parts of Poland whole families were uprooted from their native regions and transferred to regions that were foreign to them both nationally and geographically, such as the Asiatic parts of Russia, where they were doomed to perish. Even in a more congenial area of resettlement, such as the *General Gouvernement*, transferred multitudes had no chance of leading a normal life, but had to subsist with the help of relatives, chance acquaintances or charitable organizations. Deportations to the Reich for forced labor differed from mass deportations in that they affected only individuals and did not uproot entire families. The only mass population transfer carried out by the Germans took place in the Zamosc region, where 110,000 peasants from 297 communities were uprooted in order to make room for the German colonists. However, violent military counteraction by the underground, burning down of the villages where the new German settlers were installed and, finally, the setbacks suffered by the German armies on the eastern front combined to make the Germans abandon this operation.

The *General Gouvernement* also differed from territories incorporated into the Reich in that the Polish language was retained there, as were the Polish state and local governmental institutions, such as lower courts, fiscal machinery, police, and the city and county administrations. The Polish Red Cross was permitted to function, and so was a charitable organization called the Central Welfare Council. The Bank of Poland also was permitted to operate, though under a changed name, and was used by the Germans to introduce a separate currency for the *General Gouvernement*. Also permitted to function was the National Economic Bank and the Postal Savings Bank. The scope of activities of the Association of Cooperatives *Spolem* was extended to warehouse the levied food delivery quotas and to distribute among the population the scant supplies available to the Poles.

All legitimate theatres were closed, but small theatres were allowed to open with new programs, mostly pornographic, forced on them by the German propaganda. All Polish publications were banned, except for the so-called "reptile press", subservient to the Germans, whose existence, however—since it appeared in Polish—served to emphasize the difference between the *General Gouvernement* and the territories incorporated into the Reich.

Finally, in *GG* much more freedom was allowed in moving from place to place and also within the confines of one's immediate neighborhood, even though a curfew was enforced. No restrictions on travel, such as those in the incorporated territories, were imposed; control of documents, search of luggage, and arrest if anything prohibited was found, represented the only threat to those traveling by railroad. This made it possible, even though risky, to smuggle food supplies without which no larger city in Poland could have survived the years of German occupation.

The leniency of these restrictions—as compared with the hellish conditions under which Poles were forced to live in the incorporated territories—was in keeping with the provisions of "stage one" of the German plan for Poland, according to which conditions in the *General Gouvernement* were to be maintained at a level supporting a primitive existence for several millions of Polish robots. In order, however, to impress the Poles with the utter futility of all national aspirations, the Germans built up in *GG* a huge apparatus of terror, similar to that operating in the incorporated territories and dealing out the death penalty or imprisonment in concentration camps for even the most petty offenses. Of all the German-occupied countries, that part of Poland that was known as the *General Gouvernment* had the greatest concentration of the Gestapo, headed by individuals handpicked for their ruthlessness. A network of thousands of informers, recruited from among the riffraff and from the *Volksdeutsche* (i.e., Polish citizens of German ancestry, listed on special registers) was established. The Gestapo were also assisted by units of gendarmerie and by such police formations as the *Grenzschutz* (border guard), the *Bahnschutz* (railroad police), the *Werkschutz* (factory guard), and others. Every German and every Volksdeutsch had to belong to the *Selbschutz* (self-defense organization), which was also utilized against the Polish population of *GG*. In addition, German military intelligence and criminal police were also brought into the play, while the Polish police were limited to keeping general order. The German control over the Polish population was further strengthened by additional

SS units composed of volunteers from among the Ukrainians, Latvians, Estonians, Lithuanians and—during the last period of the occupation—also Russians, the so-called Vlasovites.

The terror apparatus described above operated in every city and every town in the *General Gouvernement*. To subjugate the countryside to the same extent proved impracticable, for it would have required hundreds of thousands of military and police personnel. Nonetheless, the countryside, too, was under the strict surveillance of gendarmerie units, stationed in smaller towns and villages, and German punitive and repressive measures were even more severe in the country than in the cities, because they involved wholesale destruction of entire villages by murder and fire.

4. The Pattern of Struggle

Every inhabitant of the *General Gouvernement* lived in constant awareness of the huge structure of terror. He woke up fully alerted to it; he could sense it throughout the day in the streets, in workplaces, in cafés, even in churches; he went to sleep, continuously concious of its existence, and bolted out of his bed, instantly awake, at the slightest sound in the street, in the house entrance, or on the stairway. Even if the night went peacefully by, he could never be sure on leaving his house in the morning whether he would return there at night. At any moment he could be caught in a street roundup or he could inadvertently enter a place where a trap had been set for all comers. When going away for any length of time, people always said their last goodbyes and bid their families farewell as if they were going off to wars; often they did not come back and were never heard from again.

Members of the underground movement, which flourished in the more lenient climate of the *General Gouvernement*, faced a double danger: in addition to random mass arrests, they were also threatened by planned actions, directed against particular individuals, since the Gestapo pursued the underground men with rabid doggedness. Death was the constant companion of every member of the underground. At night in the room where he hid under a false identity or without registering, he risked a Gestapo night raid, if they were looking for him; during the day, when he went out on the streets, he had to make his way past the Gestapo agents, provided with his description or photograph. Every appointment, every meeting, every delivery of messages, radio bulletins, or copies of the underground press, let alone things such as a clandestine military briefing, troup exercises, work in an underground editorial office, printing shop, broadcasting station or gun shop—generally speaking, any activity connected with the underground—required courage, alertness, utmost caution, great presence of mind, cunning and—most importantly—luck. Without these, there was an ever present threat of arrest, torture and, frequently, death.

The Gestapo hierarchy were doubtless familiar with the history of Poland, for they had foreseen far in advance that an underground organization would come into being in Poland. In a series of secret German-Soviet agreements, concluded both before and after the German invasion of Poland, there was also an agreement pertaining to mutual assistance in combatting the Polish resistance movement. According to the terms of this agreement, the Gestapo and the NKVD were to share all information that could be helpful to either of them in suppressing the underground. The Gestapo moved against the underground with the typical German thoroughness. An effort was made, with the help of a broad network of agents, to penetrate and infiltrate the underground. In a constant search for clues, a thorough study of the underground press was carried on; underground couriers, contact girls, and "mail drops" were ferreted out; broadcasting stations were tracked down, and their output monitored and decoded. Constant search went on for underground printing plants, munitions workshops and secret meeting places. Various underground groups and their leaders were assigned to particular Gestapomen each of whom concentrated exclusively on a given individual or group.

The underground fought back by means of counterintelligence, coups directed against the more prominent Gestapomen, attacks on local gendarmerie posts, assassinations of Gestapo agents, disguises, and masterly forgeries of documents such as the obligatory *kennkarten* (identity cards), birth certificates, work certificates, registration cards, various permits and passes issued by the Germans, and many other legalizing documents. Meeting places, living quarters, and overnight shelters were camouflaged and constantly shifted; varied passwords and warning signals were devised; hiding places and caches were constructed and secreted in most unlikely places; personal contacts were limited to a minimum, as was the use of any written communications or memoranda; meeting places, printing shops, and broadcasting installations were assured of a measure of security by dint of constant surveillance and frequently also by posting an armed guard. But the cardinal weapon of the resistance was silence. To keep silent and to guard the secret was the first and the most important commandment of conspiracy, and it was always included in the underground oath. Hundreds paid dearly for their fidelity to this oath, dying in torture or taking their own lives rather than to betray the secrets of the underground. (Total losses in human lives in Poland during World War II are estimated at 6 million; of this number 3½ were Polish citizens of Jewish faith.)

It was against such a background and in the midst of such a struggle that the Polish underground movement was born to wage a war whose toll was to be counted in thousands. Against all odds, it grew stronger and stronger from month to month and from year to year, until it finally evolved at its highest point into the Polish Underground State, which had its own government, administration, parliament, jurisdiction, army, education, welfare, press—in one word, all the institutions and attributes of an independent state. It came to be recognized throughout the world as the leading underground movement of World War II, and Poland was hailed as an "inspiration to the free world."

The highest recognition, however, was to come from the enemy himself: on the eve of Germany's final defeat, the question of organizing an underground resistance movement in Germany came up for consideration; various options were reviewed and the Polish model of underground organization chosen as the best to adopt.[3]

II

THE SERVICE FOR POLAND'S VICTORY (SPV)

The September campaign in Poland ended with the capitulation of Warsaw on September 28, 1939 and of Hel on October 1; General Franciszek Kleeberg's Army surrendered at Kock on October 5. This, however, did not bring the war to an end. Many Polish units continued the fight on their own and for various reasons. Some tried to fight their way to Hungary, Rumania or Lithuania; others, cut off from their command, fought on, unwilling to surrender without an order; still others continued to fight, unable to bear the thought of surrender. Among those last was the unit of Major Henryk Dobrzanski (pseudonym: Hubal), which fought on in the Kielce district until May 1940, when Major Dobrzanski was killed in battle and buried by the Germans, with military honors, in Tomaszow. A new kind of warfare, combining diversionary and combat operations and akin to guerilla warfare, was waged near Sandomierz, even before Major Dobrzanski's defeat, by the so-called "Jedrusie," a unit commanded by a student, Wladyslaw Jasinski (pseudonym: Jedrus), and later, following Jasinski's death in an engagement with the Germans, by Jozef Wiacek. Thus, symbolically speaking, armed resistance against the Germans has never ceased on Polish soil, not even for one day.[1]

Once the initial shock of the September debacle abated, secret underground organizations sprang up spontaneously throughout the country, like mushrooms after the rain. The few weeks of fighting were not nearly enough. Sustained by their unshakable faith in the ultimate victory with the help of their western allies, the Poles wanted to fight on. They began to band together in small groups of a few or several people who knew and trusted one another. Each of such groups adopted a name for their organization, drafted its rules and the wording of its oath, and began recruiting new members. In many cases these clandestine organizations were based on prewar associations, such as veterans' organizations, sports clubs, or Boy Scouts. Gradually, various political parties managed to reestablish communication between their members, with the result that local underground cells were established both in the cities and in the countryside. Within a few months, some hundreds of secret organizations emerged in the territories under both the German and the Soviet occupation; they acted independently of one another, but instinctively sought contact with other organizations in their area and upward contact with some central leadership (which, they felt sure, must have evolved in the capital), or even direct contact with the government-in-exile, reconstituted in France. Within a short time, the process of consolidation began. The central underground military organization provided the framework, but, hampered by factional and personal ambitions, this process dragged on until the outbreak of the Warsaw Rising in 1944.

The initiative to create a central leadership within occupied Poland came from General Michal Tokarzewski-Karaszewicz. As a corps commander in the army of General Tadeusz Kutrzeba, Tokarzewski retreated to the Kampinos Forest near Warsaw and reached the capital in the early hours of September 21, 1939. On the morning of the same day, General Juliusz Rommel, commandant of the capital, named Tokarzewski his deputy as well as his representative on the Defense Council of the Capital (called also the Committee for the Defense of the Capital). In accordance with the September 1, 1939 decree of the President of the Republic, the Defense Council was headed by the Civil Commissioner at the Army Headquarters; this position was held by the mayor of Warsaw Stefan Starzynski, whom Tokarzewski contacted immediately.

By September 26, the capitulation of Warsaw was already imminent. The capital was without food, water, electricity; bombing and artillery fire had turned its streets into rubble. On that day, General Tokarzewski approached General Rommel with a plan to organize in Poland armed resistance against the German occupier. General Rommel, appointed by Marshal Rydz-Smigly (who by that time had crossed the border into Rumania and was interned there) as his successor and the supreme military commander in Poland, had no chance to evade capture by the Germans. In view of this, Tokarzewski proposed that Rommel transfer the command to him.

On that same day, September 26, Major Edmund Galinat, an emissary from Marshal Rydz-Smigly, flew into Warsaw from Rumania. Anxious to learn what instructions Galinat might have brought, General Rommel deferred his decision on Tokarzewski's proposal till the following day, September 27. It turned out that Marshal Rydz-Smigly was sending Major Galinat with the suggestion that his emissary be entrusted with organizing diversionary activities in occupied Poland, in view of the fact that he was familiar with prewar preparations for such a contingency. Despite the Marshal's recommendation, General Rommel resolved to accept Tokarzewski's proposal; he assigned Major Galinat to Tokarzewski's command, recommending only that Galinat be named as the General's deputy.

At the end of their interview, General Rommel handed Tokarzewski the following note:

"The authority to command Polish military forces on all Polish territories in the war against the aggressor, given to me by the Commander-in-Chief with the approval of the Government, is hereby transferred to General Michal Tadeusz Tokarzewski-Karaszewicz, whose duty it will be to carry on the fight to maintain Poland's independence and the integrity of Poland's frontiers.

—J. Rommel, Lieut. Gen."

As former commander of the Corps VIII district in Torun, Tokarzewski was vaguely aware of the existence of plans for diversionary action, and preparations that had been made in the province of Pomorze under the direct supervision of the General Staff and Major Galinat. These activities, however, had been kept secret even from him. Tokarzewski did not follow Rommel's recommendation. He merely ordered Galinat to locate his prewar contacts and reestablish the organizational network. When this effort failed to produce the expected results, Tokarzewski permitted Galinat to return to Rumania.[2]

Transferring his command to Tokarzewski, General Rommel also passed on to his successor funds amounting to 750,000 zlotys. From Mayor Starzynski, Tokarzewski received an additional 350,000 zlotys, partly in foreign currencies. The Mayor himself refused to join the ranks of the underground organization, feeling that he should remain at his post and take care of the capital and its inhabitants as best he could. For this courageous decision Mayor Starzynski paid a heavy price. He was arrested on October 28, 1939, tortured and executed on September 17, 1943 in the Dachau concentration camp.[3]

By the time Warsaw capitulated on September 28, 1939, Tokarzewski had already prepared an outline of the underground organization and had a nucleus of the underground General Staff, composed of 15 officers among whom he divided staff functions and commands in central districts. Once the assignments were completed, communication network established, false identity documents issued, financial resources secured, weapons, ammunition and explosives collected and stored, the conspirators' attention turned to the first action planned against the Germans. It was expected that Hitler would come to Warsaw to review the victory parade of the German armies. The conspirators decided to make an attempt on Hitler's life that day. Explosives were placed at the crossing of the two main arteries: Nowy Swiat and Aleje Jerozolimskie; they were to be detonated at the moment Hitler's car passed this spot. But the coup failed. When Hitler did come to Warsaw on October 5, 1939, the streets were cleared of all people, including the observers who were to signal the proper moment to another conspirator, stationed in nearby ruins. In the absence of the prearranged signal, and unable himself to see Hitler pass by, the conspirator did not detonate the charge. Had the coup been successful, the course of history would have been altered. As it was, the conspirators were left only with the troublesome task of dismantling the explosives.

Tokarzewski's next task was to establish contact with representatives of the prewar opposition parties. In doing so, he encountered no difficulties, because he was well known and liked in those circles. His job was facilitated by the fact that he had once been a member of the Polish Socialist Party and was known for his liberal views; this earned him no favor in the eyes of the prewar government and sidetracked him to an administrative job in the army. As far as the Peasant Party was concerned, Tokarzewski's stand against the 1937 peasant strike was well known. At that time, the General held the command of the Corps VI district in Lwow and was the president of the Coordinating Office of Polish Social Organizations; in this last capacity he issued an appeal calling for the end of the strike, holding that no such action should be taking place in nationally mixed areas, where the Polish population had to maintain absolute solidarity in the face of arson and murder perpetrated by the Ukrainians.[4] Despite this appeal, he was considered a sympathizer of the Peasant Party and confirmed it in February 1938 by sending flowers to the opening session of the Peasant Party Congress in Krakow; Maciej Rataj, former Speaker of the *Sejm*, voiced his warm appreciation of the General's gesture, and the assembled delegates burst into applause and shouts of "Long live General Tokarzewski!"[5]

Tokarzewski succeeded in enlisting the cooperation of the former dean of the Warsaw Bar, Leon Nowodworski of the National Party, even though as a liberal and one of Pilsudski's legionaries he had always been considered by the National Party a sympathizer of the government they opposed. The General was equally successful in persuading Professor Mieczyslaw Michalowicz of the Democratic Party to join forces in the proposed organization.

General Tokarzewski was a man of broad vision and interests ranging far beyond the scope of his military profession. He was interested in theosophy, in social action and in politics. He was a born politician and a man of great personal charm and style, which greatly facilitated his negotiations in those critical and difficult days. Having a keen perception of the popular sentiment within the country, he decided to leave out for the time being all those political groups that

had been associated with the government before the war. He sensed
that people blamed those parties and groups—not so much perhaps
for the September defeat, which had been generally expected in the
first phase of the war, but for the shameful way in which the war
was lost within a few short weeks. The so-called *sanacja* or *Ozon*
were blamed for the errors of Polish foreign policy, for the lack of
war preparedness despite all those ringing slogans that "we won't
give up one button", for the delayed and chaotic mobilization, for
the command disarray, for the departure from Poland of the Government and the Commander-in-Chief—for everything. No such recrimi-
nations were made against the opposition parties, which had attacked sharply both the foreign and the domestic policies of the government long before the war and striven to change them. The stand
taken by the opposition parties before the war had won them great
popularity in Poland and was further enhanced after the September
defeat.

Under these circumstances, it seemed clear to Tokarzewski that if
he wanted to have the support of all the nation for his organization,
he would have to approach those political groups that were free
from the brunt of responsibility for the September debacle, enjoyed
the confidence of the people and—equally important—drew their
support from all classes of society.

The first of Tokarzewski's meetings with the leaders of the opposition parties took place "within a few weeks after September 27" in
Radosc near Warsaw. Among those present, in addition to Tokarzewski himself, were: Mieczyslaw Niedzialkowski and Zygmunt Zaremba
(Polish Socialist Party), Stefan Korbonski (Peasant Party), and
Colonel Stefan Rowecki, who had sought out General Tokarzewski
in mid-October, requesting his help in his efforts to go to France.[6]
When Tokarzewski informed him of the already existing nucleus of
an underground organization and asked him to join in, Rowecki refused, citing primarily his distaste for politics. However, when Tokarzewski ordered him to remain in Poland, Rowecki obeyed and became the Chief of Staff in the underground organization.

Another meeting was held on October 10, 1939, in Warsaw, with
Niedzialkowski, Nowodworski and Michalowicz present. According
to another source, the meeting was also attended by Kazimierz Puzak
and Zygmunt Zaremba for the Polish Socialist Party and by Maciej
Rataj, Jozef Niecko and Stefan Korbonski for the Peasant Party.[7]

In the course of these meetings the formation of a secret organization by Tokarzewski was approved. It was to be called Service for
Poland's Victory (SPV) and its organizational framework was to in-

clude the Central Political Council. Niedzialkowski became the Council's first chairman and simultaneously the Civil Commissioner alongside the SPV Commander; Nowodworski became the vice chairman, while Professor Michalowicz and former Speaker of the *Sejm* Maciej Rataj were Council members. Niedzialkowski named Stanislaw Dubois as his stand in; similarly, Rataj named Korbonski.[8]

According to the statute drafted by Tokarzewski, SPV was to be a unified, political-military organization, dedicated to: 1) struggle against the Germans until the day of Poland's liberation within her prewar borders; 2) reconstruction and reorganization of armed forces within Poland; and 3) establishment of a temporary governmental structure within the country.[9]

The SPV was to be headed by the Commander-in-Chief, who would leave political leadership in the hands of the Central Political Council, called in the statute "Central Council for National Defense"; the Commander-in-Chief retained for himself the right to preside at the Council meetings, if circumstances required, to initiate resolutions or block those he considered harmful for the country or for the organization, or which might be "contrary to the constitutional powers of Polish state authorities." The statute called upon all Poles "to join in the work of the organization" and upon all soldiers and officers to subordinate themselves to the Commander-in-Chief of the SPV.

In a professional military manner, the statute also outlined the organization of the General Staff, which included the Central Council for National Defense. The Chief of Staff was to be the second in command to the Commander-in-Chief; the chairman of the Council, serving also as the Civil Commissioner, was next in the line of command. The chairman of the Council also headed Department II, charged with "the study of the German and Soviet occupations and developments abroad; information and propaganda; building up financial resources; control of expenditures; and secretarial offices of the Central Council for National Defense."

As far as field organization was concerned, all commanders on the district and county level were to work closely with the Council for National Defense operating within their respective areas. Chairmen of these district or county Councils served as deputies to military commanders; they also headed the local branches of Department II (called Division II on the district level, and Section II on the county level) which performed essentially the same tasks as Department II, but of a more limited scope.

The smallest unit in the organizational network was to be "the post," headed by a post commander, whose second deputy would be in charge of Section II, dealing with the propaganda and financial matters.

Around the post were clustered protective, combat and special units of 25 men each; at the higher level of command only special troops were grouped: assault units, liaison and medical units; quartermaster and administration. Women were to be used in medical and liaison services.

The statute also contained detailed instruction concerning: the structure of the conspiracy (cells of five members each, with one upward contact, constant shifting of meeting places, a strict minimum of written records, control points along command channels); propaganda (penalties for contacts with the occupying forces, information on conditions in Poland and crimes committed by the Germans); intelligence; military operations; organizational deadlines; reports; communication (in principle, by word of mouth); passwords; finances; and recruiting procedures.

Rataj, who had been arrested by the Germans on November 28, 1939 and released from Pawiak Prison on February 14, 1940, was startled on hearing Korbonski's report on the development of the SPV during his absence, because certain matters in the initial stages of discussion at the time of his arrest, had in the meantime become a reality. Neither Rataj nor Korbonski were familiar with the final wording of the SPV statute or they would not have agreed to the dictatorial powers assumed by Tokarzewski in the political sector. In the winter of 1940, however, the SPV already belonged to the past: it had been replaced by a new organization, called the Union for Armed Struggle (UAS).

The nucleus of the SPV General Staff consisted of the Chief of Staff, Colonel Stefan Rowecki, and chiefs of the following departments: Sabotage and Diversion—Major Franciszek Niepokolczycki; Organization and Personnel—Major Antoni Sanojca; Finances—Lieutenant Colonel Stanislaw Thun; Propaganda and Information—Major Tadeusz Kruk-Strzelecki; Intelligence—Major Waclaw Berka; Legalization—Captain Emil Kumor; Liaison—Major Janina Karas.

Among the SPV district commanders there were, among others: in Lodz—Colonel Leopold Okulicki; in Lublin—Major Jozef Spychalski, brother of Marian Spychalski who later became a Communist Marshal of Poland.

In mid-October 1939, Tokarzewski forwarded through the intermediary of a Hungarian military attaché a report addressed to the

Commander-in-Chief, whose name, however, he did not specify. The report contained information about the establishment of an underground organization in Poland and its initial activities (SPV statute was sent to Angers, to the government-in-exile, by a courier only on January 6, 1940). The Hungarian attaché saw to it that the report reached Marshal Rydz-Smigly who was at that time interned in Rumania and who, formally speaking, continued to be the Commander-in-Chief until General Wladyslaw Sikorski's appointment on November 7, 1939.[10] Marshal Rydz-Smigly passed the report on to General Sikorski, but the fact that he had been the first to receive it was to weigh heavily on Tokarzewski's future. Tokarzewski sent three more reports, all directed to the proper addressee, but this did not improve the situation.

Toward the end of October, Tokarzewski left on a tour of the more important localities in the provinces. He was equipped with documents certifying that he was a medical doctor, and the car he was driving was flying a pennant with the mermaid, which was supposed to give it an official air. Tokarzewski embarked on this tour in order to establish personal contacts in the provinces and to subordinate to his command those resistance organizations which already existed there, and whose number he estimated at around 100. He also wanted to establish new commands and councils on the district and county levels. His adventuresome and dangerous journey lasted about three weeks and led him through the cities of Radom, Lublin, Kielce, Krakow, Tarnow, Czestochowa, and through the mining district of Zaglebie Dabrowskie. While in Krakow, Tokarzewski sought out Cardinal Adam Sapieha, the Primate of Poland, and informed him of his activities. During his stay in Tarnow, he managed through an intermediary to pass the word of SPV's existence to the chairman of the Peasant Party, Wincenty Witos, imprisoned by the Germans. Tokarzewski's trip proved fruitful. Among other accomplishments, it established a link with the underground organization in the Krakow district, headed by Colonel Tadeusz Komorowski and Colonel Klemens Rudnicki.

III

THE UNION FOR ARMED STRUGGLE (UAS)

Through various channels, the news of SPV's existence reached the government-in-exile in Angers and met with an unfavorable reception there. Tokarzewski's first report, forwarded to Marshal Rydz-Smigly, was the proverbial last straw. General Sikorski assumed that the report had been sent to Marshal Rydz-Smigly despite the knowledge that Sikorski replaced Rydz-Smigly as the Commander-in-Chief. He, therefore, viewed the sending of the report to Rydz-Smigly as an act of flagrant disloyalty to himself. In consequence, instead of lending his support to the already existing organization, he determined to liquidate it and to form instead a new organization, to be called the Union for Armed Struggle (UAS). This move also created the appearance that the initiative to start an underground resistance movement came from the government-in-exile and not from within Poland. It was decided to strip Tokarzewski of his command and to transfer him to Lwow, with an appointment as commander of Region No. 3 of the Union for Armed Struggle. This was tantamount to a sentence of death or imprisonment, because Tokarzewski was well known in Lwow, where he had served before the war as the commander of the Corps VI district; from the point of view of the conspiracy, the move was, obviously, most ill-advised. When the first emissary from the government-in-exile—Major Jerzy Szymanski (pseudonym: Konarski)—reached Poland in November 1939, he was forbidden to even meet with Tokarzewski, but ordered to contact Rowecki instead. On his second trip to Poland, Szymanski delivered to General Tokarzewski what amounted to a singular New Year's card from the government-in-exile: orders to proceed immediately to Lwow.

Simultaneously, and in accordance with the resolution of November 8, 1939, the government-in-exile established the Ministers' Committee for Homeland Affairs, which was to "watch over all matters pertaining to the homeland, over the secret striving of the nation to liberate the Republic from enemy occupation." The Ministers' Committee was headed by General Kazimierz Sosnkowski, and its members were: Aleksander Lados, Marian Seyda, Jan Stanczyk, and a scholarly historian, Major General Marian Kukiel. In principle, the decision to establish the Ministers' Committee was correct, since it limited the conduct of home affairs to a small group of people, which facilitated maintaining the required secrecy. But the choice of committee members evoked serious reservations in the minds of concerned people in Poland. Except for the two generals, well versed in the ways of conspiracy because of their activities in the years 1905-1918, no member of the Ministers' Committee had any conspiratorial experience, which disqualified them right away. Misgivings as to the caliber of some of the men chosen for the Committee were sadly confirmed by future events: in 1945, when negotiations with Boleslaw Bierut were held in Moscow, Stanczyk switched promptly to the communist side for the price of a ministerial portfolio in the so-called Temporary Government of National Unity.

Both the government instruction of December 4, 1939 (creating the Union for Armed Struggle) and the instruction voted by the Ministers' Committee for Homeland Affairs (which recommended the establishment of a network of trustees throughout Poland, a recommendation that was never carried out) rejected the concept of one, monopolistic political-military organization. Instead, "a secret military organization called the Union for Armed Struggle" was established. The UAS was to activate centers of national resistance and to advance the cause of Poland's independence through armed struggle. The UAS was to be headed not by someone from within Poland, as foreseen in the SPV statute, but by a commander remaining with the government-in-exile in Angers, and issuing direct commands from abroad to the six UAS regions within the country. This arrangement did not take into account the fact that a commander cut off from the enemy-occupied country and communicating only through infrequent courier service (as was the case at the time the instruction was issued), could not possibly be effective; neither could radio communication replace his direct contact with his subordinates; finally, the instruction disregarded the obvious truth that the commander should be where the battle is, even if not in the front line. The responsibility for this noxious and nonsensical concept must be laid at General Sikorski's door. Undoubtedly, the General was motivated by his desire to get rid of Tokarzewski, whom he did not trust as one of the more prominent of "Pilsudski's men"; Tokarzewski's report, forwarded to Marshal Rydz-Smigly by the Hungarian attaché, tipped the scales. Sikorski also realized that the men who assumed the leadership of the military underground under Tokarzewski's command, were his political enemies, strongly linked with the Pilsudski group. The General, therefore, preferred to deprive them of their home commander, a man of their own persuasion by using the old tactic of *divide et impera*. On the other hand, Sikorski also wanted to ensure their subordination by appointing as the UAS Commander-in-Chief General Kazimierz Sosnkowski, who was most highly regarded by this group. Finally, by linking General Sosnkowski with himself, Sikorski could exercise direct control over the Union for Armed Struggle and its newly appointed commander. As for General Sosnkowski, his agreement to this pernicious system of command may be explained only by his intention to return to Poland at the earliest opportunity and to exercise his command there, an intention which he voiced repeatedly. In the wake of protests coming from Poland, the situation shortly turned for the better. Tokarzewski was appointed the commander of the underground forces in the Soviet-occupied part of Poland, while Rowecki—promoted to the rank of a general—was to take command in German-occupied territories.[1]

The government instruction on the UAS made no mention of the network of civil commissioners working alongside the military commanders, or of the Councils for National Defense, operating on various levels of field organization; this, in fact, eliminated all political activity, stressing instead "the universal, national, non-party and non-class" character of the organization. The decision to depoliticize the Union for Armed Struggle was certainly correct. Undoubtedly, the civilian founders of the SPV—had it survived—would have come to the same conclusion in time: army and politics do not mix well.

Similarly to the SPV statute, the government instruction established military sectors and areas, corresponding to the administrative division of the country into counties and districts. But, in addition, six regional commands were established: No. 1 in Warsaw, No. 4 in Krakow, No. 5 in Poznan and No. 6 in Torun for the German-occupied territories; No. 2 in Bialystok and No. 3 in Lwow for the Soviet-occupied territories. The smallest organizational unit, a section, was composed of 5 members. A few sections joined to form a platoon. The instruction made no mention of larger units, but provided for joint action of several platoons for combat or training purposes.

Under the heading "Special Directives", the instruction—addressed to Rowecki and signed by General Sosnkowski—expressed an apprehension that "organizational principles outlined in this instruction may be at variance with the actual conditions already created by you." This meant that the instruction had been issued in full awareness of the fact that there was already in Poland an existing organization with which Rowecki was connected. The government instruction contained also Rowecki's appointment as commander of Region No. 1.

The concept of "preparing behind the lines of the occupying forces an armed uprising that will go into effect at the moment when regular Polish armed forces will enter the country" was advanced for the first time in this instruction. At that time no one suspected that an evil fate would strike out the words "Polish forces" and substitute instead "Soviet forces."

The government instruction pertaining to the establishment of the Union for Armed Struggle was brought to Poland in the first days of January 1940 by emissary Jerzy Michalewski (pseudonym: Dokladny), who remained in Poland and joined the UAS. It provoked Tokarzewski's understandable bitterness and caused much embarrassment to Tokarzewski's friend, Rowecki. Working closely and harmoniously together, and motivated by their interpretation of the existing conditions, the two men decided to incorporate into the Union for Armed Struggle whatever had been previously set up within the organizational framework of the SPV. Rowecki communicated this decision in his report to General Sosnkowski, requesting at the same time that a Deputy Commander-in-Chief be named within Poland immediately, since it was clearly impossible for each regional commander to send his couriers to France. The same request was also made by Tokarzewski in his report on the organizational status of the SPV, dated January 9, 1940, in which he advocated the principle of "central leadership for Poland from within Poland." Neither of these messages, however, produced any results.

Tokarzewski and Rowecki also strove to transfer to the UAS the network of civil commissioners and councils for national defense that had been established by the SPV.[2] As it turned out, however, fate itself liquidated the Central Political Council (called "Central Council for National Defense" in the SPV statute): on November 28, 1939, Rataj was arrested by the Gestapo, and the arrest of Niedzialkowski followed on December 23, 1939. Rataj was released from Pawiak Prison on February 14, 1940, but arrested again on March 30, 1940. Both Rataj and Niedzialkowski were shot in the Palmiry Woods on June 21, 1940. As for the other Council members—Professor Michalowicz withdrew from the Council and the National Party withdrew its representative, Nowodworski.

Under these changed circumstances, representatives of various political parties met again on February 7, 1940. This time the cast was somewhat different: the Polish Socialist Party (code name: Circle) was represented by Kazimierz Puzak, instead of Dubois. Puzak, a socialist since 1904, a tzarist prisoner in the Schlisselburg fortress from 1911 to 1917, became friendly with Tokarzewski while still in

Russia in 1918 and, according to the General, thrice saved Tokarzewski's life. Aleksander Debski (pseudonym: Stachurski), former
governor of the Wolyn district and political prisoner in Brest before
the war, came to replace Nowodworski as representative of the National Party (code name: Square). After Rataj's arrest by the Germans, his place was filled by Stefan Korbonski (pseudonym: Nowak),
former chairman of the Peasant Party (code name: Triangle) in the
Bialystok district. Also present at the February meeting were: Tokarzewski (pseudonym: Doktor), Rowecki (pseudonym: Inzynier) and
Major Tadeusz Kruk-Strzelecki (pseudonym: Dyrektor), chief of the
Political-Propaganda Department of the UAS General Staff. The
meeting was chaired by the senior member, Puzak. Tokarzewski presented his proposal that the Council for National Defense be formed
by those political parties that had not participated in government before the war and thus had a chance now to rally the embittered nation and win its confidence. He suggested they should demand that
the government-in-exile "either appoint a home delegate as member
of the government or else send to Poland one of its cabinet members."
The proposal that a Council for National Defense be established fell
through because of Debski's opposition; while he declared the willingness of his party to cooperate fully with the Union for Armed Struggle, Debski considered the creation of the Council premature. In all
other respects, however, the three representatives promised full cooperation of their parties with the UAS.

The next meeting was to be held on February 19, 1940, but was
postponed because of Puzak's absence till February 24. On that day,
however, Korbonski failed to show up. Living in an apartment located near the former Czechoslovak Legation on Chopin Street, where
German Governor Hans Frank took up quarters on his arrival in Warsaw, Korbonski was snatched by the Gestapo at dawn and taken to
Pawiak Prison, where he and other men from that area were held as
hostages, to be shot should anything untoward occur in Warsaw during
Frank's stay there. Secretary General of the Peasant Party, Jozef
Grudzinski (pseudonym: Waltenty) took Korbonski's place at the
meeting, where some important decisions were made that day. It was
ascertained that the three main political parties were "in total agreement and of one mind in their determination to restore Poland's independence by undertaking preparations for an armed struggle against
the two occupying powers"; that they recognized the Union for
Armed Struggle (UAS) as the sole central military organization summoned to service by the government; that they agreed to function as
the Political Coordinating Committee of the UAS, "charged with coordinating preparations of the military and the nation to take up

arms and win a victory over the oppressors." It was decided that representatives of various political parties would take turns at presiding at the Committee's meetings, each serving for one month. Kruk-Strzelecki was elected as secretary of the Political Coordinating Committee and all those present were sworn in by Tokarzewski; the wording of the oath was identical with the UAS oath, but limited to a vow to guard the secrets of the organization. The delegates pledged that all groups and units of a military character, affiliated with their parties would be subordinated to the UAS by not later than March 23, 1940; they also promised to exert their influence in persuading other political and social groups, not represented on the Political Coordinating Committee, to do the same.

Korbonski appeared at the next meeting, on March 4, 1940, and was welcomed affectionately by Puzak, twenty years his senior, as the first "prisoner from Pawiak" from among the Committee members. From then on, meetings were usually held once a week. Tokarzewski no longer attended those meetings. At the insistence of the Committee, he had at first postponed his departure from Warsaw, hoping for a change in the orders that were sending him to Lwow. When this hope failed, bitter and frustrated Tokarzewski started on his journey, with all Committee members bidding him a sorrowful farewell. He was arrested by the Soviet guards while crossing the border on the night of March 6, 1940; taken to prison, he stayed there until the outbreak of the Soviet-German war in June 1941.

All aspects of life in occupied Poland came up for scrutiny at the meetings of the Political Coordinating Committee. The Committee's decisions pertained not only to political and military matters, but also to economic and social problems, science, national culture, ethics of life under occupation, etc.

The central task of the Committee was to get the nation moving in the proper direction, hewing to the basic premise of struggle for Poland's independence. In time this led to the drafting of a "code of rights and obligations of a Pole", a set of civil struggle rules, governing relationships between the Poles and the Germans in every sector of national life. There was also the immediate need to initiate a proper reaction to current orders and measures imposed by the Germans; if they were clearly contrary to national interest, the Committee's instructions were to boycott them (the action of civil disobedience). In addition, the Political Coordinating Committee had to take a stand on current problems, involving questions such as working in enterprises taken over by the Germans, the problem of the *Volksdeutsche*, aid to people driven out of the territories incorporated into the Reich, and dozens of others.

The Committee was also concerned with foreign affairs; on the one hand, it requested from the government-in-exile information about the military and international situation; on the other hand, it sent its own recommendations pertaining to foreign policy, e.g., regarding the looming threat that the region of Wilno might be lost to Poland. Recognizing unconditionally Sikorski's government as the legitimate government of Poland, the underground leaders regarded its decisions in matters of foreign policy as binding. However, where internal homeland affairs were concerned, the government's demands or instructions were treated more as recommendations, and if they were at variance with the opinions held by the PCC, the Committee either requested a change or simply ignored them. This reflected a view held not only within the Committee, but also within far larger circles of the underground, that the government-in-exile ought to act as Poland's ambassador to the world, but that the actual decision-making center ought to be in Poland.

The Committee's decisions were circulated throughout Poland by means of organizational networks of all political parties and the UAS, which meant—as far as the *General Gouvernement* was concerned— that they were sure to reach every nook and cranny, no matter how remote. In the territories incorporated into the Reich, or into the Soviet Union, communication was not nearly as good.

At about that time, Szymanski, an emissary from the government-in-exile, arrived in Poland, bringing the government's answer to the proposal (advanced earlier by Tokarzewski and Rowecki) that the network of civil commissioners and councils for national defense affiliated with the UAS be maintained. Instead of civil commissioners, subordinate to military commanders, the government wanted to have five delegates in Poland, one of whom was to act as chief delegate. They were to hold the reins of political power, to the extent this was practicable under enemy occupation, and were to have equal rank with the respective military commanders. The government agreed to maintain a network of councils for national defense, but limited them to a purely consultative role alongside the delegates.

The government's answer was debated at the PCC meeting on March 13, 1940. The Committee concluded that the government's proposal "barred those who represent the public opinion in Poland from exercising any influence on the workings of the government"; it proposed instead that the Committee be viewed by the government as the sole source of authoritative information; that all government directives regarding homeland affairs be sent to the Committee; and that the Committee (augmented by a delegate for homeland, sent by the government from abroad) be given decision-making powers in all matters specified in the government instruction as within the competence of the delegates.[3]

In addition, Rowecki also presented a number of reservations and corrections pertaining to the government's proposal. Anticipating that the matter of delegates and councils for national defense would take a long time, he returned to Tokarzewski's plan with which he was in total agreement: he proposed that General Sosnowski nominate immediately a Civil Commissioner at the UAS Headquarters and suggested for this post either Nowodworski or Korbonski, or else Nowodworkski as Commissioner and Korbonski as his deputy.[4] This was done without the knowledge of the Committee and outside of its deliberations; neither did Korbonski, a determined and outspoken opponent of the conception of a Civil Commissioner, know anything about it.

Irrespective of this exchange of opinions and judgments, the Committee continued to carry on as the supreme political authority within the country, making decisions which under normal conditions would have been within the province of the government. Rowecki took part in all Committee deliberations. As a rule, these were lively meetings, for the opposing views presented there were not one-dimensional, i.e., involving only differences between the three major political parties. The debate was multifaceted; for instance, the three parties would on occasion unite against the position taken by the UAS, or then again both the parties and the UAS would join forces to oppose the policy of the government-in-exile. This, however, never degenerated into *bellum omnium contra omnes* (a war of all against all), but assumed instead the characteristics of a normal political process which, in most instances, resulted in a compromise.

The same was true for the counterparts of the Committee, co-ordinating various political groups on the district level. In the Krakow district—perhaps the most active—the Krakow Interparty Committee was organized; it was composed of: Zygmunt Lasocki and Stanislaw Mierzwa (Peasant Party), Stanislaw Rymar and Tadeusz Surzycki (National Party), Zygmunt Zulawski and Jozef Cyrankiewicz (Polish Socialist Party). In time, the Krakow Interparty Committee coopted also Wladyslaw Tempka and Karol Holeksa of the Labor Party. The Committee's meetings were attended by the commander of Region No. 4, Colonel Tadeusz Komorowski, and later also by the district Government Delegate, Professor Jan Jakobiec, an education official in Poznan before the war. The composition of the Committee underwent some changes later on, because of arrests and personnel shifts, but it functioned essentially the same throughout the war.

A similar organization was also formed in Wilno. It was called the Wilno District Council and was composed of the following: Rev. Romuald Swierkowski (representing the Bishops' Curia), Dr. Jerzy Dobrzanski (Polish Socialist Party), Wladyslaw Kaminski (former senator, member of the Nonpartisan Bloc of Cooperation with the Government, and now a representative of the Committee of Struggle for Liberation), Adam Galinski (affiliated before the war with the Pilsudski regime, now serving as a representative of "independent intelligentsia"), and Colonel Nikodem Sulik of the UAS.

In Poznan, too, there was a local counterpart of the Political Co-ordinating Committee. It was called the Alliance of Political Parties, and was composed of: Monsignor Jozef Pradzynski (for the organization called "Fatherland"), Jan Wojkiewicz (Peasant Party), representatives of the National Party and the Labor Party, and later on the district Government Delegate Adolf Bninski, former governor of the Poznan district. Within a short time, however, all members of the Alliance were arrested one after another, and the three men mentioned above were murdered in prison or in concentration camps. The Alliance never recovered from these blows and ceased to exist.

The relations between the three main political parties ("The Big Three") on the Political Coordinating Committee had their ups and downs. They were best between the Polish Socialist Party and the Peasant Party, because of their ideological kinship and the mutual attraction that has always existed between the peasants and the workers. Besides, the two parties shared a common tradition of political opposition to the prewar government, maintained by the "Centrolew" alliance in Poland and by the so-called Front Morges (Wincenty Witos and Wladyslaw Kiernik of the Peasant Party and Herman Lieberman of the Polish Socialist Party) outside of Poland. In line with this tradition, an agreement between the two parties was promptly reached as far as mutual consultation and joint policy were concerned. In political matters, Puzak and Korbonski usually took the same position, but they often parted company where the UAS was concerned. Korbonski opposed all political initiatives of the UAS that exceeded their immediate task of organizing the underground armed forces. Puzak, on the other hand, was far more tolerant, arguing that "those who have a hold on the army, will rule in Poland after the war." Still, in the crucial debate that came to dominate the meetings of the Committee, i.e., the question of divorcing politics from the military and abandoning the concept of a single political-military organization—both parties took the same stand. They rejected Rowecki's request for the support of his plan of having a Civil Commissioner at the side of the UAS Commander-in-Chief. Instead, they approached the government-in-exile with the proposal that Korbonski be appointed as Chief Delegate in Poland. Emissary Jan Karski was to take that proposal to France, together with the dissent of the National Party, which considered Korbonski too far to the left politically and lacking in experience. Karski, however, never made it to France; he was captured in Slovakia, while on his way to France, and never reached Paris.[5]

On September 10, 1941, the Polish Socialist Party (which had added to its party name the words: "Liberty, Equality and Independence"), withdrew from the Political Coordinating Committee, thus assuming the status of quasi opposition to the government-in-exile. The socialists disapproved of the Sikorski-Maiski agreement, concluded between Poland and the USSR on July 30, 1941, because it left open the question of Poland's eastern borders; they were also critical of the government's attitude toward the Political Coordinating Committee and of the appointment as the government's delegate of a man they did not support. The gap created in the composition of the Committee by their withdrawal was filled by the so-called "Polish Socialists," a fraction within the Polish Socialist Party, which opposed the "Liberty, Equality and Independence" socialists and supported the government-in-exile. This group was represented on the Committee successively by Adam Prochnik and Wincenty Markowski. However, in 1943, the two socialist groups reconciled their differences and in March 1943 Puzak returned to the Committee.[6]

Neither the Peasant Party nor the Socialist Party ever succeeded in developing a comparably close relationship with the National Party, represented on the Committee by Aleksander Debski. When the two parties drafted a declaration proclaiming a war against "nazism, fascism and communism," Debski demanded that the word "fascism" be deleted. On another occasion, he rejected the wording of a proclamation that stated that "future Poland should be democratic," and proposed instead that the text read: "future Poland should be nationalist."[7] Divergent views on such basic problems often produced disagreement in minor matters as well. In addition, the National Party showed some clearly monopolistic tendencies, manifested in their demands for a privileged status and a right of veto. It shunned closer ties with any other party and obviously aimed at taking over the reins the moment Poland was liberated.[8]

Dissatisfied both with the government-in-exile and with the conditions within the Political Coordinating Committee, the National Party also withdrew for a time. This made it possible to bring in the

Labor Party, whose participation had been vetoed in the past by the National Party. The fact that *tres faciunt collegium* played a major part in this decision, as did the fact that the gap left by the National Party's withdrawal from the Committee was best filled by a political group closely connected with General Sikorski who insisted on the Labor Party's admission to the PCC. Franciszek Kwiecinski (pseudonym: Karwat) became the representative of the Labor Party (code name: Rhomb) on the Committee. At the very outset he declared his willingness to collaborate closely with the Peasant Party and, consequently, with the Socialist Party ("Liberty, Equality, and Independence").

The relations between the parties and the UAS were shaped along different lines. Before the war, all three political parties within the Committee had been in opposition to the government. Men identified closely with the prewar regime (the so-called *sanacja*) and representing Pilsudski's followers and the elite of prewar Polish armed forces were in the High Command of the Union for Armed Struggle. The word from the provinces had it that here and there in the local commands of the UAS, prewar county administrators and regime activists could be found. This did not prevent the former opposition parties from cooperating with the UAS, for this was considered a national necessity; still, it prevented them—and particularly the Peasant Party—from having full confidence in the UAS. Rowecki, who had a purely military background himself, abhorred politics and often said so; he did all he could to remedy the parties' lack of confidence, but until the very end of his command over, first, the UAS and later, the Home Army, he met with indifferent success. In a way, he contributed to this lack of confidence himself by advocating repeatedly conceptions based on the law promulgated on September 1, 1939, and subordinating all political and administrative authority to military command in time of war by transferring the prime minister's powers to a civil commissioner, subject to the Commander-in-Chief. It is not known whether Niedzialkowski, Rataj and Nowodworski had had time enough to familiarize themselves with the final wording of the SPV statute and whether they agreed to such a submission of the political to the military authority at the time they were setting up the Service for Poland's Victory together with Tokarzewski. In any case, their successors—among them Puzak, usually tolerant where the UAS political initiatives were concerned—were unanimous in their negative reaction. This led to the decision to break away from the UAS and to change the Committee's name from "Political Coordinating Committee of the UAS" to "Central Political Committee."

All political parties within occupied Poland were positive in their attitude toward the government-in-exile; in principle, they all approved of its foreign policy, and particularly of its decision to carry on the struggle; they all declared their full support for the emigré government and indeed did support it until November 29, 1944, when the government of Tomasz Arciszewski assumed power and certain differences came to the fore. In practice, however, nearly all initial government decisions pertaining to homeland provoked strong objections and dissatisfaction. The strongest objections were leveled against those moves that were obviously motivated by the principle of *divide et impera* and betrayed the government's apprehension regarding the emergence of a strong central leadership within Poland, whether civil or military. Because of this apprehension, the government divided the country into six military regions, each of which was to be commanded directly from abroad; for the same reason also, the government advocated for a time the plan to appoint not five, but three coequal government delegates, each of whom was to receive his instructions directly from abroad. These moves indicated clearly that the government-in-exile either did not understand, or did not want to understand, the facts of life under enemy occupation and that it was motivated not by what was in the best interest of the homeland, but only by its desire to cement its own indivisible authority.

Ultimately, the fall of France contributed to the solution of this problem with regard to the military sector. A government dispatch, sent on June 18, 1940, still from France, named Rowecki as Deputy Commander-in-Chief of the UAS and authorized him to take independent decisions in case communication with the government was disrupted. Another dispatch, dated June 30, 1940, and sent already from Great Britain, established the Supreme Headquarters of the Union for Armed Struggle in Poland and appointed Rowecki as the Commander-in-Chief, with a recommendation that he continue close cooperation with the Central Political Committee. Even so, Rowecki's subsequent relations with the government-in-exile were marred by conflicts, resulting primarily from a lack of confidence in the Supreme Headquarters on the part of General Sikorski and his right-hand man, Professor Stanislaw Kot. One casualty of this conflict was Major Tadeusz Kruk-Strzelecki, secretary of the Central Political Committee, who was dismissed from his post on General Sikorski's orders. He was replaced by Jerzy Michalewski (pseudonyms: Dokladny, Barkowski, Piotrowski, Heller), an emissary who had arrived from abroad a short time before. This state of affairs continued until General Sikorski's tragic death on July 4, 1943, in a plane crash at Gibraltar.

IV

THE COLLECTIVE DELEGACY

A comparable balance in the relations between the Central Political Committee and the government-in-exile was not achieved equally promptly. Crisscrossing and often contradictory proposals regarding the candidates for government delegates, their number, their role and their origin (i.e., whether they were to be sent from abroad or chosen from among those who were in Poland), prompted the government-in-exile to send to Poland an Acting Delegate, Colonel Jan Skorobohaty-Jakubowski (pseudonym: Vogel) who was to evaluate and choose candidates for three coequal Government Delegates. When he reached Poland, it turned out that considerable time was needed for the "Big Three" (Polish Socialist Party, National Party and Peasant Party) to reach accord in recommending candidates for Government Delegates. Since communication with the government-in-exile was difficult because of war developments, and in view of the government sanction of the Central Political Committee's existence (dispatch from Libourne dated June 18, 1940), the following decisions were made at the meeting on June 28, 1940 (attended by Puzak, Debski, Korbonski and Rowecki), in the presence and with the approval of Acting Delegate Skorobohaty-Jakubowski:

1. To assume the functions of the Delegacy of the Government of the Republic of Poland, with the understanding that the Committee's composition will be augmented in accordance with the instruction of the government (i.e., will include the Labor Party).

2. The Delegacy, which, in addition to party representatives will also include the Commander of the UAS, will carry out its functions throughout all territories of the Republic in the name of the Government of the Republic of Poland.[1]

The first action of the Collective Delegacy was to issue on July 26, 1940, the *Commands of the Day*, signed with a cryptonym describing the nature of the issuing body: "Representation of the Polish Government-in-Exile." *Commands* set the following goals for the nation: to continue the struggle for freedom and independence; to maintain an inflexible stand against the occupiers and to reject all proposals aimed at "organizing a fictitious Polish State under the protectorate of Germany or a federated Polish Republic under the auspices of the Soviet Union." It proved to be a farsighted document, for it foresaw the possibility of a German-Soviet conflict and warned, if this should come to pass, against military collaboration with either of the two enemies through participation in any anti-Soviet or anti-Nazi legions that the occupiers might attempt to organize. *Commands of the Day* summoned all Poles to engage not only in a passive resistance, but also in an active struggle for freedom in all sectors of national life. Finally, the document stated that any services rendered to the Nazis or the Soviets would be viewed as treason.

Next, the Collective Delegacy issued a proclamation on September 1, 1940, the anniversary of the outbreak of the war, initiating the so-called Civil Struggle. The proclamation called on all Poles to refrain from participation in any forms of amusement on the anniversary day of September 1, to stay off the streets between the hours of 2 p.m. and 4 p.m., and to refrain on August 31 and September 1 from buying the daily newspapers, i.e., the German-sponsored "reptile press."

When informed of the creation of the Collective Delegacy, the government-in-exile refused to approve it, explaining that the June 28, 1940 resolution of the Central Political Committee was not in accordance with the government's instructions and decisions. Under these circumstances, the Collective Delegacy was dissolved by its own decision of September 13, 1940, thus automatically reviving the Central Political Committee (augmented by Kwiecinski); Skorobohaty-Jakubowski was acknowledged as Acting Delegate and a deadline was set to present the parties' nominees for Government Delegates by no later than November 1940.[2]

(Fate was to deal cruelly with the members of the Political Co-ordinating Committee and the Central Political Committee. Puzak died on April 30, 1950, in the communist prison in Rawicz; Aleksander Debski and his successors—Mieczyslaw Trajdos and Stefan Sacha—were arrested and murdered by the Gestapo, with Debski beheaded with an axe in the Poznan prison. Wladyslaw Jaworski, the last representative of the National Party, was the only one to survive the war. Jozef Grudzinski—who succeeded Korbonski after Korbonski's transfer from the Committee to the Headquarters of the UAS in March 1941—was killed during the Warsaw Rising in the Sadyba Oficerska district of the city. Franciszek Kwiecinski of the Labor Party was also arrested by the Gestapo on January 19, 1942, and shortly thereafter shot in the Kabacki Forest. His place on the Committee was filled successively by Zygmunt Felczak, Jozef Kwasiborski and Franciszek Urbanski.)

V

THE GOVERNMENT DELEGATES

In a partial fulfillment of its promise, the Central Political Committee advised the government-in-exile that an accord had been reached on the candidate who would serve as deputy to Acting Delegate Skorobohaty-Jakubowski. The man they had chosen was Cyryl Ratajski, former Minister of Internal Affairs and former Mayor of Poznan. The government, however, went beyond the Committee's recommendation and on December 3, 1940, appointed Ratajski not as a Deputy Delegate, but as Chief Government Delegate for the *General Gouvernement*, with headquarters in Warsaw.

Two main considerations prompted General Sikorski's decision in this matter. On the one hand, he became impatient with the Central Political Committee's inability to come to an agreement on candidates for the three government delegates. The National Party was largely responsible for the delay, because, while opposing Korbonski's candidacy (advanced by the Socialist and the Peasant Parties at an early date), they failed to present a candidate of their own, resorting in this case to the peculiar veto rights they claimed. On the other hand, Sikorski found Ratajski's candidacy very palatable. Ratajski was a member of the Labor Party (with which the General was closely connected) and had no ties to any of the "Big Three." Knowing Ratajski personally, the General also felt that he could count on Ratajski's unswerving and uncritical loyalty. Ratajski's declaration of January 18, 1940—in which he proclaimed his "subservience," voiced "expressions of hommage" to the premier, the government and the National Council, and assured them of his determination to follow all their views and instructions—proved that Sikorski's assessment was correct.

In December 1940, the Central Political Committee met in a highly dramatic session. It was Korbonski's turn to preside. Ratajski attended the meeting. At the outset he informed those present of his appointment as Chief Government Delegate, and asked to be sworn in. This brought sharp objections from the socialists and the Peasant Party. In accordance with his earlier agreement with Puzak, Korbonski was the one who stated these objections. Careful to show the 65-year old Ratajski all due courtesy and consideration, Korbonski explained that the Central Political Committee had nominated Ratajski for the post of deputy to Skorobohaty-Jakubowski; Ratajski's appointment as Chief Delegate ran contrary to the wishes of the Polish Socialist Party and the Peasant Party, Korbonski declared, and showed an insufficient knowledge of the situation on the part of the government. In view of these circumstances, Korbonski appealed to Ratajski not to accept the nomination, particularly since both the Peasant and the Socialist Party persisted in their demand that only one Government Delegate be appointed for the entire country, rather than three coequal delegates: one for the territories incorporated into the Reich, one for the *General Gouvernement*, and one for the Soviet-occupied territories.

Korbonski's appeal was not supported by Debski and Kwiecinski. Debski approved of the appointment, with the proviso that he considered it a professional and administrative, rather than a political nomination. Kwiecinski was enthusiastic, because Ratajski was a member of his own political party.

In reply, Ratajski declared that the objections voiced by Korbonski pertained not to the appointee, but to the government, and would be passed on to the government. Personally, he considered the government's decision as binding and accepted the nomination. In view of Ratajski's declaration, Korbonski administered the oath and, beginning with the following meeting, the new Delegate took over the chairmanship of the Central Political Committee, as proposed by the Committee members. This ensured regular contact and cooperation between the Government Delegate and the political leadership that had emerged within Poland, especially since Ratajski declared at one of the very first meetings that he would consider the Committee's decisions as binding. Skorobohaty-Jakubowski became Ratajski's deputy, and thus the roles originally assigned for them by the Central Political Committee became reversed by the decision of the government-in-exile. After Ratajski's arrival on the scene, General Rowecki no longer participated on a regular basis in the Committee's deliberations.[1]

Informed of the position taken by the Socialist Party and the Peasant Party, General Sikorski made his first concession to the view that only one Chief Government Delegate should be appointed for the entire country (even though he had previously named Adolf Bninski as Chief Government Delegate for the territories incorporated into the Reich). In his dispatch addressed to Ratajski (pseudonym: Wartski), Sikorski affirmed that "in case of need, the Warsaw Delegate will make decisions in matters affecting the entire Polish territory." This, however, was not satisfactory to the two parties who continued to press their demands that the government abandon its plan of dividing the country into three delegacies, which seemed tantamount to accepting the hated division of the country, carried out by the enemy. They demanded that a central governing body be established, similar to the Union for Armed Struggle. They upbraided the government for appointing Ratajski at the very moment when the three political parties had reached an agreement on the candidacy of Professor Jan Piekalkiewicz of the Peasant Party for the post of Chief Delegate. Finally, the two parties declared that they were troubled by the fact that, since both Ratajski and Bninski were to the right of the political spectrum, their nomination as Delegates did not reflect the realities of political life in Poland. The Socialist Party and the Peasant Party asserted that "solutions in liberated Poland will be reached through an alliance of peasants, workers, and other working classes." For this reason, the two parties persisted in their demand that one Chief Delegate be named for all Poland, with headquarters in Warsaw; as their candidate for the post they proposed Professor Jan Piekalkiewicz, and as his deputy—Jozef Cyrankiewicz (Polish Socialist Party). The two parties advised also that, until the final decision by the government, they would limit their participation in the Central Political Committee to military matters and matters pertaining directly to the struggle against the occupiers.[2]

The ensuing correspondence between General Sikorski and the two political parties brought some heated exchanges. Sikorski charged that the two parties failed to perceive the magnitude of the disaster that had befallen Poland and added a preachy comment that he "expected patriotism to prevail over factional or personal considerations." The Peasant Party responded that "those who remained in the country are enduring, together with the whole nation, the monstrous burden of disaster, and prove their patriotism by their active participation in the work for Poland's liberation, despite the constant threat of death. . . . The charge of factionalism is all too reminiscent of the period just ended, when much the same arguments were used in an effort to keep the nation silent." The Socialist Party accused Sikorski of resorting to lies, of advocating "ephemeral, parlor-room notions" and of taking the country by surprise with his decisions; the inappropriateness of Sikorski's preachments about patriotism was also denounced as "altogether too reminiscent of the OZON* monopoly on patriotism."[3]

The epilogue to this correspondence came with the dismissal and departure of Ratajski on September 15, 1942, and the appointment

---

* OZON—*Oboz Zjednoczenia Narodowego*—a non-party organization, supporting the prewar regime in Poland.

of Professor Jan Piekalkiewicz as Chief Government Delegate for Poland. By that time, Cyrankiewicz could no longer be appointed as Deputy Delegate: arrested by the Gestapo in 1941, he was sent to the Auschwitz concentration camp.

Dissatisfaction of the Socialist Party and the Peasant Party was not the only cause for Ratajski's dismissal. With the passing of time, the government, too, became dissatisfied with the Chief Delegate. Ratajski was 65 years old and had spent most of his life in western Poland, under Prussian domination; he had served with great distinction as mayor of Poznan, but was not well suited for conspiracy. His evident good will and patriotic devotion could not overcome his inability to solve complex problems, and his naive views and excessive optimism discouraged even his friends. Decorated by the government with the Cross of Virtuti Militari, he died in Warsaw on October 19, 1942, a few weeks after his dismissal, and was buried at the Powazki Cemetery (block 202) under the assumed name of Radwanski.

Ratajski's successor, Professor Jan Piekalkiewicz, held the post until February 19, 1943, when he was caught by the Gestapo in the street; he was murdered in May of the same year.

The next Chief Government Delegate, Jan Stanislaw Jankowski of the former National Workers' Party, took over the job on March 1, 1943. Previously, he had served as head of the Labor and Welfare department of the Government Delegacy. On May 3, 1944, Jankowski inaugurated the Home Council of Ministers (in accordance with the President's decree of April 26, 1944, regarding the temporary governmental organization on the territories of the Republic). The Council was composed of the Chief Delegate (with the rank of vice premier) and of the following ministers: Adam Bien (Peasant Party), Stanislaw Jasiukowicz (National Party) and Antoni Pajdak (Socialist Party). The Home Council of Ministers ceased to exist on March 27 and 28, 1945, after all its members had been arrested in Pruszkow near Warsaw by the Soviet NKVD. Chief Delegate Jankowski and Minister Jasiukowicz died in Soviet prisons a few years later.

Following Jankowski's arrest, Korbonski assumed the duties of Chief Government Delegate and served in this capacity until June 29, 1945 when he resigned and transferred his duties to Jerzy Braun, then president of the underground parliament, the Council of National Unity. That same night, Korbonski and his wife Zofia were arrested in Krakow by the Soviet NKVD.

VI

THE POLITICAL BUREAU AND THE CCOF

As the newly appointed Delegate, Ratajski concentrated first on liquidating government-financed diversionary activities aimed against organizations such as the Service for Poland's Victory (SPV), the Union for Armed Struggle (UAS), the Political Coordinating Committee or the Central Political Committee. These activities were directed by Ryszard Swietochowski, a confidant of General Sikorski. For his underground activities Swietochowski received from the government-in-exile 15,357,000 zlotys, even though the government already knew of the establishment of the SPV in Poland. Among Swietochowski's closest collaborators were: Franciszek Kwiecinski of the Labor Party; Marian Borzecki, formerly of the National Party; Tadeusz Szpotanski, formerly of the Polish Socialist Party; Rector of the Warsaw Polytechnic Kazimierz Drewnowski; Romuald Tyczynski and Jozef Marszalek, both from the underground organization "Raclawice." Claiming General Sikorski's authorization to represent him in Poland, Swietochowski established toward the end of 1939 the so-called Political Bureau, which usurped for itself the role of the representative of the government-in-exile, and also the so-called Central Committee of Organizations for Freedom (CCOF), which was to serve as the political representation of the nation. The CCOF gathered under its wings the Labor Party, "Raclawice," the National Radical Organization—ABC, the Union of Reserve Officers, the so-called Secret Polish Army (SPA), the "Musketeers" and other small groups.

In an indirect confirmation of the authorization given to Swietochowski, General Sikorski advised Rowecki that Swietochowski had his full confidence and that the two should cooperate. At the same time Korbonski received a letter from Professor Stanislaw Kot, minister of internal affairs in the government-in-exile (charged by General Sikorski with the supervision of homeland affairs, bypassing the Committee of Ministers for Homeland Affairs). In his letter Kot reproached Korbonski for his unwillingness to cooperate "with General Sikorski's people." The cooperation between Rowecki and Swietochowski never came to pass, either, because Swietochowski refused to acknowledge that the UAS had a mandate from the government to organize the underground armed forces and to consolidate various underground military organizations. On the contrary, Swieto-chowski encouraged such organizations to refuse consolidation and financed the activities of those who did refuse to subordinate themselves to the UAS. All this created great confusion in the underground and a pressing need for intervention with the government-in-exile.

At the root of these diversionary activities lay a lack of confidence felt by both Sikorski and Kot. Both men belonged to the so-called "Front Morges," fiercely hostile to the prewar government and anyone ever connected with it, such as the "Pilsudski men" who dominated the UAS Supreme Command, or those representatives of the Socialist and Peasant Parties on the CPC who had no ties with Front Morges. Among those were Niedzialkowski and Rataj, as well as their successors on the Committee; Kot thought them all guilty of too conciliatory an attitude toward the UAS.

Developments in the underground forced Kot and Sikorski to reckon more and more with first, the Political Coordinating Committee and, later, the Central Political Committee and the UAS. Dissatisfied with such a turn of events, Swietochowski decided to leave Poland in order to see Sikorski personally. He left in April 1940, taking the customary route of the emissaries; he was arrested in Slovakia and died in Auschwitz in July 1941. The Labor Party, which had long been trying to gain admission to the PCC, now withdrew from the weakened CCOF. The Labor Party's drive for admission got a strong boost from General Sikorski, who charged Acting Delegate Skorobohaty-Jakubowski with the task of bringing the Labor Party into the Committee. As a result of these pressures—and following the temporary withdrawal from the CPC of the National Party, dissatisfied with the government's policies—the Labor Party joined the Central Political Committee in July 1940. The appointment of Ratajski (also a member of the Labor Party) as Chief Government Delegate in Poland, turned out to be the proverbial coffin nail for the Political Bureau and the CCOF, since he was authorized to take over the funds they had received from abroad. Swietochowski's collaborators withdrew one by one from the two organizations. A commission appointed by the Chief Delegate (and including Michalewski) found a total of 10,122,030 zlotys in the Political Bureau's treasury; this money, however, was never turned over to the Delegate.[1]

The CCOF diversion was paralleled by a shortlived but similar action conducted from the opposite end of the political spectrum, by members of *sanacja*, affiliated with the prewar regime. On July 26, 1940 there appeared in Warsaw an issue of *The Journal of Laws* and

Monitor, published in its prewar format. It carried the announcement that an underground government was established in Poland, composed of a premier, six ministers and a viceminister for military affairs. When this action was disavowed by the Acting Delegate and the Union for Armed Struggle, it petered out without a trace.[2]

VII

THE GOVERNMENT DELEGACY

1. The Scope of the Government Delegate's Activities

The Delegate's position in relation to the Political Coordinating Committee and the political parties was outlined in the resolution of the Ministers' Committee for Homeland Affairs of April 17, 1940, which acknowledged the "central coordination of the parties," i.e., the PCC, and its role in "coordinating the political life of the country, maintaining contact with the Government and making decisions in all matters of a political, economic and social nature." According to the resolution "the Government Delegate serves as a liaison between the Government and homeland in political matters; he collaborates with the political parties, but does not direct them."

The Delegate's relationship with the UAS was defined in the MCHA resolution of April 16, 1940 and modified by the resolution of April 10, 1941. Both resolutions drew a strict dividing line between politics and the military, prohibiting all political activity by the UAS, while instructing the Delegate to extend all aid to the organization, especially in the matter of subordinating other military groups to the UAS. Even more important, they authorized the Delegate—acting either alone or in concert with the Central Political Committee—to give political directives to the UAS command, to control the UAS budget, to comment on appointments at Headquarters or on a regional level of command, and to receive periodic reports on the organizational status and activities of the UAS.[1]

In this manner was the conception of a single, unified, political-military organization—such as the SPV—finally laid to rest. Rowecki's participation in the Collective Delegacy was its last manifestation.

2. The Presidium Office

Within this framework, the Delegate embarked on the task of setting up the Government Delegacy. Following the pattern of prewar governmental structure, he began by establishing various ministries, each with its own area of competence, and the Presidium Office. The Presidium Office was headed at first by Jerzy Michalewski, who served until the end of Ratajski's term, and then, successively, by Jan Domanski (Peasant Party), serving with Delegate Piekalkiewicz;

Stefan Pawlowski and Tadeusz Miklaszewski, serving with Delegate Jankowski; and Miklaszewski, serving with Korbonski.

The reestablishment of prewar governmental structure was dictated by the conviction, voiced already by the Political Coordinating Committee, that not only the military, but every sector of national life should come within the Delegacy's purview. Inevitably, this led to an effort to reconstruct in the underground some tested governmental patterns.

The main task of the Presidium Office was to support the Delegate in every area of his activities. Conditions of life under occupation made it mandatory to give precedence to efforts aimed at ensuring the personal safety of the Delegate. He had to be provided with illegal identity papers that were not only faultlessly forged, but also "sure," i.e., of the kind that would protect him from street roundups or accidental random arrests; he had to have at his disposal several hideouts, different from the network of apartments and rooms used by the Presidium Office, or as "mail drops," or as hiding places for the underground archives; he also had to have an absolutely trustworthy team of contact—women to maintain liaison within the organization, and administrative personnel to take care of the necessary paperwork (reduced to bare minimum) and handle the funds, both sent from abroad and collected within the country.

Considerable trouble was caused by the many requests from various underground people to see the Delegate in person. They all felt entitled to it, and Ratajski was unwilling to deny such personal contact to anyone. It was the responsibility of the Chief of the Presidium Office to sift those requests ruthlessly and to admit before the Delegate only those who had a valid reason to see him personally.

The budget-finance section functioned in conjunction with the Presidium Office. The funds it managed were received from the government-in-exile and were forwarded in the beginning by various land routes and later by aerial drops. In addition, small sums were contributed by local sources, through voluntary contributions and donations. No data are available as to the final total of monies received by the budget-finance section throughout the occupation years. There are, however, some fragmentary data, showing that in 1941-42 the civil or political authorities of the underground movement received through the military liaison channels about 900,000 German marks; in 1942-43—about 3 million dollars and 3 million marks; in 1943-44—about 5.5 million dollars and about 12 million marks, 164 pounds sterling in gold and about half a million zlotys in occupation currency, the so-called *mlynarki*. The budget-finance section paid out monies to various departments, prepared the budget of the Government Delegacy, drafted financial reports, and kept all accounts. The section was headed from the very beginning until the end of the occupation by Wincenty Bryja of the Peasant Party, president of the Association of Peasant Intelligentsia "Orka."

The final word on financial matters belonged to the Central Auditing Office, similar to its prewar counterpart and charged with keeping tabs on the finances of the Delegacy and its subordinate departments, auditing their accounts, and passing on the appropriateness of their expenditures. The Auditing Office was headed by Stanislaw Peszynski, a Labor Party attorney, and, following his death at the hands of the Gestapo, by former senator Waclaw Januszewski of the Peasant Party.

Also connected with the Presidium Office was the Delegate's Advisor for Foreign Affairs, with functions defined by his title. This post was filled successively by: Roman Knoll, former Polish Ambassador in Berlin, and—after his withdrawal because of disagreements with Delegate Jankowski—by Tadeusz Chromecki, former official of the Ministry of Foreign Affairs.

3. Department of Internal Affairs

Of all the departments, the Department of Internal Affairs was the most clearly linked with the Delegate. Its tasks were both current and future. Among its current tasks was to organize and staff the delegacies established throughout the country (parallel to the administrative division into counties and districts). All appointments were usually approved beforehand by the Central Political Committee and were made according to the so-called "party key," which ensured the democratic character of the delegacies and the use of party-affiliated underground organizations.

Fifteen district delegacies were established: *Warsaw-City*—Delegate Marceli Porowski, Labor Party; *Warsaw-District*—Delegate Jozef Kwasiborski, Labor Party; *Krakow*—Delegate Professor Jan Jakobiec; *Lublin*—successively: Wladyslaw Cholewa and Jan Chmielewski, both from the Peasant Party; *Radom-Kielce*—former mayor of Piotrkow Fiszer, Polish Socialist Party; *Lwow and part of the Tarnopol district*—Professor Franciszek Bujak, Professor Kulczynski (pseudonyms: Szary, Lipowski, Lotny), followed by Assistant Professor Adam Ostrowski who in later years served under the communist regime as the Krakow District Governor and the regime's envoy in Sweden; *Poznan*—successively: Adolf Bninski, killed by the Gestapo; Jan Wojkiewicz, Peasant Party, killed by the Gestapo; Marcin Poprawa, Peasant Party; and a merchant from Gniezno, Leon Jedrowski,

National Party; *Wolyn*—Kazimierz Banach, Peasant Party; *Polesie*—Jozef Barski, Labor Party; *Wilno*—successively: Dr. Zygmunt Federowicz, National Party; Dr. Jerzy Dobrzanski, Polish Socialist Party; Adam Galinski, affiliated with the followers of the late Marshal Pilsudski; *Nowogrodek*—Jan Trzeciak; *Bialystok*—successively: former *Sejm* representative Kazimierz Laszkiewicz, Peasant Party, and Jozef Przybyszewski, National Party; *Torun*—Antoni Antczak, Labor Party; *Katowice*—successively: Ignacy Sikora, president of the metallurgical union, and attorney Jerzy Lewandowicz, son-in-law of Wojciech Korfanty, the Labor Party leader; *Lodz*—Piotr Rychlik, Peasant Party.

The district and county delegacies were set up primarily to carry out instructions and directives received from the central leadership, and to cope with all manner of local problems, frequently with the help of a body composed of representatives of the same political parties of which the Political Coordinating Committee was composed. In theory, district delegacies were organized along the same lines as the Government Delegacy and included similar counterpart departments. In practice, however, local conditions of life under occupation determined the actual pattern of organization. The same was even more true on the county level.

Among the "tasks for the future" assigned to the Department of Internal Affairs, preparations were to made for the takeover of the country following Germany's defeat. With this in mind, a complete administrative structure was developed underground, ready to go into action and assume control at the propitious moment. The final form for these activities was provided in the President's decree of April 26, 1944, pertaining to the establishment of a temporary governmental structure on the territories of the Polish Republic.

In conjunction with other departments, the Department of Internal Affairs also concentrated on working out the best ways to weather the critical days of transition from occupation to independence, salvage as much as possible of wealth and funds left behind by the occupying power, protect state property, industries, farms and estates that had been taken over by the Germans or abandoned by their original owners, as well as hospitals and public utilities, such as power plants and gas works. The problem of the *Volksdeutsche* was studied jointly with the Department of Justice; more lenient procedures were determined for the territories incorporated into the Reich than for the *General Gouvernement*.

The Department of Internal Affairs also organized future police, called the State Security Corps. It numbered several thousand men who were to come out into the open at the time of the takeover.

The Department of Internal Affairs was headed by Leopold Rutkowski, who had worked with Ratajski before the War in the Ministry of Internal Affairs. Rutkowski was followed, successively, by Kazimierz Baginski and by Stefan Korbonski, both of the Peasant Party.

Connected with the Department of Internal Affairs, the Bureau for the New Territories was established in 1942 in order to pave the way for the Polish takeover of East Prussia, West Pomerania, and the Opole Silesia, which—it was correctly assumed—would become part of Poland after the war. The Bureau tackled the gigantic task of working out detailed plans for the takeover in every sector of life and of mobilizing a few thousand experts, each of whom received specific assignments where to go, what to do, and how to proceed when the proper moment arrived. In 1945, the Bureau for the New Territories was absorbed by the Department of Internal Affairs. At the end of the occupation, and with the approval of the underground authorities, the director of the Bureau, Waldyslaw Czajkowski, turned over to the new Ministry for the Recovered Territories all the plans that had been prepared by his office, as well as trained cadres of thousands of functionaries. At that time, the Ministry was headed by Wladyslaw Gomulka; Czajkowski was given the post of vice minister.

4. Department of Information and Press

The main task of the Department of Information and Press was to provide the people with true information and to build up an illegal press that would serve as the organ of the underground authorities. The huge German propaganda machine—making use of, among others, daily Polish-language papers published in the *General Gouvernement*—strove to undermine people's faith in the ultimate victory; it sought to convince them that Poland's independence would never be restored and that their own survival depended on their blind obedience to the German master race. Slander was heaped on Polish history and Polish culture, and ridicule on the Polish government-in-exile. Every means was used to destroy the nation's faith in itself and in a brighter future. To that end, false information was circulated, which, in a country cut off from the free world, deprived of a free press, divested of radios that had been confiscated, was practically impossible to check. It was the Department's job to counteract this propaganda and they succeeded in doing it brilliantly. First of all, a service was organized monitoring the Polish-language broadcasts of the British Broadcasting Corporation (BBC) and later of the Voice of America. Based on these broadcasts, a daily news bulletin was published, called "strips" in popular parlance. In time, the scope of the monitoring service was enlarged to include programs broadcast by neutral and allied stations in English, in French and in Italian. A roundup of the week's news, culled from the "strips" appeared in *The Weekly Review*, published by the Department. A compilation of the most important news of the month, together with the stenotyped programs of the Polish Radio, broadcast by the BBC, was put out by the Press-Information Agency *Serwis* (APIS). All three publications were delivered first of all to the underground leaders, providing them with daily information on world events and the developments on the war fronts. In addition, the Department supplied its publications to all underground organizations linked in one way or another with the Government Delegacy and the Union for Armed Struggle, which assured them the widest distribution. A similar pattern was followed on practically all levels of the underground movement, especially by organizations affiliated with the various political parties, so that within a short time the provinces, too, were humming with their own monitoring services and broadcast bulletins. Many people also did not give up their radios, but kept them hidden, risking their lives to listen to allied broadcasting stations, above all to the BBC and the Voice of America, and sharing the information with their families and trusted friends. As a result, people in occupied Poland were extremely well informed about what was going on in the world and scoffed at the clumsy enemy propaganda.

The Department of Information and Press also published the official organ of the Delegacy, a biweekly called *The Republic of Poland*. Its editorial staff was headed by Franciszek Glowinski and included: Tadeusz Kolski, Witold Zarski, Stefan Krzywoszewski, Marian Grzegorczyk, Leon Brzeski and Jan Mosinski. Among *The Republic*'s contributors were professors Andrzej Tretiak, Waclaw Borowy and Zygmunt Wojciechowski. *The Republic of Poland* contained six regular sections. The official section featured the proclamations, announcements and communiqués of the Government Delegate, the Commander-in-Chief of the Union for Armed Struggle (or, later, of the Home Army), the Directorate of Civil Resistance and the Directorate of Underground Resistance and, after the two organizations were merged, the Directorate of Underground Struggle. Articles presenting the Delegacy's point of view on various political problems were printed in the second section. The third section was devoted to the activities of the government and the emigré National Council, and to the Polish armed forces fighting in the west. The fourth section gave news of the world, especially political news, and of global war developments. The fifth section provided information about the conditions and events in the terrirories incorporated into the Reich and territories under the Soviet occupation. Later on, the Department issued special publications focusing on this subject—*The Western Territories* and *The Eastern Territories*—and put out as supplements to *The Republic of Poland*. The sixth section contained a review of the underground press.

The Republic of Poland appeared from March 1941 until July 1945, that is, until the dissolution of the Government Delegacy.[2]

Finally, the Department of Information and Press prepared for the government-in-exile quarterly reports of the Delegacy on conditions within the occupied country. They provided information on every aspect of national life, spotlighting—among others—policies of the occupying powers; the general reign of terror; economic, social and cultural affairs; the moods and the attitudes of the people, etc. In addition, the Department forwarded periodically separate reports on the territories incorporated into the Reich and territories under the Soviet occupation. All the reports mentioned above made up six volumes of about 1,000 pages each.

From the very beginning until the end of the occupation, the Department of Information and Press was headed by Stanislaw Kauzik (Labor Party),former Department Director in the Ministry of Finances and president of the Publishers' Association.

5. Department of Education and Culture

The Department of Education and Culture was established in order to provide an organizational framework and uniform standards for clandestine instruction. Initiated by the teachers, underground schools sprang up spontaneously in nearly every locality where the Germans had closed the existing institutions, allowing only limited programs in primary schools and a few vocational schools,and banning the teaching of history and geography. According to Himmler's prescription, the Poles were to provide a reservoir of physical laborers for the Reich; all they needed to learn, therefore, was "to count up to 500, to write their name, and to know that by divine order they owed obedience to the Germans."[3] The existing Polish intelligentsia class was to be physically destroyed and not to be ever regenerated again.

Even before the Department of Education and Culture was established in the Delegacy, various teacher and educational groups had formed in December 1939 the so-called Clandestine Study Center and began secret instruction on high school and university levels, as well as supplementary programs for younger children. In time, this action grew into the largest of the underground organizations, with vast armies of pupils and students who had to observe strict rules of conspiracy to attend clandestine classes or lectures. In case of detection, prison or concentration camp awaited both the students and the teachers. Still in 1942, one million and a half children took part in the supplementary educational programs on the primary school level; if found out, their parents were held responsible by the Germans. Underground high schools had over 100,000 students in 1944; in certain counties of the Warsaw school district, high school attendance almost tripled, compared to before the war. Underground universitiees enrolled over 10,000 students in 1944; of these, 748 pursued their studies at the University of Warsaw, 600—at the University of the Western Territories in Warsaw; and 500—at the Jagiellonian University in Krakow. The universities of Lwow and Wilno were also reestablished underground. In addition, there were 10 clandestine pedagogical institutes, training new teaching cadres for the day of Poland's liberation.[4]

The underground schools were an impressive manifestation of the instinct of self-preservation in a nation condemned by the enemy to illiteracy and serfdom.

The results cited above were achieved due to the collaboration of students and teachers under the guidance of, first, the Clandestine Study Center and, later, the Department of Education and Culture of the Government Delegacy. The Department instituted a network of district and county offices, working with their respective delegacies; in certain townships, it even established Township Commissions for Education and Culture. With the approval of the Department, the Educational Office for the Western Territories, organized by Rev. Professor Maksymilian Rhode and transferred to Warsaw because of German terrorism, retained its autonomy.

The main task of the Department was to prepare programs and examinations for the underground schools and to draft future plans for an educational system in independent Poland. The Department also financed underground education; in 1942, for instance, it dispensed for this purpose 3,525,700 zlotys (this did not include subsidies for university professors, paid from the budget of the Department of Welfare.

The cultural section of the Department, headed by the director of the national museum in Warsaw Stanislaw Lorentz, focused primarily on the task of salvaging the works of art and monuments of Polish culture. It also gathered documentation and kept records of the tremendous cultural losses, caused by enemy looting and destruction, in the fields of art, museums, archives and libraries. Because of their

work, most of the cultural treasures taken to Germany were returned to Poland after the war.

Institutions of higher learning were under the supervision of Professor Kazimierz Drewnowski, rector of the Warsaw Polytechnic, and then,
successively, Boleslaw Miklaszewski, rector of the Central School of
Commerce, and Professor Stanislaw Pienkowski from the University
of Warsaw. In Krakow, similar functions were performed by Professor
Wladyslaw Szafer from the Jagiellonian University.

Throughout the entire period of its existence, the Department of
Education and Culture was headed by Czeslaw Wycech (Peasant
Party), president of the Union of Polish Teachers before the war,
and Speaker of the *Sejm* in postwar Poland.

6. Department of Labor and Social Welfare

The main task of the Department of Labor and Social Welfare
was to provide assistance and aid to all political prisoners and to
their families; this was done through an organization affiliated with
the Department, called "Patronage." The Department also helped
scholars, professors, writers, artists, and other people who were considered particularly valuable in national life. To this end, it exerted
its influence through philanthropic organizations such as the Central
Welfare Council, established with the approval of the occupying
authorities and directed by Adam Ronikier, or the Polish Red Cross,
which was also permitted to carry on its activities. Similar operations
were conducted in the provinces by specially trained officers connected with the county or district delegacies.

After the Warsaw Rising, the work of the Department increased
manyfold. Help was needed for hundreds of thousands of the inhabitants of Warsaw, driven out of the city by the Germans. The Department also financed directly over a hundred temporary hospitals, located in improvised quarters, private houses and apartments in the
vicinity of the capital, and caring for thousands of sick and wounded
people.

Plans were made, with regard to the future, for taking over or
running those areas of state administration that lay within the competence of the Department of Labor and Social Welfare.

Of all the departments of the Government Delegacy, the Department of Labor and Social Welfare had the highest budget. In 1942,
for instance, it amounted to 4,540,500 zlotys.

The Department was headed successively by: Jan Stanislaw Jankow-
ski, former Minister of Labor and Social Welfare and later Government
Delegate in Poland; Judge Stefan Mateja (Labor Party), shot by the
Germans on the roof of a burning house during the Warsaw Rising,

while he was trying to extinguish the fire, and Franciszek Bialas (Polish Socialist Party).

7. Department of Industry and Commerce

In regard to the current problems, the Department of Industry and Commerce prepared a register of industrial and commercial enterprises taken over by the Germans, and worked out a plan, in conjunction with the Department of Internal Affairs, to reclaim and safeguard them at the end of the occupation. The Department also followed closely all German policies pertaining to industry and commerce, and prepared relevant reports for the Delegate and the government-in-exile.

With a view toward the future, the Department prepared cadres of personnel and drafted administrative measures needed to reestablish immediately after the war the Ministry of Industry and Commerce and its subordinate agencies.

The Department of Industry and Commerce was headed by Boleslaw Rutkowski, director of the Chambers of Commerce and Industry Association before the war. He was killed during the Warsaw Rising.

8. Department of Agriculture

The Department of Agriculture was established together with the autonomous Administration of State Forests, headed by Teofil Lorkiewicz, former Administrator of State Forests from Poznan. The Department studied German agricultural policies and prepared pertinent reports for the Delegate and the Government. It trained cadres of future personnel and drew up the measures required for the speedy reestablishment of the Ministry of Agriculture and its subordinate agencies. It also worked on a project of postwar government agrarian policy, particularly the agrarian reform.

The Department of Agriculture was headed successively by Witold Maringe, an agriculturist and economist, and Zygmunt Zaleski (Peasant Party), also an agriculturist.

9. Department of Justice

Similarly to other departments of the Delegacy, the Department of Justice observed closely German policies in its own area of competence and prepared relevant reports and plans for future legislation. But it also had another, different task. Since the lower courts were permitted to continue their functions, the Department exerted its influence to impress upon the judges their obligation to be guided in their decisions, both in civil and criminal cases, not by enemy pressures, but by the best national interest.

The Department did not feel competent to establish the under-ground courts of justice and left this task to the Directorate of Civil Resistance. However, it assisted in working out the legal aspects of this problem with reference to the Polish prewar criminal law, supplemented by the resolution of the Ministers' Council for Homeland Affairs of April 16, 1940, pertaining to underground courts.

The Department of Justice was headed successively by: Leon Nowodworski (National Party), former dean of the Warsaw Bar, and, following his death, by Feliks Zadrowski, an attorney from the Labor Party.

10. Department of Liquidating the Effects of War

The Department was primarily concerned with the registration and compilation of losses inflicted by occupation and war in every area of national life. The reports it prepared were to form the basis for demands for appropriate reparations after victory was won. An impressive amount of work was accomplished in this regard.

The Department was headed successively by: Antoni Olszewski, former Minister of Industry and Commerce, and by Bronislaw Domoslawski, a fiscal expert.

11. Department of Public Works and Reconstruction

The Department compiled a register of destruction suffered by Polish cities, ports, railroads, highways, etc. in the course of war operations or during the occupation. It also prepared a comprehensive program of rehabilitation and reconstruction after the war.

The Department of Public Works and Reconstruction was headed successively by: Stefan Bryla, professor of the Warsaw Polytechnic, and, following his death at the hands of the Gestapo, by Bronislaw Ziemiecki (Polish Socialist Party), former Minister of Labor and Social Welfare; following Ziemiecki's arrest by the Gestapo in February 1944 and his execution in the ruins of the Warsaw Ghetto, the post was taken over by Stanislaw Araszkiewicz of the Peasant Party.

12. Department of National Defense

The Department of National Defense was established very late—in November 1944, i.e., after the Warsaw Rising, which constituted such a critical turning point in the existence of the underground armed forces. However, the question of the advisability of establishing such a department had come to the fore as early as 1941. It was raised by parties' representatives on the Political Coordinating Committee, who feared the dangerous tendencies within the Union for Armed Struggle to assume the reins of power at the critical moment.

In order to forestall such a possibility, it was argued, a superimposed Department of National Defense should be created, and it should be headed by a civilian. This initiative was backed most forcibly by the National Party whose misgivings were strong enough to prompt it to build up its own military units, known as the National Military Organization. The example of the National Party was shortly followed by the Peasant Party, which organized its Peasant Battalions, and by the Polish Socialist Party, which reconstituted its Socialist Fighting Organization, harking back to the events of 1905. However, in the wake of long negotiations with the Union for Armed Struggle and its successor, the Home Army, all three party military organizations were subordinated to the High Command and merged in the Home Army.

In 1941, the National Party submitted to the Political Coordinating Committee a detailed plan for the establishment of a Department of National Defense. The plan was approved—with the Socialist representative abstaining—but was never implemented because of the vehement opposition from General Rowecki, who considered the PCC initiative as unwarranted meddling in strictly military affairs. Rowecki also argued that all the offices that had been grouped before the war in the Ministry of Military Affairs, were now included in the High Command, and that to create the Ministry's counterpart at this point would be superfluous and a duplication of organizational efforts.

The debate went on for nearly three years and ended in November 1944 with the appointment of Jerzy Michalewski as director of the Department of National Defense, charged with establishing the Department. The appointment was made by Delegate Jankowski, with the concurrence of General Leopold Okulicki, at that time Commander of the Home Army. However, the swift turn of events precluded the need for the establishment of the Department, and Michalewski restricted his activities to maintaining contact between Delegate Jankowski and General Okulicki; following their arrest, he performed the same services for Jankowski's successor—Stefan Korbonski, and Okulicki's successor—Colonel Jan Rzepecki.

13. Other Departments

Other departments—such as the Department of Finances (headed, first, by the former Minister of Finances Czeslaw Klarner and later by a former official of the Ministry, Jozef Zajda), the Department of Postal and Telegraph Services (headed by Dziekan), or the Department of Communications (headed by former Vice Minister of Communications Czapski)—limited their operations to the close study of German policies in their respective areas of competence and to the preparation of substantive reports. With an eye to the future, they worked on readying personnel cadres and drafting plans and measures required for the instant takeover and operation of pertinent agencies and ministries once the occupation ended. The limited scope of the Department of Communications and the Department of Postal and Telegraph Services was undoubtedly due to the fact that they both were duplicated by the military.

VIII

DECREES, PRONOUNCEMENTS AND PROCLAMATIONS
OF THE GOVERNMENT DELEGATES

Developments in occupied Poland were reflected, among others, in the following pronouncements of the Government Delegates:

1. The pronouncement of Delegate Piekalkiewicz of October 1, 1942, warned all Polish functionaries against collaborating with the Germans in roundups and forced deportations to the Reich.

2. The appeal of Delegate Piekalkiewicz of November 20, 1942, called on all Poles to give help and assistance to one another.

3. The decree of Delegate Jankowski of July 7, 1943, proclaimed national mourning following the death of General Sikorski.

4. The pronouncement of Delegate Jankowski of September 1, 1943, regarding the governmental crisis in London in the wake of General Sikorski's death.

5. The pronouncement of Delegate Jankowski of September 14, 1943, proclaimed the completion of the task of political consolidation in Poland.

6. The protest of Delegate Jankowski of October 22, 1943, against mass executions and manhunts.

7. A warning from Delegate Jankowski (December 15, 1943) against irresponsible, wildcat operations.

8. The declaration of Delegate Jankowski of January 9, 1944 announcing the formation of the Council of National Unity.

9. The declaration of Delegate Jankowski of May 3, 1944, in connection with the anniversary of the Constitution of May 3, 1791.

10. A dispatch, sent on May 24, 1944 by Delegate Jankowski and the Council of National Unity, congratulating General Wladyslaw Anders on the victories of the Polish Second Corps in Italy.[1]

IX

THE HOME ARMY

1. The Organization

By an order of the Commander-in-Chief, dated February 14, 1942, the name of the Union for Armed Struggle was changed to the Home Army. It was commanded by General Stefan Rowecki (pseudonyms: Rakon, Grabica, Inzynier, Kalina, Grot). Following Rowecki's arrest by the Gestapo in Warsaw, in his hideout at 14 Spiska Strreet, on June 30, 1943, the command was taken over by Tadeusz Komorowski (pseudonyms: Bor, Korczak, Lawina), promoted in the meantime to the rank of general. The organization of the underground army, initiated by General Michal Tokarzewski-Karaszewicz, underwent certain changes with the passing of time and, in the last phase of its development, appeared as follows:

At the head of the Home Army stood the Commander, assisted by his Chief of Staff, Colonel Janusz Albrecht. Following Albrecht's arrest by the Gestapo, his release, and his suicide, General Tadeusz Pelczynski (pseudonym: Grzegorz) became the Home Army's Chief of Staff. The High Command was composed of 31 staff units, of which the most important were the following: organization, operations (including intelligence and reconnaissance), liaison, quartermaster services, communications, diversion (*Kedyw*), army offices, and the bureau of information and propaganda (BIP). The entire territory of Poland was divided into three regions—the Bialystok region, the Lwow region and the western region; after 1944, these were changed to: the Warsaw region, the Lwow region and the western region. Following the lines of the administrative division, each region was divided into districts (corresponding to administrative districts), each district into sectors (corresponding to counties), and each sector into posts (corresponding to townships). Districts in Central Poland were subject directly to the High Command of the Home Army. Their commanders—down to the county level—had their own staffs. A platoon constituted the lowest rung of the organizational ladder; commanded by a platoon leader, it comprised three squads, each divided in turn into three sections of five men each. On occasion, several platoons would join to form a company, or several companies to form a battalion. At its peak, the Home Army numbered

380,175 men, including 10,756 officers, 7,506 cadet officers and 87,886 noncommissioned officers. In fighting the Germans, the Home Army lost 62,133 men: 4,970 officers, 29,075 noncommissioned officers and 28,088 soldiers. These figures do not include losses suffered during the Warsaw Rising, in the course of which about 10,200 Home Army soldiers and about 150 to 200 thousand civilians lost their lives.[1]

2. Consolidating the Underground

The single most important organizational task of the underground High Command was to complete the consolidation of dozens of conspiracies of a military character. This job had been started already by General Tokarzewski, in accordance with the instructions from the government-in-exile or the Commander-in-Chief, recognizing the Union for Armed Struggle (later, the Home Army) as the Polish Army. In the process of consolidation, which lasted almost until the time of the Warsaw Rising, the following larger underground organizations or military units affiliated with various political parties, were either subordinated to or incorporated into the Home Army: the Peasant Battalions, the military force of the Peasant Party; the National Military Organization, established by the National Party, the Socialist Fighting Organization, recreated by the Polish Socialist Party; the Camp of Fighting Poland, started by Pilsudski's followers; the military organization founded in southern Poland by Colonel Tadeusz Komorowski and Colonel Klemens Rudnicki; the Secret Polish Army; the "Unia," affiliated with the Labor Party; the Union for Military Action; the "Raclawice," organized by the Central Association of Rural Youth SIEW; the Polish Military Organization; the Freedom and People Union; the Armed Confederacy; the Association of the Reserve Noncommissioned Officers; the Secret Military Organization; and those units of the National Armed Forces that had originated in the National Military Organization.

The following organizations refused to recognize the authority of the Union for Armed Struggle or, later, the Home Army: the radical leftist Polish People's Army; the communist People's Army (at least part of which, however, fought later under the Home Army's command during the Warsaw Rising); and, on the extreme right, those units of the National Armed Forces that gave their allegiance to the Rampart Group, the underground continuation of the prewar National-Radical Camp.

Parallel to this consolidating action there developed particular services, which combined to make up that underground army which, on the one hand, had to face the German enemy daily—within a few days after the outbreak of the German-Soviet war on June 21, 1941, the Germans took over all the territories occupied previously by the Soviets—and on the other, had to prepare for the day of reckoning when the whole nation would rise up in arms.

3. Liaison

One of these services was liaison, organized with the outstanding participation of women. Among others, regular contact was maintained with the government-in-exile by means of clandestine radio stations (which suffered heavy losses in men and equipment because of the counteraction by the German goniometric teams), and also by dozens of couriers and emissaries who generally used the land routes, taking advantage of the underground bases established in Budapest, in Bucharest and in Kaunas (this last one was later transferred to Stockholm). Among the emissaries, the most important role fell to Jan Kozielewski (pseudonym: Karski) who had been one of the first government emissaries to arrive in Poland. On his return to the west, Karski could provide eyewitness information about conditions in Poland—and particularly about the German terror and the extermination of the Jews—not only to the government-in-exile, but also to such western leaders as Franklin Delano Roosevelt and the British Foreign Secretary Anthony Eden, both of whom he saw personally. After Karski came other emissaries: Jan Nowak, who twice made the long journey from the west to Poland and back, Jerzy Lerski, Czeslaw Raczkowski, and many others. Among the military emissaries, the most important mission was that of Colonel Kazimierz Iranek-Osmecki, a member of the High Command of the Home Army.

In connection with maintaining liaison with the government in London, three landings of allied aircraft were made in Poland. The planes landed on secret airfields, hidden in the forests. Known as "bridges," these were difficult and extremely risky operations, requiring utmost precision and closest cooperation with the local Home Army units.

The first "bridge" took place on the night of April 15, 1944. A British plane, taking off from Brindisi in Italy, landed on the secret airfield near Belzyce in the Lublin district. It brought to Poland two officers from the Supreme Headquarters and took off on its way back west carrying aboard: Zygmunt Berezowski of the National Party (who shortly became a member of the Polish government in London); Stanislaw Oltarzewski, an emissary of the Government Delegate in Poland; and three officers from the High Command of the Home Army.

The second "bridge" landing was made on the night of May 29, 1944. Another British plane, also starting from Brindisi, landed in the vicinity of Zaborow near Tarnow. This time the plane brought to Poland General Tadeusz Kossakowski and took back Jan Domanski, a political emissary of the Peasant Party.

The third "bridge" operation was carried out on the night of July 25, 1944. A British plane, starting from Brindisi, landed again near Zaborow, bringing three officers from the Supreme Headquarters. It took off for the West with the following aboard: Tomasz Arciszewski, leader of the Polish Socialist Party, who later served as premier of the Polish government in London; Dr. Jozef Retinger, a British-Polish emissary, who had parachuted into Poland earlier and was now returning on the completion of the missions assigned to him by, on the one hand, the British government and, on the other, by the Polish government; Captain Jerzy Chmielewski of the Home Army, who carried with him drawings and parts of the German V-1 rocket.[2]

4. Training

The underground army training programs provided five months of schooling for the officer cadets of infantry reserves and four months for the noncommissioned officers. In 1941 and 1942 these schools trained 1,162 students; in 1943—3,110 students; and in 1944—4,275 students. In addition, special training courses were organized such as: diversion (completed by 832 students), assault, mechanics, artillery, armaments, propaganda, and many others.

At the end of the course, each student took an examination including both the theory and the practice of the subject given. As a practical exercise in one case, for instance, a group of cadets (observed by the school commander) stole at night to a German airfield and burned all the planes, then withdrew under German fire without a single casualty.

Some schools operated in the forests, alongside the partisan units. Graduation exercises at one of the training centers of the Peasant Battalions were held in the forest near Zamosc. They began with the field Mass, attended also by the local people from the area, and ended with a march-past of the students and a soldiers' meal—all under the watchful eye of German Stork reconnaissance planes, patrolling the woods.

The underground training programs included also new subjects, which in the curricula of military schools before the war belonged to historical, rather than practical studies. Among these were diversion, guerilla warfare, and—above all—the principles of insurgency warfare, vastly different from the regular army operations.

5. Intelligence

At the request of the Commander-in-Chief and the allied military leaders, the intelligence operations of the Polish underground were extended beyond the borders of Poland to include also the neighboring countries, i.e., the German Reich and the USSR. In 1941 and 1942, these operations ranged as far as the German armies, i.e., to Leningrad, Moscow, the banks of the Volga, and the Caucasia. The most striking feature of these operations was their universality. Everybody in Poland, it seemed, watched the Germans closely and passed on information to proper channels. In the Reich, intelligence relied primarily on the Poles who had been deported as forced labor and were working in Germany's numerous war industries. In Russia, it utilized the Todt organization, which hundreds of agents joined as volunteers on orders of the Polish underground authorities. Polish railroad men, who often rode their trains deep into the Reich or the USSR, also played a major role in collecting intelligence information.

German preparations for an attack on Russia did not escape the attention of the Home Army intelligence, which kept the Soviets abreast of the developments through the intermediary of the British military mission in Moscow. In April 1942, i.e., after the outbreak of the Soviet-German war, the Russians even proposed that direct communication be established for intelligence purposes between the radio station of the Polish military mission (located in Srebrny Bor near Moscow) and the radio station of the Home Army's High Command. When the Polish Army under General Wladyslaw Anders was about to leave the Soviet Union, this communication was broken off at the Soviets' request.

The work of the Polish intelligence service was rated very highly by the allied General Staffs.[3]

Among its most important accomplishments, the Polish intelligence discovered that a new, secret weapon (as it turned out later: rockets) was being tested at Peenemünde in Germany, and forwarded to London the plans of the site. As a result, several hundreds of British bombers were sent over the testing grounds on the night of August 17, 1943, demolishing the station completely. Chief of Staff of the German Luftwaffe, General Oberst Jeschonek (born in 1900 in Inowroclaw, undoutedly of Polish extraction) perished during that air raid. According to other sources, he committed suicide.

The Polish intelligence service made a vital contribution to ultimate victory by providing the allies with the drawings and parts of the German rockets. Tests of the new weapon were moved from Peenemünde to Poland, to a small place called Blizna, near Mielec. Rockets fired from these new testing grounds exploded most frequently in the vicinity of Sarnaki, near Siedlce, close to the Bug River. German patrols were dispersed throughout that area beforehand in order to collect all splinters after the explosion, so as to leave no fragments of the missile. But the Home Army intelligence units were also on the lookout and sometimes managed to beat the Germans in a race to the site of the explosion. Once there, they collected all remaining fragments—warheads, tubes, parts of mechanism, and splinters—and recorded the observations of the local people pertaining to the flight of the rocket, the strength of explosion, etc. Not infrequently, there were skirmishes between the Home Army units and the Germans at those sites. All the material collected was forwarded to Warsaw, where a team of experts conducted further studies, measurements and evaluations.

At the end of May 1943, one of the rockets came down in the vicinity of Sarnaki, but failed to explode. The Home Army patrol was the first to arrive on the scene. They heaved the rocket off the bank and dumped it into the river. When the German patrol left after a fruitless search, the Home Army soldiers came back and hauled the rocket out of the water. Experts arrived from Warsaw disassembled the rocket, took hundreds of photographs of various parts, made drawings, took measurements, prepared detailed descriptions, and—most important—took with them a number of original parts. All this was turned over to Captain Jerzy Chmielewski of the Home Army, who boarded a British plane at a secret airfield on the night of July 25, 1944 (Operation "Bridge III"), and reached London safely, bringing with him his precious cargo. Detailed knowledge of the construction and characteristics of V-I thus acquired, facilitated and speeded up British defense preparations against the German rockets.[4]

Recently revealed secrets of the intelligence services of France and Great Britain brought to light the most crucial Polish contribution: In July 1939, the Poles gave to the Allies a duplicate of the German coding machine "Enigma" constructed by the Polish intelligence service; this made it possible for the Allies to read the dispatches of Hitler and his commanders throughout the war.

A separate section of "counterintelligence" concentrated on defense against the penetration of the underground by the Gestapo or by the German police or administration. It was also its task to ferret out information about future German plans and proposed moves, in order to mount appropriate counteraction. On its part, the German intelligence "offensive" attempted to penetrate the underground and to paralyze its activity by wresting its secrets, through arrests and executions. A fascinating duel of intelligence services ensued, in which both sides won victories and suffered defeats. The work of the Polish intelligence, which had established in minute detail the patterns of habits and movements of SS General Franz Kutschera, commandant of the SS and police in the Warsaw district, made it possible to carry out his assassination on Aleje Ujazdowskie on February 1, 1944, in an action that took only 1 minute and 40 seconds. On the other hand, a split second identification by a German agent, Eugeniusz Swierczewski, of General Rowecki crossing the street, led the Gestapo to the General's hideout at 14 Spiska Street, where he was arrested on June 30, 1943.

6. Arms and Equipment

Weapons that the Home Army had at its disposal came from four different sources: arms buried by the Polish armies on the battlefields of the September campaign; arms purchased or captured from the Germans; arms manufactured by the Home Army; and arms received from the air drops.

As far as the first source of supply is concerned, a tally of buried arms produced the following count: 614 heavy machine guns and 535,765 rounds of ammunition; 1,193 light machine guns and 203,505 rounds of ammunition; 33,052 rifles and 2,999,988 rounds; 6,732 pistols and 1,548,144 rounds; 28 antitank light field guns and 3,083 rounds of ammunition; 25 antitank rifles and 1,406 rounds of ammunition; 43,154 hand grenades. Because of inadequate conservation, due to lack of proper materials, most of these guns were in poor condition; when they were dug up—mainly in 1944, in preparation for Operation Tempest—only 30% were usable.

Arms purchases from the German soldiers, especially after it became obvious that Germany was headed for defeat, were conducted on a "grass roots" level at prices established by the Home Army Command. Purchases were made by individual units, and sometimes even by individual soldiers of the Home Army. All such deals were dangerous, because the Gestapo, aware of the existence of this Polish-German trade in arms, tried to check it by sending their agents provocateurs to the trading points that were usually fairly well known. Ordinarily, the trade was limited to sidearms, submachine guns and grenades, but occasionally light and heavy machine guns could also be purchased.

It was much easier to trade with the Italian and Hungarian units stationed in Poland, who willingly sold arms to the Polish underground. However, negotiations regarding the purchase of large quantities of arms, including artillery and antitank weapons, were broken off by the Hungarians, who feared the consequences of such a deal.

On the other hand, efforts to capture weapons from the Germans proved highly successful. Raids were conducted on transport trains, carrying arms to the front lines, on guardhouses and gendarmerie posts. On occasion, a Home Army soldier would tackle a German soldier and deprive him of his arms. Sizable quantities of machine guns, including heavy machine guns, were captured, as well as ammunition. There were also some instances of captured armored cars and antitank guns, and during the Warsaw Rising even a few tanks were captured.

Underground manufacture of arms was carried on in three kinds of workshops: those that were run by the Germans, those that were merely controlled by the Germans, and those that were run by the Home Army. In the first category, there were the prewar Polish armaments factories, whose employees and workers belonged to the underground movement. In order to procure arms for the Home Army not only did they take advantage of every slip-up in the German system of controls, but also they managed occasionally to bring from Germany needed precision tools and parts, requisitioned on official German forms. In this production were involved three foundries of iron and semi-precious metals, ten mechanical and chemical plants, nineteen technical workshops of various kinds, three laboratories, one steel mill and rolling mill, and indirectly also: Junkers in Dessau, Zeiss in Jena, Famo in Breslau, Magdeburg Werke in Magdeburg, Bruhn Werke in Braunschweig and Stock in Berlin.

Smaller shops (under 100 workers) were usually placed under German control, rather than outright management, and work conditions there were somewhat easier. They produced mostly automatic pistols and flamethrowers, which were to be used so extensively during the Warsaw Rising. The quality of arms they produced for the underground was so high that German suspicions turned toward the armament plants which, they thought, were the only ones capable of such excellence.

The Home Army's own clandestine arms production was carried out in five mechanical shops, two shops that manufactured pistol barrels, two assembly shops for automatic pistols, two testing ranges, two assembly and development shops, and four shops producing explosives.

In addition to automatic pistols (of Blyskawica and Sten type) and cartridge magazines, flamethrowers, bombs, road mines, and hand grenades, these shops produced also all sorts of explosive devices—detonators of various kinds, time fuses and percussion caps. Hundreds of people worked in these shops, and all of them, without an exception, were members of the underground organization.

One of these shops, located in the Jarnuszkiewicz factory in Warsaw and equipped with a subterranean rifle range, was designated after the war as a national and historical monument.

As for the supplies received through allied air drops, the most eagerly sought after were the antitank weapons (PIAT) and an explosive substance ("plastic"), neither of which could be produced in occupied Poland. Along with matériel, the allied planes also parachuted money and highly qualified instructors and officers who were to play an important role in the struggle against the Germans; finally, they also brought couriers and emissaries.

Altogether, 485 drops were made, delivering to Poland: 346 parachutists (one of them, a woman), 28 political couriers, 4,802 containers, 2,971 packages, and 58 receptacles with a total weight of 600.9 tons. In the course of these operations, 70 planes were lost and 62 crews (of which 28 were Polish), as well as 11 parachutists. In a separate operation, carried out on the night of December 26, 1944, a five-man British military mission, led by Colonel D. T. Hudson, parachuted near Zarki in the Radom district.[5]

In a different kind of endeavor, one hundred thousand maps were provided for the Home Army by four printing shops, three drafting shops and eight depositories. Supplies such as gloves, underwear, blankets, and the all-important medical kits, were also produced by the underground or obtained by various means from the German warehouses.

7. Finances

Funds used by the Union for Armed Struggle or the Home Army came mainly from remittances sent by the government-in-exile, first, by underground land routes and later, by air drops. Money was carried in specially made, sealed, silk belts worn by the parachutists. Only a small percent of the money came from local sources, e.g., remnants of prewar government funds, public donations (collected, for instance, by an organization called "Uprawa"), or money captured from the Germans. Altogether the following sums were transmitted to Poland for the use of civil and military authorities: 34,823,163 dollars in paper and in gold; 1,775 British pounds in gold; 19,089,500 German marks; 40,569,800 Polish zlotys (in occupation currency); 10,000 Hungarian pengös.[6] All military funds were passed on to the Bureau of Finance and Audit, subject directly to the Commander of the Home Army.

Disbursements were made in two categories: personnel and matériel. Included in the personnel outlays were monthly subsidies for those who worked full time for the underground and thus were unable to earn their living in other ways. The Home Army soldiers, generally speaking, received no pay, and thousands of them lived in utmost poverty. Subsidies for people in leadership positions amounted to the equivalent of $16-18 per month, for middle level—$10-12 per month, and for the lower level—$6-9 per month.

Expenditures for matériel were larger by far and amounted to 80% of total outlays. They included purchases of materials needed for the production of explosives; of arms, ammunition, and other military supplies and equipment; of printing presses, paper, and printing inks; of medicines and medical instruments; they also included the cost of intelligence and diversion operations, the construction of hiding places, etc.

Both the receipts and the outlays were verified by a special auditing commission, which sent in its reports to the High Command of the Home Army, and copies to the Commander-in-Chief's staff in London.

In 1943, the coffers of the Home Army were handsomely replenished due to the spectacular capture of 100 million zlotys from the truck of the German-controlled bank of issue.

8. Information and Propaganda

The purpose and the activities behind the creation of the Department of Information and Press in the Government Delegacy pertained to the entire country. The Bureau of Information and Propaganda (BIP), a special Section VI of the High Command of the Home Army, reaching out to the provinces through subordinate district BIPs, was set up specifically for the rank and file of the underground army. Propaganda was recognized as an extremely valuable weapon in the struggle against the invader and was conducted on three different levels. "Positive propaganda" was aimed at the Home Army rank and file and at the prisoner of war camps; "diversionary propaganda" was used against the enemy; "counterpropaganda" served to counteract the German propaganda efforts. In accordance with the means used, it was classified as "written" (leaflets, inscriptions on the city walls), broadcast (bulletin containing monitored broadcasts from the West), and "whispered" (spread by word of mouth).

The main object of the "positive propaganda" was to instill the spirit of citizenship and patriotism in the Home Army ranks. This was done by disseminating accurate information on the international situation and war operations (especially those in which the Polish forces in the West were taking part), and on positions taken by the government-in-exile and the underground leadership, as well as instructions issued by them; finally, discussions were held pertaining to international problems and educational-military matters. There was no need, however, to exhort those soldiers to carry on their struggle against the invader. If anything, it was rather necessary to restrain their ardor on occasion.

The Home Army press, with a circulation of over 200,000 throughout the country and some 50 publications (to count only the more important), was the primary means used. The most influential among the underground publications was *Biuletyn Informacyjny* (The Information Bulletin), a weekly which came out first on November 5, 1939. At its peak, the Bulletin had a circulation of 50,000. Next in popularity was the biweekly *Wiadomosci Polskie* (The Polish News), which had also begun its publication in November 1939 and was aimed at a more highbrow readership. The Polish News was the organ of the High Command of the Home Army and presented the Headquarters views on basic issues. Circulation of The Polish News reached 10,000 at its highest point.

In addition, the following periodicals were published: the monthly *Insurekcja* (circulation: 7,000) focused on professional military matters; another monthly, *Zolnierz Polski* (The Polish Soldier) (circulation: 12,000) was of an educational character; *Agencja Prasowa* supplied weekly review of news from Poland and abroad for the entire underground press; *Agencja Wsbodnia* (Eastern Agency) and *Agencja Zachodnia* (Western Agency), first published in 1943 and merged in 1944 into *Sprawy Polskie* (Polish Affairs), were devoted to the problems of Polish eastern and western territories respectively; *Glos Ojczyzny* (The Voice of the Fatherland) was published for the Polish soldiers in German POW camps and Polish laborers deported to Germany; biweekly *Glos Polski* (Voice of Poland) was geared specifically to counteract German propaganda. Three other special publications should also be listed here: a monthly for Silesia, a weekly for Lodz and vicinity (incorporated into the Reich), and a weekly for Wolyn (under Soviet occupation).

Finally, the keen need for current, up-to-date news was filled by *Dziennik Radiowy* (The Radio Daily), a mimeographed publication, bringing daily monitored BBC broadcasts and the news from the Reuters Agency.

In addition to the publications received from the Headquarters, individual Home Army districts also produced their own publications. In Krakow, *Malopolski Biuletyn Informacyjny* (Information Bulletin for Malopolska) and *Malopolska Agencja Prasowa* were published; in Lwow—*Biuletyn Informacyjny Ziemi Czerwienskiej* (Information Bulletin for the Czerwien Lands) and *Kobieta w Walce* (Women at War) of which only eight issues appeared; in Wilno—*Niepodleglosc* (Independence); in Polesie—*Przeglad Polityczny* (The Political Review); in Lublin—*Twierdza* (The Fortress) and the "forest sheets" of the local partisan units.

Books were also published by the Bureau of Information and Propaganda. The first to appear was *Rocks for the Rampart*, by Aleksander Kaminski, a scouting leader using the pseudonym of "Juliusz Gorecki;" it described the activities of the underground Boy Scouts, particularly the so-called "little sabotage." The book was tremendously popular in the underground, and after the war it was published again, both in Poland and abroad (as one of the emigré publications).

BIP also printed two songbooks, one of which—*Songs in Arms*—contained words and music of 19 songs born in the underground, and the other—sixteen. In addition, BIP issued a number of pamphlets dealing with current problems; 50 thousand White Eagle stickers for a national holiday; three pictures of "Our Lady Expelled," "Our Lady of Ostra Brama," and "Saint Barbara, Patroness of the People of the Underground;" leaflets in Ukrainian, Byelorussian, Lithuanian and Czech (these last ones, with a picture of Masaryk), appealing for a reconciliation and collaboration with these national groups.

One special section of BIP, called "Akcja K" (and later "R"), concentrated on fighting the communist propaganda. It put out the biweekly *Glos Ludu* (Voice of the People), intended for the countryside, and *Wolnosc Robotnicza* (Workers' Freedom) for the workers; another biweekly, *Agencja*, provided anticommunist materials for the underground press. Throughout the city, on houses, fences and walls, inscriptions were placed: "PPR—Platne Pacholki Rosji" (Polish Workers Party—Paid Flunkies of Russia). All BIP publications were produced by the Clandestine Army Press, which—in Warsaw alone—operated five printing shops. Some of these shops were located in deep dugouts, lined with brick and equipped with ventilation and precision alarm systems. In addition, there was a photochemigraphy department, a lithography department and a bindery. In the spring of 1944, these operations suffered a heavy blow; following their detection by the Germans, most of the printing shops were lost, and many of the typesetters arrested. These losses, however, were made up within a short time. Distribution of all BIP publications, whether produced in Warsaw or in the provinces, was handled by the Liaison Section of the Bureau of Information and Propaganda. Hundreds of contact-girls and carriers were involved in the distribution of the underground publications, crisscrossing the country by every conceivable means of communication, on foot, by train and by car. Distribution on such a massive scale resulted in heavy losses over the years of occupation. Hundreds of distributors perished at the hands of the Gestapo and the gendarmerie.

A courtesy copy of each issue of The Information Bulletin was regularly sent by mail to Dr. Fischer, the German Governor of the Warsaw district.

Throughout the period of occupation, the Bureau of Information and Propaganda was headed by Colonel Jan Rzepecki (pseudonyms: Sedzia, Rejent, Jan).

9. Military Bureaus Administration (code name: Briefcase)

The Polish Underground State was founded on two tenets: national self-defense and ceaseless struggle against the invader, culminating in the general rising. The first mention of such a rising may be found already in General Sosnkowski's instruction sent to Rowecki on December 4, 1939, that is, barely two months after the September war had ended.[7] Purely military preparations for the national rising began when the Service for Poland's Victory was born, and went on uninterruptedly for nearly five years, carried on by the Union for Armed Struggle and the Home Army. In addition to military preparations, there was also the need to prepare the country for the uprising. Primarily, there was the need of ensuring a measure of safety behind the fighting lines and of providing the Home Army with arms, uniforms, provisions, medicines, and all other needed supplies. This required the setting up of a state administration and police, maintaining communication lines by rail and other means, establishing liaison, operating various war industries, taking over banking, organizing food deliveries—briefly, creating a viable administrative and economic apparatus. In order to realize these goals, General Rowecki decided to set up the office of the Military Bureaus Administration, basing his action on the decree on the state of war. He proposed that Military Bureaus be established on the ministerial level, Military Departments—on the district level, and Military Divisions on the county level.

Rowecki's proposal met with a determined opposition on the part of the Government Delegate and members of the Political Coordinating Committee who feared this was the first step toward the complete military takeover of the country when the moment arrived. Also, to carry out Rowecki's plan meant to duplicate the work of the Government Delegacy departments, since they were preparing for precisely the same tasks Rowecki had in mind: to step in at the decisive moment and take over the reins of state administration at all levels.

Rowecki argued that delegacies in districts and counties were staffed "according to a party key," that is, by incompetent people, who made but little progress in preparing the future administrative machinery. Accordingly, Rowecki went on with his plans and created eight Military Bureaus, corresponding to the underground Departments of the Government Delegacy; 16 Military Departments on the district level (including three for the territories, which—it was foreseen—were likely to be within Poland's borders after the war: East Prussia, Gdansk, the Teschen Silesia and the Opole Silesia); and about 40 Military Divisions on the county level. Altogether, about 15,000 future functionaries were assembled within the framework of Operation Briefcase.[8]

From its beginning until the end, the Military Bureaus Administration was headed by the former county administrator Ludwik Muzyczka (pseudonym: Benedykt).

In time, however, the Commander of the Home Army ordered the consolidation of the Military Bureaus Administration with the administrative network set up by the Government Delegacy (August 1, 1943). This was brought about by the pressure exerted, first, on Rowecki—and after his arrest on General Komorowski (Bor)—and also by the considerable growth of the district and county delegacies. The chiefs of the military bureaus at all levels became deputies to the corresponding functionaries of the Delegacy. Only the railroads, the postal and telegraph services, and the war industries (about 40 production units) remained under military management. Jerzy Strowski, a high official in the prewar administration, was appointed by the Government Delegate as the coordinator of the consolidating activities.

The task of consolidation was completed by the decree of the President of the Republic, issued on April 26, 1944, and pertaining to the establishment of a temporary governmental structure on the territories of the Polish Republic. The Decree placed supreme powers in the hands of the Government Delegate and at the same time authorized the Commander of the Home Army to bring before the Delegate his own proposals regarding all matters connected with the military operations. By subordinating the military to the political authorities, the Decree affirmed an important principle, while at the same time giving the military the right to present to the Delegate their demands and proposals, which he was bound to respect.

X

CIVIL RESISTANCE

1. Code of Rights and Obligations of a Pole under Occupation

The universally implacable stand of the Polish people and their determination to carry on the fight against the German occupiers made it necessary to establish the principles of the struggle and to provide its organizational channels. The old Polish penal code was still in force, as was all Polish legislation. But, in addition, new rules were drawn pertaining to Civil Resistance. Civil Resistance went far beyond the activities of the underground organizations. The term applied to the universal resistance against the Germans—both passive and active—of the entire nation. The rules of Civil Resistance regulated the Poles' conduct with regard to the Germans and defined the do's and don'ts of life under German occupation. A universal boycott of all German orders and measures that were socially harmful or damaging to the national substance, was the basic command of Civil Resistance. Equally important was the injunction to engage in all kinds of sabotage that would result in material and moral losses to the Germans. A further basic dictate was the duty of obedience to the Polish underground authorities which—following the clarification of their relations with the government-in-exile—represented the Polish Government within the occupied country.

Based on these fundamental principles, detailed instructions were drafted for all segments of society and also, in particular, for workers, industrialists, farmers, office employees, doctors, lawyers, judges, railroadmen, priests, women, and the young people. Among the first such instructions were: the ban on registering as *Volksdeutsche*; the boycott of forced labor in the Reich; the ban on maintaining any sort of social relations with the Germans, buying German lottery tickets, attending the movies ("only pigs go to flicks"), gambling establishments, theatres and concerts conducted by the Germans; all Poles were also enjoined to collect materials pertaining to German crimes in Poland. Among the more particular directives: farmers were instructed to sabotage the German-imposed delivery quotas of meat, grain, eggs and dairy products; workers and office employees were permitted to remain on their jobs in factories and plants taken over by the Germans, but were instructed to carry on sabotage within the limits prescribed by their own personal safety; doctors were instructed to issue false medical certificates in cases where such certificates could prevent forced labor draft; priests were directed to issue false baptismal certificates for Jews and others hounded by the Gestapo; judges were forbidden, as a rule, to transfer cases from a Polish to a German court. And so forth.

With the passing of time, these initial directives were supplemented with Civil Resistance proclamations, instructions and warnings, serving the needs of each given moment. They dealt, for instance, with the obligation to help the homeless Jews, uprooted Poles, deserters from the Hungarian, Italian, Rumanian or Slovak units; they prohibited the spreading of alarming news that might touch off panic; they warned against the possibility of a communist provocation on May Day or against the impending mass roundup of reserve officers; they ordered a counteraction to prevent the evacuation to the Reich of Polish institutions and enterprises.

The basic rules of Civil Resistance—assembled in a "code of rights and obligations of a Pole"—as well as specific proscriptions, orders, instructions and warnings were disseminated widely through all available underground channels of communication, through the huge network of underground publications, and also through the BBC and the broadcasting station SWIT, whose programs were heard everywhere in Poland, even though listening was punishable by death.

Only a few of these rules were deemed applicable and binding in the territories incorporated into the Reich. German saturation of these provinces, and the mass terror raging there, allowed no more than to observe those rules of Civil Resistance, which stressed the need to maintain a dignified posture in dealing with the Germans, to boycott German orders, and to engage in the so-called "little sabotage," limited mainly to carelessness in servicing machinery and equipment and wasteful use of raw materials.

2. Directorate of Civil Resistance

The Chief of Civil Resistance was appointed jointly by the Government Delegate and the Commander of the Home Army.[1] Adopting for his organization the name of Directorate of Civil Resistance, he headed, together with his deputy, a number of departments whose names indicated their functions; these were the Departments of Justice, Sabotage and Diversion, Radio Information, Armaments, Chemicals, Legalization, and Registration of German Crimes. A biweekly, *The Chronicle of Civil Resistance* was the organ of the Directorate. Directors of Civil Resistance were attached to Government Delegates on the district and county levels. In addition, the General Commission of Civil Resistance was established, serving the Directorate of Civil Resistance in both a consultative and an executive capacity. The General Commission was composed of representatives of the same political parties that were included in the Political Coordinating Committee, hence it was nicknamed the "little PCC." Its tasks included, on the one hand, serving the Directorate of Civil Resistance with counsel and assistance, and on the other, transmitting through the party organizational networks all instructions of the Directorate of Civil Resistance. Later, the General Commission was also joined by a representative of the Civic Self-Defense Organization, an association of about twenty smaller underground groups, of which the more important were: "Pobudka," headed by Witold Rosciszewski, member of the prewar radical right ONR; "Raclawice," headed by Jozef Marszalek and Romuald Tyczynski; and "Front Odrodzenia Polski," headed by the well-known writer, Zofia Kossak. Simultaneously, a close cooperation developed between the Directorate of Civil Resistance and the following groups: the Socialist Fighting Organization, led by Leszek Raabe and, after Raabe's mysterious death, by Wlodimierz Kaczanowski, who was later killed during the Warsaw Rising; the Union of Polish Syndicalists, headed by Stefan Szwedowski and by Professor Kazimierz Zakrzewski, who was executed at Palmiry on March 11, 1941; and, finally, "Zryw," headed by Zygmunt Felczak and by Dr. Feliks Widy-Wirski. Moreover, three special commissions—of clergy, women, and the young people—were appointed in order to carry out the tasks of Civil Resistance in these special settings.

From its inception and throughout its entire existence, the Directorate of Civil Resistance was headed by Stefan Korbonski (pseudonyms: Nowak, Zielinski). Korbonski's deputy was Marian Gieysztor, a professor of the Warsaw University (pseudonym: Krajewski). The following served as district directors of Civil Resistance: Krakow district—Professor Tadeusz Seweryn; Warsaw district—Wojciech Winkler; Wilno district—Adam Galinski; Lodz district—Boleslaw Scibiorek, murdered by the Security Police in 1945; Kielce-Radom district—Stanislaw Jagiello; Lwow district—Professor Adam Ostrowski; Lublin district—Mieczyslaw Tudrej.

Government Delegate Professor Jan Piekalkiewicz announced the creation of the Directorate of Civil Resistance in his proclamation, published, among others, in "The Information Bulletin" (no. 47; December 3, 1942). He wrote:

"I call upon all Poles to give unqualified obedience and support to all directives, pronouncements, and recommendations of the Directorate of Civil Resistance."[2]

3. Underground Courts of Justice

The first task before the Directorate of Civil Resistance was to familiarize the people with the Civil Resistance rules of conduct. The second was to ensure that these rules were adhered to. To this end, underground courts of justice were established and maintained by the Directorate of Civil Resistance, as well as court commissions of Civil Resistance, a kind of citizens' courts, which heard all cases of less serious transgressions and infractions of Civil Resistance rules.

The basis for the establishment of the underground courts had been provided by the resolution of the Ministers' Committee for Homeland Affairs of April 16, 1940, which stated that "it is within the competence of the special courts to pronounce death sentences on oppressors, traitors, spies, and *agents provocateurs* . . . ."[3]

In consequence of this resolution, the government-in-exile drafted a code for the underground courts, or rather legislated their structure, defining their composition, procedure, and the manner of carrying out court sentences.

Accordingly, the court consisted of three judges, one of whom had to be a professional judge or a lawyer or—at the very least—a graduate of a Law School. The court based its deliberations on the depositions of witnesses and other evidence, e.g., documents, photographs, and opinions of experts if needed. The hearings were held in secret. The presiding judge determined whether the defendant was to be called or brought before the court, provided this did not endanger the court or the underground. If absent, the accused was defended by a court-appointed attorney. There was no appeal from the sentence passed by the court, but each sentence had to be approved by the respective District Government Delegate.[4] Both the resolution of the Ministers' Committee for Homeland Affairs of April 16, 1940, and the code of May 1940 conferred on the underground courts the status of state courts.

In pronouncing death sentences, the courts were guided by the Polish Penal Code of 1932 (Articles 99-113), special statutes, and the code for special courts, which provided that "whosoever commits the crime of treason, espionage, instigation or oppression of the Polish people—is liable to the penalty of death."

There is no data on the exact number of death sentences pronounced by the underground courts and carried out, as a rule, by shooting. But the number is known to be no more than 200 for the entire country, a very small percentage of the thousands of cases brought before the underground courts of justice. In any case, there were no instances of attempts to reverse these sentences after the war through court actions initiated in the People's Republic of Poland. There were, on the other hand, a great many cases which ended in acquital or deferment until after the war.

Death sentences were carried out by the so-called "executive" of the Directorate of Civil Resistance, subject to the Director of Civil Resistance in a given district, or by special units, either detached from the local Home Army or provided by the underground groups cooperating with the Directorate of Civil Resistance. Boy scouts and juveniles were not permitted to take part in these actions.

The first death sentences were pronounced and carried out in Warsaw on Roman Leon Swiecicki, a lieutenant in the "blue police" (for his part in street roundups and his work with the German police court, sentencing Poles to death) and Izydor Ossowski, an employee of the German Labor Office (for the extraordinary zeal with which he pursued those among his compatriots who attempted to evade the compulsory labor requirements). Both sentences were promulgated in the underground press and radio and also by means of big, red posters, of which some 3,000 were plastered on the Warsaw walls on the night of March 4, 1943, which made a deep impression on the inhabitants of the city.

There were also some cases of lynchings, either by individuals or by various groups, pretending to act on behalf of the Directorate of Civil Resistance. As a result, a proclamation was issued by the Directorate of Civil Resistance, protesting the criminal abuse of its name; it was published in "The Information Bulletin" (no. 20; May 20, 1943).

Some underground organizations usurped for themselves the prerogatives of the courts and passed their own sentences, liquidating those they deemed guilty. For instance, the "court" of the National Armed Forces group condemned to death their own commander, Lieutenant Colonel Stanislaw Nakoniecznikoff-Klukowski (pseudonym: Kmicic), and the sentence was carried out on the spot.[5]

Court Commissions of Civil Resistance consisted each of three Polish citizens of irreproachable probity. They dealt with lesser offenses and infractions deserving of infamy, censure or reprimand. Sentences of infamy and censure were published in the underground press; reprimands were delivered to the culprit only.

Among the most renowned cases was the sentencing to infamy of the conductor Dolzycki for his servility to the Germans, and of four actors—Samborski, Kondrat, Plucinski and Chodakowska—for acting in a German film slandering Poland. Three other actors—Dymsza, Perzanowska and Malicka—were censured for maintaining social relations with the Germans.

Penalties of flogging and head-shaving were also used by Civil Resistance, particularly in the countryside and in cases where the sentences of infamy or censure would not necessarily act as a deterrent. Flogging was used, for instance, in cases of misappropriation of Polish property; head-shaving was the penalty for women who consorted with the Germans and attended German parties.

4. SWIT Radio Station ("Anusia")

The Directorate of Civil Resistance operated its own, carefully guarded transmitters, which permitted daily contact with the government in London. This had been approved by Government Delegate Ratajski, who permitted the head of the Directorate of Civil Resistance to contact the government-in-exile directly in urgent matters requiring immediate BBC broadcasts to Poland. Ratajski informed the government of this arrangement in his dispatch of April 14, 1942. Somewhat connected with this was the establishment near London, under the shroud of greatest secrecy, of the radio station SWIT, which pretended to be broadcasting from within occupied Poland. The head of the Directorate of Civil Resistance was the only one in Poland who was let in on the secret. He was responsible for furnishing SWIT daily with up-to-date news from Poland without which it would have been impossible for SWIT to maintain the pretense of being an underground station in Poland.

Due to this scheme, SWIT received daily news from Warsaw and the provinces, as well as a brief digest of the underground press and the German-sponsored "reptile press," whose propaganda could thus be instantly and effectively rebutted. In its evening broadcast, SWIT could, for instance, comment at length on events that had taken place that very morning in Warsaw; in this way, it could masquerade successfully as a radio station broadcasting from within Poland. SWIT—which used the cryptonym "Anusia" in its messages to the Directorate of Civil Resistance—also became one of the weapons of Civil Resistance, broadcasting to Poland directives, proclamations, instructions, warnings, threats and communiqués of the Directorate of Civil Resistance, transmitted earlier that day to London. Here are some samples of dispatches sent to SWIT by Korbonski (pseudonym: Nowak):

October 3, 1943. Prepare Anusia for evening broadcasts of same-day news from Warsaw. Will have morning transmissions occasionally (e.g., German posters), but afternoons more likely: 'The New Warsaw Courier' comes out between 1 and 4 p.m. . . .

November 1, 1943. Talked with someone who had been picked up in a street roundup and now freed from Pawiak Prison. He claims that some of those arrested in a roundup are shot on the spot, once they are brought to Pawiak. Broadcast this item as an interview of your own correspondent.

October 27, 1943. Martin Fuldner, sentenced by the special court for the murder of the Horodynski family and their guests at a wedding in Zbydniow, was shot on October 13, at Charzewice-Rozwadow. The execution was carried out in the presence of two *General Gouvernement* officials from Krakow, who were set free. Fuldner's wife and child were also killed in reprisal for the murder of women and children in Zbydniow. Make sure Anusia includes this item in Saturday p.m. broadcast; those who carried out the execution will be listening.

October 26, 1943. Today, 35 hostages were shot in Leszno Street. The usual procedure. Street roundups continue, with the participation of young German fliers, considered reliable as members of the *Hitlerjugend*. Streets, trolleys and stores are deserted. Confidential. We're preparing retaliation. Will let you know the results.

October 1, 1943. Please threaten the commandant of the detention camp in Lublin, at Fabryczna Street. The commandant, *Untersturmführer* Thumann, beats up every prisoner he meets. Those who are incapable of work and selected for the gas chambers, are gassed by *Oberscharführer* Andress himself.

September 22, 1943. The following, sentenced to death by the special civil court in Warsaw, were shot: Eugeniusz Magalas, Ukrainian, employee of the Labor Office, for his part in the street roundups conducted in order to provide labor; Czeslaw Wiechcinski, employee of the railroad investigative office in Warsaw, for his ruthless pursuit of sabotage operations connected with the railroads and for tormenting prisoners; Zdzislaw Landycz, a sergeant of the criminal police from the detention camp at Gesia Street, for tormenting the prisoners.

The radio section of the Directorate of Civil Resistance had started the work on its own broadcasting station even before the onset of SWIT. In its dispatch no. 45, dated April 1, 1943, specific terms of cooperation were proposed:

April 1, 1943. Starting with April 15, we can begin broadcasting from our own station. We can broadcast once every two weeks, as radio station Warsaw, or instead of Anusia, using the same wave length. What do you prefer? The first program: one speech in Polish and two in English, aimed at foreign countries, to be taped and transmitted by the BBC. In view of Anusia's existence, Rakon's permission to transmit appears superfluous. Both the Delegacy and the Army think you are Station III [i.e., broadcasting station within Poland], so be sure to guard your secret. You're creating a sensation here. Nowak.

As it turned out, however, only one program, taped in part by the BBC, was broadcast by the new station. The radiophonic equipment of the Directorate of Civil Resistance was stolen by a Polish diversionist group, which put an end to all efforts to broadcast from within occupied Poland.[6] Broadcasting was taken up again during the Warsaw Rising, in a liberated section of the city, by the Home Army station "Blyskawica."

The secret of SWIT remained undiscovered for about a year and a half, because only five people in Poland knew about it: Government Delegate Jankowski and General Rowecki, whose inclusion the chief of the Directorate of Civil Resistance considered necessary; the chief of the DCR himself; his wife Zofia, who coded all dispatches to SWIT; and Jozef Stankiewicz (Ziutek), who had built the equipment and who was shot by the Germans within a short time, taking the secret of SWIT with him to his grave.

SWIT was first unmasked in England, following General Sikorski's death, when its secret was revealed to General Sosnkowski. Eventually, this revelation reached the High Command of the Home Army, but not the people of Poland, who generally believed SWIT to be broadcasting from within Poland to the very end.

5. *Actions Taken by the Directorate of Civil Resistance Against Forced Labor, Agricultural Quotas, Cinema and Lottery*

According to German plans, Poland was to serve as a granary, providing the Reich with food supplies, and a reservoir of labor, badly needed for war production. This presented a double threat—of starvation and of depopulation, especially with regard to the younger people. In order to counteract this twin danger, the Directorate of Civil Resistance issued a number of specific instructions within the general framework of directives pertaining to the sabotage of delivery quotas and the boycott of forced labor. Dispatches to SWIT for the years 1941-43 provide a comprehensive review of these measures:

Please broadcast repeatedly uniform instructions pertaining to action directed against delivery quotas. Deliver grain only as a last resort, the least you can, the worst you can, and the latest you can. Hide as much as possible, or sell in the free market. It is forbidden to burn your wheat in the fields, in stacks or in the barns. All pertinent documents and quota lists should be burnt by the organizations. Falsify receipts, wherever available. Burn down the warehouses, but only when empty. Contaminate all temporary warehouses with non-poisonous substances, such as kerosene. Destroy all threshing machines at German collection points, but not those that belong to individual farmers. Township administrations, quota commissions, personnel of the agricultural-trade cooperatives, township and village agricultural agents—should all engage in appropriate sabotage. Excessive compliance will be punished. Confidential. Communists want to burn everything. We do not call for full boycott, because this would inevitably result in an open battle. Nowak.

Repeat several times that we are opposed to burning standing crops in the fields. They should be harvested and hidden away, to the extent possible, for the use of the Polish population, while delivery quotas should be boycotted. Confidential. Soviet diversionary groups are setting fires in Grojec county and others. The peasants don't know how they should behave. Nowak.

The Directorate of Civil Resistance appealed to all farmers to deliver as much food as possible to starving cities in accordance with the rule: "As little as possible to the enemy, as much as possible to people in the cities." A system evolved whereby the same grain was delivered time and again to collection points, receipts for the supposedly delivered grain or cattle were falsified, secreted cattle were falsely tagged, officials were bribed, etc.

A total prohibition on all quota deliveries for the *General Gouvernement* (and partial prohibition for the territories incorporated into the Reich) was issued only during the Warsaw Rising, on September 6, 1944, and promulgated throughout the country by means of allied broadcasting stations, particularly SWIT.

In an effort to counteract the enforcement of German compulsory labor decrees, the Directorate of Civil Resistance issued—within the general framework of boycott—a number of specific instructions, indicating practical ways of avoiding forced labor. All employers were requested to pay their employees more than the official low rates, calculated to make the workers apply voluntarily to the German Labor Office. Employers were also instructed not to select from among their workers those who were to be sent to the Reich. In addition, the Directorate of Civil Resistance prohibited all Poles from working as recruiters for labor in the Reich and threatened reprisals against the "blue" policemen who took part in street roundups of labor. A total boycott was proclaimed of work in Germany for underage youth; on the walls of technical and industrial schools in Warsaw and other cities, Civil Resistance organizations posted warnings against labor deportations to Germany, calling on all students to leave their schools, not to stay overnight at their homes, but also exhorting them against joining the partisan groups prematurely. All these instructions were published by the underground press, broadcast by the BBC and SWIT and they were well known throughout the country.

Simultaneously, the Directorate of Civil Resistance, aided by SWIT, resorted to terror and threats against functionaries fulfilling the labor quotas and pursuing those who evaded forced labor. Here are a few samples:

March 29, 1943. Threaten the head of the Labor Office in Piotrkow Trybunalski, Reis. He will be punished for his bestiality during the roundup on March 5. He was beating people and threatening them with his gun. Nowak.

June 26, 1943. Threaten Dr. Schön, Kreishauptman in Sochaczew, who personnally sets fire to farms that have failed to deliver their quotas on time. Nowak.

At the same time, the "executive" of Civil Resistance, along with the combat units of the Home Army and the Peasant Battalions, carried out attacks on quota commissions and the gendarmes assigned to their protection, halted trains to let the cattle out and to spill out the grain, and administered the punishment of flogging to "cattle taggers."

The crowning achievement in the sabotage of delivery quotas and the boycott of forced labor was the destruction in the township offices of all documents pertaining to delivery quotas (when necessary, this was done by burning down the township buildings), setting fire to saw mills, putting the dairies out of commission, and burning down Labor Offices. In this action, coordinated by the Directorate of Civil Resistance and calculated to take the enemy by surprise, the following results were obtained up to June 30, 1944, by the combat units of the Home Army, the Peasant Battalions and other organizations cooperating with the Directorate of Civil Resistance:

14 Labor Offices burned down

41 other German offices burned down

300 township offices burned down

113 dairies immobilized

30 saw mills burned down

132 threshing machines burned down or damaged on farms administered by the Germans

2 warehouses burned down[7]

This action was carried out in 28 counties; it disorganized completely the German apparatus of exploitation, which never recovered from the blow.[8]

Actions such as the boycott of compulsory labor and delivery quotas probably were responsible for the opinion voiced after the war by German generals, who claimed that "well organized civil resistance in occupied Europe gave us much more trouble than military actions."[9]

Appeals to boycott the movies were published by the underground press and radio. But, in addition, various organizations cooperating with the Directorate of Civil Resistance, regularly flooded the theatres with appropriate leaflets and spread malodorous chemicals, which sometimes even damaged the clothing of the patrons. When such activities failed to bring the expected results, an all-out attack against the theatres was mounted by the "Zryw" group. On a prearranged day, and at the same prearranged hour, "Zryw" fighting units burst into six Warsaw movie houses and destroyed or seriously damaged their films and equipment. Similar actions were also carried out in Czestochowa (where two movie projectors were destroyed) and in other localities.

The same "Zryw" units forced their way on October 28, 1943, inside the six lottery offices in Warsaw, destroyed their records, and took away all lottery tickets; inscribed with an appeal to boycott the lottery, these tickets were later scattered through the streets of Warsaw, strewn from a fast-moving car.

6. Demonstrations Organized by Civil Resistance

It was one of the tasks of the Directorate of Civil Resistance to maintain the morale of the Polish population and to depress and dishearten the Germans. Another task was to promote demonstrations of patriotic feelings whenever required by the events. On May 3, 1943 (a Polish national holiday), the "executive" of the Directorate of Civil Resistance used the loudspeakers installed along the streets to broadcast a patriotic program and to play the Polish national anthem. A huge crowd of passers-by gathered. People bared their heads when they heard the national anthem. Anxious Germans slunk away quickly. A similar broadcast took place in Warsaw on July 31, 1943, during the conference of district directors of Civil Resistance, who heard it on Nowy Swiat Street. This time, the Germans started running off the streets.

The same purpose was served by the publication, in March 1943, of a forged, special supplement of *Nowy Kurier Warszawski* (The New Warsaw Courier); its appearance was the same as that of the German-sponsored "reptile daily," but it contained information about the Polish armed forces in the west and poked unmerciful fun at Hitler and the supposed German victories. Distributed on the streets of Warsaw by the paper boys, the same as usual, the supplement sold like hot cakes and promptly became a prized collector's item. This feat of the underground propaganda was repeated again, and with similar results, on May 6, 1944.

An action undertaken in the wake of General Sikorski's death on July 4, 1943, in an airplane crash at Gibraltar, may serve as an example of promoting demonstrations of patriotic feelings. In his order of July 7, 1943, Government Delegate Jankowski proclaimed the national mourning and appealed to all Poles to refrain from participating in any form of amusements during the time of grief over the painful loss. In pursuance of the Government Delegate's order, 200 obituary notices were posted in the streets of Lublin—to take one example—announcing General Sikorski's passing and signed by the

Directorate of Civil Resistance. The following night, identical obituary notices were posted by the Germans, also signed by the Directorate of Civil Resistance, but with one added sentence, claiming that General Sikorski had been murdered by the agents of the Soviet GPU.[10]

Similar obituary notices were also posted by the Civil Resistance people in Krakow.

In response to the obituary notices posted in Warsaw and signed "The Nation," the Germans put up placards with the caption: "Sikorski, the last victim of Katyn," implying that the General had been killed by the British, in cahoots with the Soviets. A final touch was added when new metal plaques were put up on all street corners of one of Warsaw's main thoroughfares—Aleje Jerozolimskie—proclaiming that henceforth it would bear the name of General Sikorski. Streets were also similarly renamed in other cities of the *General Gouvernement*.[11]

DIRECTORATE OF UNDERGROUND STRUGGLE

1. Sabotage and Diversion

Sabotage and diversion were the Home Army's first contributions to the struggle against the Germans. Sabotage consisted of surreptitious, covert destruction or damaging of whatever was useful to the enemy in the conduct of war—factories, warehouses, machinery, means of transportation—and also of efforts to disorganize the German war machine. The rule of "covering all tracks" was strictly observed in order to prevent the enemy from finding out who was responsible for a given act of sabotage. Diversion, on the other hand, was an overt attack and destruction of property and persons, and, if fighting ensued, it became a combat diversion. The enemy then had not a shadow of a doubt as to who the attackers were. Both sabotage and diversion went through a few successive phases.

In the first phase, a special sabotage-diversion unit was formed in 1940 within the framework of the Union for Armed Struggle. It was called *Zwiazek Odwetu* (Union for Revenge) and operated until 1942. Following the outbreak of the Soviet-German war, a second sabotage-diversion unit was formed, also within the general framework of the Union for Armed Struggle. This second unit was called *Wachlarz* (The Fan) and was to operate exclusively on Soviet territories, occupied by the German armies. With the quickening pace of combat activities, both units were subordinated to the Directorate of Diversion ("Kedyw"), which—together with the Bureau of Information and Propaganda, section "N" (psychological warfare), counterespionage, and the fast developing guerilla activities—was, in turn, placed under the Directorate of Underground Resistance, established in the fall of 1942 and headed by the Commander of the Home Army.

There was a confusing similarity of names between the already existing Directorate of Civil Resistance and the new Directorate of Underground Resistance. There was also an inherent duality and overlapping, which created confusion in the underground. The Government Delegate and the Commander of the Home Army agreed, therefore, to consolidate the DUR and the DCR under one common name—the Directorate of Underground Struggle. The Directorate of Underground Struggle consisted of: the Commander of the Home

Army, General Rowecki (and, following his arrest, General Bor-Komorowski); the Chief of Staff, General Tadeusz Pelczynski; the chief of "Kedyw," Colonel Emil Fieldorf (pseudonym: Nil); the chief of BIP, Colonel Rzepecki, and Stefan Korbonski, as Director of General Resistance. On July 5, 1943, a joint declaration of the Government Delegate and the Commander of the Home Army informed the nation and the underground about the fusion. From that moment on, all actions against the Germans were directed exclusively by the Directorate of Underground Struggle.

Decisions and directives of the new central leadership were implemented by the "Grey Ranks," a name adopted by the Polish scouting movement. They formed a discretionary unit of "Kedyw," operating under varying appellations, the last of which was the Diversionary Brigade ("Broda"). The unit consisted of 20 officers, 43 cadet officers, 64 noncommissioned officers, 344 soldiers, 79 women, and 113 cooperating individuals.[1] Alongside "Broda" operated also several other organizations subordinated to "Kedyw," such as the Socialist Fighting Organization or "Pobudka." In the districts, there were teams organized by the local commands of "Kedyw." All these groups, well-trained in sabotage, diversion, and combat (underground commandos), were supplied with matériel and diversionary weapons produced by separate manufacturing units, linked with "Kedyw."

In addition, "Kedyw" also operated its own medical service, organized by its own section called "Rola" (later, "Skiba"). Hospital facilities were either secreted in the existing regular hospitals, or camouflaged in private homes. All combat units were accompanied in action by a doctor and nurses. Starting with Autumn 1943, underground hospitals were established, with their own operating rooms and personnel on duty.

No compilation exists of combined total results of joint sabotage-diversion activities, conducted by all these organizations. The report for the period of three and a half years—January 1, 1941 to June 30, 1944—comes the closest. It provides the following statistics:

*Locomotives damaged 6,930
*Locomotives delayed in overhaul 803
*Transports derailed 732
*Railroad cars damaged 19,058
*Transports set afire 443
*Disruptions of electric power in Warsaw. 638
*Military vehicles damaged or destroyed 4,326
*Railroad bridges blown up. 38
*Aircraft damaged. 28

*Gas storage tanks destroyed. 1,167
and tons of gas destroyed 4,674
*Oil shafts incapacitated. 3
*Carloads of wood wool burnt. 150
*Military warehouses burnt. 122
*Military food storage houses burnt 8
*Production in factories brought to a standstill. 7
*Defective parts for aircraft engines produced. 4,710
*Defective cannon barrels produced 203
*Defective artillery shells produced. 92,000
*Defective aircraft radios produced. 107
*Defective capacitors   for electronic industry 570,000
*Defective lathes produced 1,700
*Important plant machinery damaged 2,872
*Various acts of sabotage 25,145
*Attacks on Germans. 5,733

Sabotage and diversion differed from actions involving self-defense, retaliation, terror, or procuring arms. Again, information available is not complete. But fragmentary data pertaining to self-defense operations show that 2,015 Gestapo agents were liquidated during the 18-month period between January 1, 1943 and June 30, 1944,[2] and that in 1943 and 1944 several hundreds of prisoners were rescued from prisons in Bialystok, Kielce, Konskie, Opatow, Dabrowka, Wizna, Jaslo, Wysokie Mazowieckie, Dabrowa Wielka, Mielec, Garwolin and Bilgoraj. In Warsaw, prisoners were once rescued from the Hospital of the Holy Child, and twice from Saint John the Divine. Rescuers used either subterfuge (Gestapo uniforms) or terror. The most spectacular perhaps was the rescue in Warsaw of 25 prisoners on March 26, 1943, at the corner of Bielanska and Dluga streets, near the Armory; five Gestapomen and two civilian agents were killed in that encounter. Two wounded soldiers of the Home Army were similarly rescued from the Hospital of the Transfiguration, after they had been arrested there by the Gestapo, following the attempt on the life of the SS General Kutschera.

Struggle against banditry should also be classed as self-defense. The Germans befriended bands, gangs and common criminals, whose misdeeds they tried to blame on the underground, in an effort to discredit the movement in the eyes of the Poles. In 1943, the underground liquidated 231 bandits; 695 bandits were killed in the first six months of 1944.

In actions of terror or retaliation, 361 gendarmes were killed in 39 attacks carried out on gendarmerie patrols in 1943; from January through June 1944, 584 gendarmes were killed in 130 separate engagements. Also, in individual reprisal for exceptional brutality, the following Germans were assassinated in Warsaw only:

* February 1, 1944 (Aleje Ujazdowskie)—SS General and chief of police for the Warsaw district, Kutschera;

* May 6, 1943 (Mokotowska Street)—Gestapoman Schultz;

* May 22, 1943 (Square of the Three Crosses)—Gestapoman Lange;

* September 7, 1943—the cammandant of the Pawiak Prison, Gestapoman Buerckel;

* September 24, 1943—Gestapoman Kretschman;

* October 1, 1943—Gestapoman Ernest Wefels;

* October 2, 1943 (vicinity of the Gestapo Headquarters)—Captain Lechner of the Gestapo;

* June 12, 1944 (corner of Zurawia Street and the Square of the Three Crosses)—Gestapomen Peschel and Leitgeber;

* June 15, 1944 (Zoliborz)—Gestapomen Jung and Hoffman.

In retaliation for the persecution of the people of Warsaw, the following were also shot: director of the Labor Office Hoffman (March 1943) and the functionaries of the same office, Hugo Dietz and Geist (April or May 1943); social security inspector Bruno Kurt; director of the Warsaw Housing Office, Braun; and director of the Trust Properties Administration, Fleming.

Outside of Warsaw, the main event was the attempt on the life of SS General Krüger, head of the security police for the entire *General Gouvernement*. It took place in Krakow, on April 20, 1943. Krüger was not killed, but after the coup he disappeared without a trace, which indicated that he had either sustained serious wounds or suffered a mental breakdown. General Kurt Renner was killed in the Lublin district in the course of the pacification action; and two Gestapomen, Pottebaum and Flaschke, were killed in Rzeszow on May 25, 1944.

On the orders of the Directorate of Underground Struggle a massive operation was conducted in the districts of Warsaw, Lublin and Kielce (June 2-10, 1944), in the course of which 136 Gestapo agents and informers were shot, among them: Willi Holze, August Gering and Kammertentz.

In reprisal for the ousting of Polish villagers, particularly in the Zamosc district, two villages occupied by German colonists were burned down (Cieszyn and Wierzby) and several German colonists were shot. In reprisal for the execution of 280 Poles, the German village of Siedliska was burned down in June 1943, and 69 German colonists were killed. In another reprisal action near Wilanow, in the vicinity of Warsaw—where four soldiers of the Home Army had been turned over to the Gestapo—22 German colonists, 7 gendarmes, and 3 Polish collaborationists were killed in the fighting.

No data are available that would permit the presenting of a complete picture of considerable operations aimed at procuring arms and munitions. At the grass roots, the disarming of individual German soldiers was widely practiced, particularly in the cities and under the cover of darkness. A single German soldier would be set upon from behind—the barrel of a gun (or, sometimes, a finger) pressed between his shoulder blades—forced to raise his hands, and disarmed. Local German commands warned their soldiers against this practice through leaflets distributed at every larger railroad station. At the opposite pole was the capture of military magazines or transports. Fragmentary data available provide some instances of such operations:

* in October 1943, a Home Army unit gained control of the town of Janow Lubelski for a few hours, and captured arms and other military provisions;

* in February 1944, eight raids were made to procure arms and the following were obtained: 179 rifles, 38 submachine guns, 13 light machine gunes; 7 heavy machine guns, 52 pistols and 160,000 rounds of ammunition, 410 hand grenades, 1,500 meters of blasting fuse, two radio stations, and one antitank gun;

* in April 1943, thirty-seven railroad transports were attacked and six carloads of arms were captured;

* in May 1943, fifty-three excursions were made to procure arms, and twenty-six sorties were made the following month.

But nothing could stop the well-planned and well-executed attack on the bank truck, en route from the bank of issue to the railroad station. It happened in Warsaw, on August 12, 1943, in broad daylight, at the crossing of Miodowa and Senatorska streets. A handcart was pushed in front of the bank truck, forcing it to stop; the gendarmes escorting the transport were shot; one of the Home Army soldiers got behind the wheel of the truck and drove it to a hideout, where it was unloaded. The booty amounted to 100 million zlotys. In an effort to find those responsible for the robbery, the Germans posted a reward of 5 million zlotys, but without any success.

The Union for Armed Struggle managed to set up in Berlin the Territorial Command, directing sabotage-diversion operations in the Reich. During its existence (often interrupted by arrests), it directed the sabotage activities carried on in German industry and agriculture by Polish workers who had been forcibly deported to Germany. The

work of the men in the Territorial Command was made doubly difficult by the fact that they had no job ties or housing assignments
legalizing their stay in Berlin. Despite these difficulties, 12 trains and
16 locomotives were derailed in October-November 1941 and 33
loaded railroad cars were burned; in January and February 1942,
two trains were derailed and 11 oil storage tanks were set afire.

Independently of these operations, one of the discretionary units
of "Kedyw" (code name: "Kosa") managed to plant bombs in railroad stations in Gdansk and in Berlin. A team of three (one of them,
a woman), equipped with *Volksdeutsche* documents, left Warsaw in
the Spring of 1943, taking a train reserved for Germans only; reaching Berlin via Bydgoszcz, they got out at the Friedrichstrasse station.
Working in the station washroom, they prepared a two-kilogram
bomb, concealed in a leather briefcase, and planted it on a platform
just before the arrival of two passenger trains. The bomb exploded at
the moment when the passengers began to leave the trains—14 people
were killed and 27 injured. Within minutes the station was surrounded by the Gestapo and the gendarmerie, but the conspirators managed
to leave ahead of them and four days later they were back in Warsaw.[3]

The sabotage-diversion activities of the Fan (*Wachlarz*) had a twin
object. First, it strove to improve the chances of the future uprising
in Poland by making it impossible—through acts of sabotage and diversion, particularly with regard to railroads—for the German armies
engaged in Russia to come to the aid of German forces battling the
Polish   insurgents. Second, current sabotage and diversion, while
preparing the Fan for future tasks, also complicated and rendered
more difficult the Germans' struggle against the Soviets. The western
Allies were most interested in this second aspect of the Fan activities;
even so, they failed to supply the Fan with air drops designed specifically to assist its operations, which weakened its effectiveness.

Activities of the Fan were greatly hampered by the eradication of
all Polish elements in Russia and by the German mass reprisals for
every act of sabotage or diversion. Besides, the whole area behind
the front lines was swarming with Gestapo agents (Ukrainian, Byelorussian and Lithuanian), bands of cutthroats, and Soviet diversionary
groups, hostile toward the Fan soldiers (four of whom were killed by
the Russians). Finally, the entire area was crisscrossed by well-
guarded frontier lines, dividing it into German occupation zones
such as the Ukraine, Byelorussia, Lithuania, Latvia, and the front
zone; restrictions were imposed even on movements from one township to another.

As of February 1943, the Fan consisted of 10 officers (most of
them, parachutists trained in Great Britain) and 268 soldiers, trained

in the *General Gouvernement*. They were divided into groups, ranging from platoon to company, and were located in Kiev, Berdichev, Zviahl, Zhitomir, Rowne and Shepetovka. These groups, in turn, were divided into diversionary patrols of 4 to 6 men each, placed along the railroad lines, linking these towns. Ostensibly, the soldiers of the Fan were employed by German firms, supplying the German armies. In Kiev, the Fan succeeded in taking over the management of a German transport firm; in Rowne, they infiltrated the auxiliary unit, responsible for the protection of German communication lines: out of 205 men in this unit, 120 were the Fan soldiers (including three officers, parachuted from England).

There is no complete data on the Fan's activities. Fragmentary data for May-June 1942 report 16 diversionary actions, with the following losses: 12 men killed, 7 missing, 4 wounded, and 14 men arrested.

One of the most daring operations of the Fan, was the rescue of three Fan officers, imprisoned in Pinsk. On January 18, 1943, in a model textbook exercise that took but a few minutes, a detachment of Fan soldiers seized the prison, shot the resisting German guards, freed all prisoners, and drove away with the three officers, who returned to Warsaw within a short time.

As the German armies withdrew, the soldiers of the Fan gradually changed from sabotage-diversion to combat activities, forming the nucleus of Polish partisan units in the east.

2. Partisan Warfare

The first military actions after the September defeat were undertaken by a group of soldiers under the command of Major Henryk Dobrzanski (pseudonym: Hubal) and by the so-called "Jedrusie," commanded at first by Wladyslaw Jasinski, and later—following Jasinski's death on the battlefield—by Jozef Wiacek. "Jedrusie" also tracked down the Gestapo informers and put out their own publication called *Odwet* (Revenge).

All these were spontaneous, wildcat operations. A planned partisan warfare, following organizational principles and serving the Home Army's strategic aims was to increase sabotage and diversionary operations and to prepare the Home Army for the uprising. It was hastened by the expulsions of peasants from the Zamosc district, designated as the first German colonization area.

The decision to resist those German actions with force of arms, was implemented through partial mobilization of the Home Army in the Lublin district; a few guerilla groups were organized—about 850 men in all—who proceeded immediately to burn down the newly settled villages and to kill the German colonists. Superior German forces, supported by planes and armored cars, tried to encircle the partisans. The battle began on February 4, 1943 and lasted for 10 days. The Germans failed to hem in the partisans, and lost 60 men in the battle.

The main burden of counteracting the expulsions was, however, assumed by the Peasant Battalions, which promptly set up guerilla units, using the same methods, i.e., setting fire to German-held villages and liquidating German settlers. They fought the German army and gendarmerie in three major engagements: on December 30, 1942, near Wojda; on February 1, 1943, near Zaboreczne; and on February 2, 1943, near the village of Roza. Several smaller engagements were also fought in various localities. Out of a total of some 1,500 used in this action, the Germans lost 161 killed and several hundred wounded. Taken aback by the violence of the counterattack, the Germans abandoned their expulsion activities in the Zamosc district, never to renew them again.[4]

Local emergencies were also instrumental in the rise of partisan warfare in the districts of Nowogrodek, Wilno, Wolyn and Lwow. In the first two districts, an urgent need arose to protect the local population against the German mass reprisals and the marauding bands of cutthroats and robbers. In the districts of Wolyn and Lwow, the growing incidence of killings of Poles by the Ukrainians also assumed mass proportions. With the open or tacit approval of the Germans, the Ukrainians began to liquidate the Polish population of southeastern Poland and part of the Lublin district, in an effort to eliminate the Polish element in these areas. The Home Army began the rescue operations by assembling the Polish population in fortlike bases, surrounded by trenches and wire entanglements, and guarded by the Home Army soldiers.

Simultaneously, in eastern Poland fighting broke out between the Home Army units and the Soviet partisans who demanded their total submission; in addition, the Home Army had to fight against the Germans who strove to surround and destroy them and also against the Byelorussian and Lithuanian communist bands. In this many-faceted struggle, the difference between the discretionary units of the local "Kedyw" and the partisan units was quickly obliterated. Usually, the "Kedyw" units developed into full-fledged partisan detachments.

Partisan warfare was also on the rise in central Poland. It was waged everywhere by soldiers-volunteers—primarily, local peasants—but it included also men from all social strata—city intelligentsia, school youth, craftsmen, workers, and the landed gentry. Command was usually assumed not by men who held an officer's rank, but by men of proven leadership ability. Some partisan detachments were led by noncommissioned officers, who had officers serving under their command. Partisan units were given names and numbers of regular infantry or cavalry regiments, stationed before the war in the areas in which the partisans were operating. This practice created the appearance of a regular army, or nuclear cadres of future regiments. In practice, however, they were usually known by the pseudonyms of their commanders, e.g., the units of Ponury, Kmicic, Zapora, etc.

As a rule, these were infantry units, but they often used horses for liaison, and larger groups maintained cavalry platoons, which were used for reconnaissance. Liaison service was performed by women. Every unit had a sapper team, indispensable for diversionary actions. Uniforms were a hodgepodge of miscellany. Nearly everybody wore a military cap (either the traditional four-cornered army cap or the soft overseas cap), adorned with the Polish eagle emblem. As for the rest, it depended on circumstances: Polish uniforms, made-over German uniforms, civilian suits, military tunics with civilian trousers, or, for that matter, civilian jackets with military trousers, cycling caps, round caps, German helmets, etc. Arms were also a mélange of weapons salvaged from the September 1939 fighting, captured or bought from the Germans, and also obtained from air drops or from warehouses and transports seized by the Home Army; in eastern Poland, there were also Soviet arms. Rifles, hand guns and hand grenades were the most easily available. But light and heavy machine guns were rare and much sought after, and every soldier would give his eyeteeth for the much coveted submachine guns, particularly the German *Schmeiser*. Against tanks and armored cars, the partisans used special grenades ("gamony"), captured German "armored fists" (*Panzerfaust*) and—all too seldom—the splendid PIAT antitank weapons provided by allied air drops.

Food provision varied. The partisans ate whatever food was available to the local population, who shared gladly. In addition, they confiscated food from estates administered by the Germans. Some provisions were also purchased. In 1944, the High Command of the Home Army paid out 40 zlotys per soldier per day for food, which was very little. As far as medical services were concerned, it was rare for a partisan unit to have its own doctor. Usually, his place was taken by fairly well qualified nurses. Operations were performed covertly in makeshift field hospitals, located usually in local manor houses, or—more seldom—in forest dugouts.

The partisans were imbued with patriotic and fighting spirit. Many of the soldiers had personal scores to settle with the Germans—

murdered relatives, expulsions, loss of property. Generally speaking, discipline was adequate; much depended on the kind of authority the leader exercised. Rare cases of banditry or desertion were punished by death.

In mid-1943, the fighting strength of the partisan units of the Home Army was as follows:

* Radom area—4 partisan units;
* Krakow area—8 small partisan units (from squad to platoon);
* Subarea Rzeszow—1 small partisan unit;
* Area Lodz—3 partisan units;
* Area Bialystok—a few partisan units in the Szczuczyn, Augustow, Bialystok and Grodno sectors;
* Area Polesie—4 partisan units;
* Area Nowogrodek—8 partisan units;
* Area Wilno—2 partisan units;
* Area Wolyn—a few partisan and local self-defense units;
* Area Lublin—11 partisan units (platoon strength each);

Other partisan units were active in Pomerania, in the Tucholski Forest, and there were also 7 units in Silesia, ranging from a squad to a platoon in strength.

The average fighting strength of a partisan unit ranged from a platoon to a company, that is, from 30 to 100 men, and was subject to frequent variations.

A year later, when Operation Tempest began and the Warsaw Rising broke out on August 1, 1944, Polish forests were full of partisan units; they dominated their areas, with the exception of cities and towns, where the Germans barricaded themselves at night in buildings surrounded by bunkers and barbed wire entanglements, which they did not dare to leave before daybreak.

3. Diversionary Propaganda (Action "N")

Action "N" concentrated on undermining the morale of the German armies by imbuing the soldiers with the conviction that Germany would lose the war, would be plagued by disaster and destruction, and that they should—first of all—think of themselves and how to escape from the snares in which they were trapped. If they wanted to leave Poland safe and sound—the argument went—and to return to their families and homes, they should lay down their arms the moment the Poles rose, and wait to be sent back to Germany.

Action "N" conducted psychological warfare in the full meaning of this term. It strove to disarm German soldiers spiritually; it endeavored to set them at loggerheads with the Nazi party, whose members—it was claimed—"goldbricked" far from the front lines, enjoying luxuries at the expense of frontline soldiers and their families; it sought to drive a wedge between combat soldiers and the Gestapo, the gendarmerie, the SS formations—those legions of privileged praetorians, those uppity bastards, looking down their noses at frontline soldiers who froze and bled to death on the eastern front.

Weapons in this psychological warfare were publications written in impeccable German and signed with names indicating they had emanated from the German underground, e.g., *Soldatenbund, Hindenburg*, or *Oesterreichische Freiheitsfront*; the technical level of production of all those publications was very high.

First of all, there were five periodicals in the German language, and one in Polish: *Der Soldat* and *Der Frontkämpfer*, published from 1941 through 1944, were aimed at German soldiers on the eastern front; *Bilder für die Truppe* presented photographs calculated to produce despondency and gloom; *Der Klabautermann* (1942-43) was an illustrated satirical magazine; *Der Hammer* (1941), later renamed *Der Durchbruch* (1942-43), was intended for the German population of the Reich and the incorporated territories; *Die Ostwache* was published for Germans in the *General Gouvernement; Die Zukunft-Przyszlosc* (1943-44), published in Polish, was aimed at the *Volksdeutsche* and threatened them with dire consequences of their conduct.

Three booklets were also published in German, with misleading covers that implied their anti-Soviet or anti-British contents. The cover of *Der Rote Terror* (The Red Terror) featured Stalin trampling prostrate human bodies, while inside the reader could find an account of German atrocities in Poland and shocking photographs of executions of Poles by the Germans. The second booklet was called *Der Grosste Lügner in der Welt* (The Greatest Liar in the World) and showed on its cover Churchill, holding the British flag and stamping on human skulls inscribed "Belgium," "Denmark" and "Holland;" inside the reader could find a compilation of mutually contradictory quotations from Hitler's speeches and writings. The third booklet, entitled *Der Windmacher* (The Windmaker), ridiculed Hitler and the Nazi Party.

Hundreds of leaflets were printed, purportedly by German underground organizations (e.g., Rudolf Hess' group). They called for the overthrow of Hitler, encouraged separatism, mimicked to perfection the style of German ordinances, and though they struck at German authorities, they were often preserved by the soldiers as authentic German publications. Other leaflets brought appeals and proclamations which were written in a style that simulated the language of some well-known Nazis, but were in fact attacking the Nazi party; one such leaflet, for instance, appeared on May 1, 1943, signed ostensibly by Goebbels (and an excellent forgery it was). One kind of leaflets resorted to pornography to show the soldiers the lusty life of Nazi bigwigs and SS-men far from the frontline. Another kind specialized in mocking and ridiculing Hitler.

Placing inscriptions on the walls and cleverly changing and twisting German propaganda slogans, were also within the province of Action "N." For instance, the German slogan: *Deutschland siegt an allen Fronten* (Germany wins on all fronts) was changed by substituting "l" for "s" in the word *siegt*, with the result that the slogan read: "Germany is flat on her face on all fronts"—which created considerable merriment among the Polish passers-by. Similarly, the name of the SS General von Moder on a German poster was changed to *Mörder* (murderer).

In remembrance of the German defeat in World War I, in October 1918, the word "October" was painted at night by thousands of underground people throughout the country. This provoked the Germans to counteraction: they painted "26" before "October" and added "*vier Jahre des GG*," which made it read: "October 26, four years of the *General Gouvernement*." This, in turn, provoked a further addition by the underground: "and not a day longer." That was one round the Germans lost.

Forgeries of German orders and ordinances—uncannily plausible in contents and form—created much confusion among the Germans, weaned on obedience and respect for all official pronouncements. In Krakow, for instance, an announcement was posted in the streets and mailed to all German offices; printed both in Polish and in German, it was signed by the chief of propaganda for the *General Gouvernement*, Ohlenbusch. The announcement proclaimed that the manner in which thousands of Polish officers had been killed by the Soviets near Smolensk, showed clearly how primitive Soviet technology of murder was; the Department of Propaganda will, therefore, organize popular excursions to Auschwitz, Majdanek, and other similar places to acquaint the Polish population with such humanitarian installations, used by the Germans, as steam and gas chambers, electric shock plates, and the Auschwitz crematory, capable of processing 3,000 people within a 24-hour period. Many German functionaries actually posted this announcement!

Other false ordinances instituted registration of cats in the *General Gouvernement*, made changes in delivery schedules (which created an unholy bedlam), informed that new passes had been introduced, marked with a green slash across, which exempted all vehicles from the mandatory load control. Before this last ruse was detected, hundreds of cars had managed already to transport arms, ammunition, food and medical supplies from or to the Home Army warehouses; at the sight of passes "with the green slash," the gendarmes saluted and urged the drivers on.

But the greatest coup of Action "N" came with the posting on February 24, 1944, of an order, purportedly from General Koppe, chief of police for the *General Gouvernement*, in which he directed all Germans to withdraw immediately from the *General Gouvernement*; panic ensued, but a swift counteraction by phone succeeded in preventing a mass exodus.

Action "N" was headed, from its inception until the end, by Tadeusz Zenczykowski (pseudonym: Kania).

XII

NATIONAL POLITICAL REPRESENTATION

Following the self-dissolution of the Collective Delegacy in September 1940, the Central Political Committee was automatically revived. It survived until March 1943, when its name was changed to "National Political Representation," although its composition and the scope of its activities remained the same. In the course of its existence, this body issued several declarations and proclamations to the Polish nation. Among these were the following:

1. The declaration of March 14, 1943 proclaimed that the Polish nation stood steadfast and united in its support of the inviolability of Poland's eastern borders as of September 1, 1939. The Polish people desired good, neighborly relations with the Soviet Union, provided the Soviets recognized unequivocally Poland's eastern borders as of 1939 (determined by the Treaty of Riga) and refrained from interference in Poland's internal affairs.

2. The appeal of March 20, 1943 called on the Polish youth to be on guard against the enemy and to join the ranks of the underground armed forces.

3. The declaration of May 9, 1943 stated that the Soviets had used the Katyn affair as a pretext to break off diplomatic relations with the Polish government (note of April 25, 1943), anticipating that this action would facilitate the Soviet annexation of Poland's eastern territories. The Polish nation was unalterably resolved to support the integrity of Poland's territories.

4. The declaration of May 9, 1943 rejected with scorn the Soviet charge that the Polish underground movement was collaborating with the German invader.

5. The proclamation of July 30, 1943 appealed to the Ukrainian nation to coexist in peace with the Polish nation.

6. The declaration on the Political Agreement of Four Parties (August 15, 1943) pertained to the harmonious interparty collaboration, at least until elections could be held for a constitutional legislative body in free Poland. The declaration called on the emigré counterparts of the four parties to do likewise and to maintain a coalition government. It announced the imminent establishment of the Council of National Unity and a representative governmental structure devoid of totalitarian and prewar regime elements. The

declaration also promised the political parties' full support for the Home Army. Finally, the declaration defined the Polish war aims: inviolability of the eastern borders; western and northern borders that would guarantee Poland broad access to the sea and ensure her complete security; a confederation of states situated between Germany and the USSR, based on a Polish-Czech alliance; solution of the national minorities problems in accordance with the principles of freedom and equality. In addition, the declaration contained a number of proposals pertaining to the transition period: immediate implementation of agrarian reform; development of the cooperative movement; repatriation of Poles who had been deported abroad; and achievement of full employment.

The Declaration set forth for the first time the platform of the body serving as a surrogate Parliament of the Polish Underground State.

7. The appeal of November 1, 1943, calling on other political groupings to cooperate with the National Political Representation on the basis of the Declaration on the Political Agreement of Four Parties of August 15, 1943.

8. The proclamation of January 8, 1944, to all nations of the world, explaining the legal and political status of Poland's eastern territories (based on the Treaty of Riga of March 18, 1921, the decision of the Council of Allied Powers of March 15, 1923, confirming Poland's frontiers in the east, and the Polish-Soviet Non-Aggression Pact of July 25, 1932). The proclamation appealed to the Allied Nations to support the Polish demands that the Soviets respect Poland's sovereignty and territorial integrity, including the Polish eastern frontier, as determined by the Treaty of Riga.[1]

XIII

THE COUNCIL OF NATIONAL UNITY

The Council of National Unity was established on January 9, 1944 by the decree of the Government Delegate. A successor to—in order—the Political Coordinating Committee, the Central Political Committee and the National Political Representation, this authentic parliament of underground Poland was composed of 17 people: 3 representatives of each of the four parties within the National Political Representation (the Polish Socialist Party, the Polish Peasant Party, the National Party, and the Labor Party); 1 representative of the Democratic Alliance—a union of the Democratic Party, the Union for the Republic's Reconstruction, the Organization for Independent Poland, and the Pilsudskite Group of Olgierd (Henryk Jozewski); 1 representative of "Raclawice," a peasant youth organization; 1 representative of "Fatherland," autonomous National Party active in the western territories; 1 representative of the clergy; and 1 representative of the cooperative movement. Between the plenary meetings, the work was carried on by the General Commission of the Council of National Unity. Kazimierz Puzak of the Socialist Party served as chairman of both the Commission and the Council. The most important of the proclamations, pronouncements and resolutions of the Council of National Unity was the declaration issued on March 15, 1944, under the meaningful title: "What the Poles Are Fighting For." It reflected faithfully the constitutional, political, economic and social views of a nation crushed under the most cruel occupation ever known to mankind, which strove to stamp out all thought and all hope. It also mirrored aspirations and illusions of the Poles in the fifth year of the war.

In its introduction, the Declaration outlined the program of proposed postwar arrangements—both international and internal—far more comprehensive and universal than that contained in the Declaration on the Political Agreement of Four Parties of August 15, 1943. The basic goals formulated in the program were "freedom, integrity, sovereignty, power, security, and vigorous internal development of the Republic," as well as an enduring and just peace. The Program anticipated the total military and moral disarmament of the German Reich, the breakup of German territories and punishment for war criminals, long years of international control (with Poland's participation), the establishment of an international organization guarding the peace, and a federation of smaller countries in central and southeastern Europe. It asserted that Poland would base its foreign policy on a close alliance with England, the United States, France, Turkey, and would maintain good relations with the USSR, provided the Soviets recognized the integrity of Poland's prewar frontiers and refrained from interference in Poland's internal affairs. It demanded the incorporation of East Prussia into Poland and a shifting of Poland's frontier westward; it proposed that the Polish-Czechoslovak frontier follow the line established by the agreement of November 5, 1918.

The government structure of postwar Poland was to be that of a parliamentary democracy, with a strong executive, a decentralized administration and an apolitical army.

National minorities were to enjoy full political equality and to have cultural autonomy.

Poland's economic life was to be rebuilt along the lines of more widespread private ownership, larger and more fairly distributed national income, nationalization or collective ownership of enterprises of public utility, and planned economy. Private property in postwar Poland was to be considered a social function rather than a personal privilege.

A change was also to take place in the agrarian structure of the country. The state would assume control of all forests and all privately owned land over 50 ha. (about 125 acres), which would be used to establish new farms with an area of 20-37 acres each or to enlarge the existing undersize farms.

The extension of private ownership in towns was to be assisted by the government through an extensive building program to provide the working class with their own homes, and through government aid for new enterprises, both industrial and commercial, as well as crafts.

Social policy would be aimed at liberating the workman and ensuring his social rise; at eliminating differences between the blue-collar workers and the white-collar workers; at providing jobs for all; at making it possible for the workers—through labor unions and self-government—to have a voice in controlling the economic life of the country; at introducing a comprehensive insurance program and a program of child-and-mother care.

In the field of education the program foresaw a rapid and extensive reconstruction, free schools for the peasant and working class youth, broad development of out-of-school courses, and a democratization and universalization of culture.

The Declaration ended with a rebuttal of the unjustified claims of Poland's eastern neighbor and an appeal to the Polish nation to maintain its unity and to have faith in its own powers, in the righteousness of Poland's cause and in a bright future.

From among other proclamations and pronouncements of the Council of National Unity, the following should be mentioned:

1. An appeal to the Polish-Americans, asking for their help (March 15, 1944).

2. A dispatch to General Anders, dated May 24, 1944, and signed also by Government Delegate Jankowski, congratulating the Polish Second Corps on its victories in Italy.

The Council of National Unity also passed several resolutions pertaining to current problems in occupied Poland and various decisions taken by the government-in-exile. It also issued a number of proclamations and statements, e.g., on Soviet troops entering the Polish territories, on the Katyn affair, and in connection with the Warsaw Rising. These will be discussed in the following chapters.[1]

XIV

UNDERGROUND ORGANIZATIONS OF
THE *BBWR* AND THE *OZON**

1. *The Assembly of Organizations for Independence*

There were some political groups which did not join the Political Coordinating Committee, the National Political Representation or the Council of National Unity and, while recognizing the government-in-exile, chose to assume the stance of opposition. Among these were the Assembly of Organizations for Independence and the Camp of Fighting Poland.

The Assembly was initiated in Poland by the former leaders, members and adherents of the Nonparty Bloc of Cooperation with the Government (*Bezpartyjny Blok Wspolpracy z Rzadem*—BBWR) and its former chief, Colonel Walery Slawek. These men were critical of the Block's political successor, the Camp of National Unification (*Oboz Zjednoczenia Narodowego*—OZON), headed by Colonel Adam Koc; they decried the fascistic tendencies, introduced by the Camp in Poland in the wake of the Constitution of 1935. The Assembly endeavored to vindicate the prewar regime of the earlier BBWR period and established close ideological ties with the Democratic Party, advocating a return after the war to a truly democratic structure. Their views were propagated by a wide range of publications, the most important of which was *Mysl Panstwowa* (Reflections of State).

In its activities, the Assembly relied on groups with ties to the prewar regime: former state or local functionaries, teachers, members of various organizations originating in the early days of struggle for Poland's independence before World War I, etc. The Assembly was headed by two prominent Pilsudski followers: Zygmunt Hempel and Mikolaj Dolanowski; they were joined later by Dr. Waclaw Lipinski, who returned to Poland from Hungary in 1942.

The Assembly declared its adherence to the Union for Armed Struggle at the very outset. However, because of the generally negative attitude within the country toward men previously associated with the prewar regime, and because of the pressure from General Sikorski, Zygmunt Hempel (who served as chief of the Bureau of

---

* BBWR and OZON—organizations affiliated with the prewar regime in Poland, followers of Marshal Pilsudski and his successors.

Information and Propaganda for the Warsaw district) was removed from the Union for Armed Struggle. As a result, the Assembly switched to open opposition; this was signaled in an article which appeared in *Mysl Panstwowa* of May 12, 1942, entitled "Food for Thought," in which it was charged that the underground army was subject to political party influences.

Similarly, former District Governor Henryk Jozewski was removed from the Union for Armed Struggle in January 1940. In spite of this, he organized in July 1940 the so-called Group of Olgierd (Jozewski's pseudonym), which gathered former Pilsudski's legionnaires and published a periodical called *Polska Walczy* ("Poland Fights On"). This group was eventually subordinated to the Union for Armed Struggle and in 1944 joined the Democratic Alliance, which had a representative on the Council of National Unity.

2. The Camp of Fighting Poland

The initiative to organize the Camp of Fighting Poland came from a group of men prominent in the prewar regime, who had left Poland during the war and were left stranded in Hungary and in Rumania. They were led by former Vice Minister Julian Piasecki, who coordinated his plans for an underground organization based on the ideology of the prewar OZON with Marshal Edward Rydz-Smigly, when the Marshal arrived in Budapest, following his escape from the Rumanian internment camp in Dragoslavele on December 10, 1940. The group managed to maintain a regular contact with the occupied country and within a short time Marshal Rydz-Smigly left for Poland, where he was to assume the command of the Camp of Fighting Poland, leaving the base in Hungary in the hands of General Dr. Stefan Hubicki. At a great personal risk, the Marshal—accompanied by a mountaineer-guide and a former District Vice Governor Bazyli Rogowski—crossed the Polish border on the night of October 26, 1941, and reached Warsaw by way of Krakow. In Warsaw he found quarters at the home of the widow of General Maksymowicz-Raczynski. He began his activities by requesting a meeting with General Rowecki. However, Rowecki avoided the meeting, fearful that it would strain even further his already strained relations with General Sikorski. On December 7, 1941, five weeks after his arrival in Warsaw and deep in the underground work, Marshal Rydz-Smigly suffered a fatal heart attack. He was buried at the Powazki cemetery under the name of Adam Zawisza.

Julian Piasecki, who arrived in Poland shortly after Rydz-Smigly, assumed the leadership of the Camp of Fighting Poland. For its membership, the Camp reached out to the same circles as did the

Assembly, vying for greater influence. Among its several publications, the most important was its official organ, *Przeglad Polityczny* (The Political Review). In contrast to the Assembly, which maintained close contact with the liberal Democratic Party, the Camp of Fighting Poland leaned more to the right, and by 1944 established a close working relationship with the National Party.

Similarly to the Assembly of Organizations for Independence, the Camp of Fighting Poland assumed the stance of opposition to the government-in-exile, the Government Delegacy and the underground parliamentary bodies. An article in *Przeglad Polityczny* (November 20, 1943) launched an attack against the agreement of the four parties (Polish Socialist Party, Peasant Party, National Party and the Labor Party) for supposedly monopolizing political power in Poland and eliminating from political representation other groups, which—the article claimed—had the support of the majority of the population. This accusation had no foundation in reality, since neither the Assembly nor the Camp had ever acquired any large following, and both remained in effect elite organizations.

The Warsaw Rising marked the end of both organizations. Zygmunt Hempel and Julian Piasecki were killed during the Rising. Dr. Waclaw Lipinski was arrested after the war by the security police and sentenced to death; though reprieved, he died later in the prison at Wronki. Henryk Jozewski is still living in Warsaw at the present time.[1]

XV

UNDERGROUND ORGANIZATIONS OF THE *ONR*

1. *National Armed Forces (Narodowe Sily Zbrojne—NSZ)*

A political organization called the Rampart Group (*Grupa Szanca*) was established in the underground by members of that fraction of the National-Radical Camp (ONR) which, before the war, gathered around the daily *ABC*. The Rampart Group was headed by Tadeusz Salski, Otmar Wawrzkowicz and Jerzy Olgierd Illakowicz. The same group also established a military organization called the Union of Salamander (*Zwiazek Jaszczurczy*), led by Wladyslaw Marcinkowski. Both groups acknowledged the government-in-exile as Poland's lawful government. The Rampart Group, however, did not recognize the Government Delegacy as the sole representative in Poland of the emigré government, and demanded an equal status for itself; similarly, the Union of Salamander refused to recognize the Union for Armed Struggle as the official Polish underground army, and pretended to a status equal to that of the UAS. Both organizations drew their membership primarily from the cities, from among the adherents of the prewar *Oboz Narodowo-Radykalny* (ONR). In their publications—the most important of which was *Szaniec* (The Rampart)—they advocated the "ONR ideology," patterned after the Italian fascist movement, hostile not only toward the communists, but also toward all liberal democratic groupings, and imbued with an intensely nationalistic and antisemitic spirit. In 1942, the Rampart Group formed a quasi underground government, with departments of the army, propaganda, administration, security, justice, and finances.

In 1942, the National Party subordinated its military organization, *Narodowa Organizacja Wojskowa* (NOW), to the Union for Armed Struggle. This decision met with the opposition of nearly half of the members of the National Military Organization and provoked a split. The dissidents joined with the Rampart Group and the Union of Salamander to form a military organization called *Narodowe Sily Zbrojne* or NSZ (The National Armed Forces), subject to the Provisional National Political Council, headed by Zbigniew Stypulkowski. The Council operated military, administrative and propaganda departments, which absorbed the quasi government of the Rampart Group.

The establishment of the National Armed Forces was tantamount to rejection of the consolidation action, ordered by the government-in-exile and the Commander-in-Chief. Accordingly, Professor Jan Piekalkiewicz, the Government Delegate in Poland, issued a statement, published in the "Information Bulletin" on March 11, 1943, in which he branded the formation of the National Armed Forces as seditious factiousness and reasserted the status of the Home Army (which meanwhile evolved from the Union for Armed Struggle as its successor) as the official underground army of Poland. This pronouncement provoked a series of attacks, mounted by the nationalist underground press against the Government Delegate and the Home Army.

Under these circumstances, General Bor-Komorowski (who succeeded General Rowecki as Commander of the Home Army, following Rowecki's arrest by the Gestapo on June 30, 1943) notified the National Armed Forces that the organization should be subordinated to the Home Army by October 15, 1943. When this deadline passed and no action was taken, General Bor issued an order, dated November 9, 1943, stating that:

1. Membership in the National Armed Forces is not tantamount to active service in the ranks of the Armed Forces of the Republic;

2. Members of the National Armed Forces are dutybound to withdraw immediately from that organization and to report for active service in the ranks of the Home Army.

Meanwhile, a detachment of the National Armed Forces became responsible for the first military underground operation that resulted in a fratricidal warfare. On August 9, 1943, they attacked a unit of the communist People's Guard in the village of Borowo (Krasnik county), killing 26 guardsmen and four local peasants who had come to visit the soldiers. The incident forced the Commander of the Home Army, General Bor, to issue on November 9, 1943, a statement denying the Home Army's participation in the murder committed by the National Armed Forces.

Various units of the National Armed Forces were also responsible for instances of murder of Jews, who were hiding in the forests. And on June 13, 1943, a squad of the National Armed Forces, bent on "cleaning out the Jews" from the Bureau of Information and Propaganda of the High Command of the Home Army, killed two officers of the High Command—Professor Ludwik Widerszal and Jerzy Makowiecki, an engineer, whose wife was also killed. Another worker of the Bureau of Information and Propaganda, an engineer by the name of Czarnomski, was also murdered by the National Armed Forces storm troopers. Finally, on July 14, 1944, two other BIP workers—Professor Marceli Handelsman and a well-known writer, Halina Krahelska—were abducted from their office by the National

Armed Forces and delivered to the Germans, who put them in prison.[1]

Action aimed at liquidating those whom the National Armed Forces considered objectionable, was to terminate with a "Saint Batholomew's Night," though, as it turned out, nothing came of these plans. Long lists were prepared of proscribed persons, who were to be liquidated at a propitious moment, e.g., at the time of disintegration of the occupation authorities. Prominent socialist leaders, well-known liberals and democrats, men suspected of being Freemasons, etc., could all be found on that list. Most of them were active in the underground; their liquidation was to pave the way for a nationalist coup d'état and assumption of control in Poland.

Negotiations pertaining to the consolidation of the underground were renewed in January 1944. This time around they were successful. On March 7, 1944, an agreement was signed, subordinating the National Armed Forces to and merging them with the Home Army. Pleased with this development, General Bor issued an order of the day on April 13, 1944, welcoming the soldiers of the National Armed Forces into the ranks of the Home Army. General Bor's order was published in the Home Army's organ, "The Information Bulletin" (April 13, 1944) and in the National Armed Forces' organ, "The Rampart" (April 15, 1944).

But the signing of the agreement failed to put an end to the problems of consolidation. On the contrary, it brought a new split, this time in the leadership of the National Armed Forces. Those among the leadership who were connected with the National Party or the National Military Organization (among them, Zbigniew Stypulkowski) supported the implementation of the agreement; others—linked with the Rampart Group or the Union of Salamander—refused to obey its terms. As a result, some 10 to 15 thousand soldiers of the National Armed Forces joined the ranks of the Home Army, while many more remained in the non-merged military organization. To take the place of the Provisional National Political Council, the Rampart Group instituted the Political Council of the National Armed Services, headed by Wladyslaw Marcinkowski. The Council appointed Lieutenant Colonel Stanislaw Nakoniecznikoff-Klukowski as Acting Commander General of the National Armed Forces.

In view of these developments, General Bor ordered on June 5, 1944, a unilateral incorporation of the non-merged units of the National Armed Forces into the Home Army. To carry out this assignment, he appointed Lt. Col. Albin Rak, acting Commander General of the National Armed Forces. The NAF retaliated by sentencing Colonel Rak to death. This sentence was never carried out. But a few months later, an identical sentence was passed on Lieutenant Colonel Nakoniecznikoff-Klukowski under the pretense that he was scheming to subordinate the National Armed Forces to the communists, but actually because he intended to subordinate the National Armed Forces to the Home Army. He was shot in Czestochowa, on October 18, 1944. (His assassin, Otmar Wawrzkowicz, emigrated to Canada after the war, and eventually died by his own hand.) Wladyslaw Pacholczyk, a former member of the National Party, was also shot.

Further, though still partial, consolidation came with the outbreak of the Warsaw Rising on August 1, 1944. The non-merged NAF units joined the merged units (800 men in all), and they fought together under the command of the Home Army.

Meanwhile, the remainder of the National Armed Forces concentrated in the Kielce district and, following a reorganization, was renamed the Holy Cross Brigade (and after the local Holy Cross Mountains). Establishing contact with the German occupation authorities (represented by Paul Fuchs, head of the *Sonderkommando* IV A in the Radom district), the Brigade, 850-men strong, began on January 13, 1945—with German approval and even under German protection— the long trek westward through Silesia to Czechoslovakia. Once there, and again with the collaboration of the German Army, two patrols of parachutists were sent to Poland, which, however, were intercepted by the security police. On May 6, 1945, the Holy Cross Brigade made its way to the American-occupied zone of Germany. It then established contact with the Polish Second Corps of General Anders, but did not come under his command. As a result of their total isolation, the soldiers of the Brigade eventually formed the core of the Guards' Battalions, established by the Americans and commanded on behalf of the Americans by Franciszek Sobolta, a colonel in the Polish Army.

Meanwhile, those units of the National Armed Forces that remained in Poland were officially dissolved on July 5, 1945, by the order of Major Broniewski, at that time the Commander of the NAF. In spite of this, scattered remnants of the NAF went on fighting the security police for the next few years (similarly to the remnants of the Home Army). Their political leaders either managed to escape to the west, like Wladyslaw Marcinkowski, or were caught by the security police, sentenced to death and executed, like Stanislaw Kasznica and Lech Neyman.

In consequence of the events described above, service in the non-merged formations of the National Armed Forces has not been recognized by the government-in-exile as service in the Polish Armed Forces.

2. The National Confederation

One faction of the prewar National-Radical Camp (ONR-Falanga), headed by a Polish fascist, Boleslaw Piasecki, endeavored at first to work out some form of collaboration with the Germans. These efforts ended with Piasecki's arrest by the Gestapo, whereupon the movement descended underground and established an organization, bearing the high-flown name of the National Confederation, even though it had no more than one thousand members. Among Piasecki's closest collaborators were: Jerzy Rutkowski (who, however, left Piasecki within a short time and joined the Home Army), Andrzej Swietlicki, Wojciech Ketrzynski, Aleksander Bochenski and Stanislaw Briesemeister (chief of intelligence service of the National Confederation). In its ideological declaration, issued in October 1940 and followed by other pronouncements, the Confederation stated that—as far as internal affairs were concerned—it would not permit the rule of political parties or groups in Poland; in foreign affairs, the main goal, according to the Confederation was the break up of the USSR, in order to build on the rubble of Russian defeat a "Great Slavic Imperium," in which the leading role was to be played by Poland. This program of Piasecki's policy in the east was advocated on the pages of the Confederation's organ *Nowa Polska* (The New Poland). To propagate his program and to give it added weight, Piasecki decided to begin guerilla operations beyond the Bug River, in the eastern territories. To this end, he organized a group called "Striking Battalion Cadres," or—for short—"Strike." On Piasecki's orders, about 300 men showed up at the concentration point in Sterdynskie Woods in October/November 1942. This attracted the Germans' attention. They surrounded the group and smashed it to such an extent that barely 60 men managed to cross the Bug River. Pursued by the Germans, they scattered. The surviving remnants returned to Warsaw, bringing the news of the disaster.

Piasecki's subsequent initiatives were equally unsuccessful. In June 1943, the Germans surrounded another "Strike" group (about 200 men) near the Bialowiez Forest and destroyed it completely. According to one source, 30 soldiers—heralds of defeat—were saved; according to another source, there were only two survivors. A third "Strike" group was similarly annihilated in August, 1943, in the Augustow forests. After these three defeats, in which some 500 young men were killed, Piasecki decided to forego further efforts and, toward the end of 1943, recognized the authority of the High Command of the Home Army, but not the Government Delegacy, with regard to which he maintained an ambivalent attitude. Even efforts to have the National Confederation join "Civil Resistance" ended in a fiasco. The head of the Directorate of Civil Resistance, Stefan Korbonski, met with Piasecki twice, but heard nothing from him except empty assurances.

In November 1944, Piasecki was arrested by the Soviet NKVD. Threatened with death, as Russia's Enemy No. 1, Piasecki saved his life by coming up with a plan of disintegrating the Catholic Church in Poland from within, with the help of lay Catholic activists and recruited priests. This plan was approved by Ivan Serov, a general of the NKVD. Not only did it win Piasecki his freedom, but also various political and economic privileges, which permitted him to build a powerful, pseudo-Catholic political organization, PAX, based on an economic empire developed—in a communist system—along the classic capitalistic lines. With the passing of time, Piasecki became the Soviets' most trusted tool in Poland.[3]

THE COMMUNIST AND PRO-COMMUNIST UNDERGROUND
AND THE CIVIC ANTICOMMUNIST COMMITTEE

1. The Polish Workers Party

The Polish Communist Party, founded on December 16, 1918, was dissolved in 1938 by the Executive of the Communist International, because of the supposed infiltration of the party by the agents of the Polish political police. Those leaders of the Polish Communist Party, who happened to be in the Soviet Union, were put to death by Stalin's orders. Three years after Stalin's death, i.e., in 1956, the Polish Communist Party was rehabilitated and its past dissolution declared groundless.

After the outbreak of World War II, the few Communists that remained in Poland showed no great inclination to rebuild the party along the old lines. Only after the outbreak of the Soviet-German war on June 22, 1941, did the initiative come from the Soviet Union. In the USSR at that time there were many Polish communists, who had escaped from the territories occupied initially by the Soviets before the advance of the German armies. From among these men, the so-called "initiative groups" were formed for diversionary purposes. Properly instructed and trained, they were parachuted into Poland. They established contact with the remnants of the Polish Communist Party and initiated together—on January 5, 1942, in Warsaw—the Polish Workers Party. They shunned the old party name in order to mislead the Polish population, which hated Russia passionately for its attack on Poland on September 17, 1939, and for its participation together with the Germans in the fourth partition of Poland.

The Polish Workers Party (*Polska Partia Robotnicza*—PPR) was run by the Central Committee, headed by the First Secretary Marceli Nowotko. According to the information provided by Jozef Swiatlo— a colonel in the security police, who escaped to the west in 1955— Nowotko was shot on November 28, 1942, by Edward Molojec (parachuted into Poland together with Nowotko on December 28, 1941), after Molojec had discovered that Nowotko's men supplied the Germans with names, pseudonyms and addresses of members of the underground, connected with the Government Delegacy or the Home Army. Nowotko was succeeded by Pawel Finder, who was caught by the Gestapo on November 14, 1943, and shot. Finder's successor, Wladyslaw Gomulka, remained as First Secretary until the end of the war.

In January 1942, the Polish Workers Party issued its first declaration, outlining its program. Brandishing patriotic slogans and following instructions from Moscow, it called for an immediate "mass armed action" in Poland, i.e., for a universal uprising, disregarding the fact that at that very moment victorious German armies stood at the gates of Moscow and Leningrad, and that an uprising in 1942 would have been tantamount to national suicide. Since this ran contrary to the policy of the Government Delegacy and the High Command of the Home Army, who were preparing for an uprising timed to coincide with the reversals or defeat of the German armies, the communists coined an accusation that was to be reiterated time and again until the outbreak of the Warsaw Rising, that the Home Army "stood with arms at ease."

In April 1943, the Polish Workers Party established a military organization called People's Guard (*Gwardia Ludowa*—GL), headed by Franciszek Jozwiak and Marian Spychalski.

On February 18, 22 and 25, 1943, meetings were held by the representatives of the Government Delegacy and the High Command of the Home Army with the representatives of the Polish Workers Party, probing the feasibility of cooperation. The Delegacy and the Home Army were represented by Stefan Pawlowski, director of the Presidium Office, and by Eugeniusz Czarnowski, a functionary of the Bureau of Information and Propaganda of the High Command of the Home Army. The Polish Workers Party was represented by Wladyslaw Gomulka and Jan Strzeszewski. Representatives of the Delegacy and the Home Army advanced the following conditions of cooperation: recognition by the Polish Workers Party of the government in London and submission to the government representatives in Poland; formal declaration by the Polish Workers Party that the party was not an agent of the Komintern or of any foreign government and that it supported the inviolability of Poland's eastern frontiers. Representatives of the Polish Workers Party put forth their counterproposals, formulating their own conditions of cooperation: creation of a new government in Poland (thus reducing the government in London to the role of a representative abroad); granting the People's Guard organizational autonomy and equal status with the Home Army; leaving open the question of Poland's eastern frontiers. In view of these diametrically opposed positions, no agreement was reached.

The fiasco of negotiations signaled for the Polish Workers Party the beginning of a political and organizational action against the government, the Delegacy, and the Home Army. In two basic declarations entitled "What Are We Fighting For?", the Polish Workers Party proclaimed a "socialist"—actually, communist—program for Poland (March and November 1943), discarding a constitutional government in favor of a "government of the people." This program was expounded in the party's main organ *Trybuna Wolnosci* (Tribune of Freedom) and other publications, as well as broadcasts of the radio station "Kosciuszko," located in Russia but pretending to be broadcasting from within Poland. Until the very end of the occupation, these propaganda organs of the Polish Workers Party continued to denounce the government, the Delegacy, and the Home Army, as "tools of capitalist reaction, seeking to enslave the people of Poland" and to exhort the Poles to "revolt and cast off the yoke, with the help of victorious Soviet armies, advancing steadily closer to the Polish border."

Military offensive was complemented and bolstered with a new political offensive. In April 1943, the Soviets organized in Moscow the Union of Polish Patriots in USSR, a body composed of Polish communists living in Russia at that time. The Patriots' immediate concern was the creation of a Polish army in Russia, to be commanded by Zygmunt Berling, a colonel in the Polish army before the war, now promoted to the rank of general.

In Poland, too, a new organization came into being. On December 31, 1943, the National Council of the Homeland was born. It consisted of the Polish Workers Party and a group called the Workers Party of Polish Socialists, led by Edward Osobka (Morawski); to create the appearance of universal support, a few fictitious groups were added for good measure. Boleslaw Bierut—a Komintern agent and a Soviet citizen, totally unknown in Poland—became the chairman of the Council. One of the first acts of the National Council of the Homeland was to change the name of the People's Guard to People's Army (*Armia Ludowa*—AL). The command of the People's Army was given to General Michal Zymierski (pseudonym: Rola), drummed out of the service before the war and later rejected by both the Home Army and the Peasant Battalions. The guerilla activities of the People's Army were limited; it was more concerned with penetrating the pro-government underground—e.g., the Peasant Battalions—than with fighting the Germans. It was more active east of the Bug River, where it was supported and supplied by the Soviet partisans. After the war, most of the soldiers of the People's Army were assigned to service in the security police.

When the Soviet armies entered the town of Chelm Lubelski, the Union of Polish Patriots was transformed on July 21, 1944 into the Polish Committee of National Liberation (*Polski Komitet Wyzwolenia Narodowego*—PKWN), a national representation. The Committee began by issuing the so-called "July Manifesto," which elaborated on theses set forth in the two declarations, issued by the Polish Workers Party in March and November 1943, and outlined specifically the new form of government, repudiating the Constitution of 1935 and the government-in-exile, and proclaiming the National Council of the Homeland as the only "lawful" authority in Poland. The Manifesto guaranteed to all citizens such democratic freedoms as freedom of religion, press, association, etc., but with one proviso—that these could not be exploited by the "enemies of democracy." This clause provided the basis for the strong-arm rule of the security police and the terror prevailing in the territories occupied by the Soviet armies and directed against the Polish population, which was nearly unanimously anti-communist.

Government Delegate Jankowski and chairman of the Council of National Unity Puzak reacted to the establishment of the Polish Committee of National Liberation by issuing on July 26, 1944 a proclamation to the Polish nation. They denounced the Committee as a creature of Russia and called for the support of the state authorities, represented in Poland by the Government Delegate (who was also the vice premier of the government-in-exile), the Home Cabinet, and the Council of National Unity.

On the day this proclamation was issued, i.e., on July 26, 1944, the Soviets extended their recognition to the Polish Committee of National Liberation as an official representative of Poland, and on December 31, 1944, its name was changed by a decree of the National Council of the Homeland to "Provisional Polish Government." The process of building a government apparatus, ruling Poland on behalf of the USSR, was now completed.[1]

2. Centralization of Democratic, Socialist and Syndicalist Parties

After the WRN fraction of the Polish Socialist Party had left the Political Coordinating Committee in September 1941, and until their return in March 1943, their place on the Committee was occupied by the Organization of Polish Socialists, spiritual descendants of Stanislaw Dubois, publisher of the "Bulwark of Freedom." Adam Prochnik was the first chairman of the Polish Socialists. On April 11, 1943, the Polish Socialists held a meeting in Warsaw and subsequently changed the name of their organization to "Workers Party of Polish Socialists" (*Robotnicza Partia Polskich Socjalistow*—RPPS). The new name was better suited to their radicalized program. After Proch-nik's death, on May 22, 1942, some of the leaders of the organization, led by Edward Osobka (Morawski), joined the communist National Council of the Homeland, created on December 31, 1943. A majority, however, followed the Central Committee of the organization in an ef-fort to consolidate the radical left. This led to the creation, in February, 1944, of the Centralization of Democratic, Socialist, and Syndicalist Parties ("Centralization"). In addition to the Workers Party of Polish Socialists, two fractions of the Democratic Party also joined the Cen-tralization: the Polish Democratic Party, led by attorney Waclaw Bar-cikowski, and the Party for Polish Democracy. Other groups that joined the "Centralization" were: the Union of Polish Syndicalists, headed by Stefan Szwedowski and Professor Kazimierz Zakrzewski, the Jewish So-cialist Organization BUND, and a few smaller groups of no great signifi-cance. The Centralization's executive, People's Central Committee, chaired by Romuald Miller, announced the new organization's program in March 1944. It demanded that the Government, the Delegacy and the High Command of the Home Army eliminate from their ranks all those affiliated with the National Party, the prewar regime (*sanacja*), and the National-Radical Camp, and be limited to the central-leftist representation. As regards the foreign policy, the Centralization de-manded the establishment of close relations with the USSR, but re-frained from any pronouncement on the subject of Poland's eastern frontier.

In April 1944, the Centralization formed its own military organiza-tion, called the Polish People's Army (*Polska Armia Ludowa*—PAL), headed by Colonel Julian Skokowski and consisting mostly of rather ambitious and broadly developed staff network. Actually, the few hundred men of the People's Militia of the Workers Party of Polish Socialists represented the total military strength of the Centralization.

Shortly, the Centralization began to negotiate—on the one hand, with the Delegacy and the High Command of the Home Army, and on the other, with the communist National Council of the Home-land. All this negotiating proved fruitless. On the one hand, the de-mand to abandon the concept of national unity, represented in Po-land by the four-party agreement, and to replace it with a central-leftist concept, was totally unacceptable. On the other hand, nego-tiations with the communist National Council of the Homeland were blocked by the Union of Polish Syndicalists, which—though support-ive of changes outlined in the program—had long since recognized and cooperated with the Government Delegacy, the High Command of the Home Army and the Directorate of Civil Resistance.

Despite the initial setbacks, with the advance of the Soviet offensive the Centralization began to lean more and more toward the National Council of the Homeland and the Polish Workers Party. For instance, it joined the Polish Workers Party in setting up secret committees in plants and factories. Finally, in September 1944, i.e., toward the end of the Warsaw Rising, it entered—together with the Polish Workers Party and the Corps of Security (established by the Council for National Defense, a cluster of a few small groups)—into a compact called the Insurrectionary Democratic Agreement, which promptly extended recognition to the Moscow-spawned National Council of the Homeland and the Polish Committee of National Liberation as the only lawful ruling authority in Poland.[2]

3. Civic Anticommunist Committee

The underground leadership did not sit idly by while the Polish Workers Party engaged in activities bordering on treason. The first initiative was taken by the High Command of the Home Army in 1942, when Section "K" was established. It was to keep a watchful eye on the Polish Workers Party and to counteract its propaganda, mainly by providing the underground press with information items, and often even articles, that revealed the real aims and nature of the Polish Workers Party. By the end of 1943, the growing need for counteraction forced the High Command to enlarge Section "K" into a separate division of the Bureau of Information and Propaganda, which produced special publications, pamphlets and leaflets, showing the Polish Workers Party for what they were—a tool of Soviet policy. It was during this period that the slogan "PPR—Paid Flunkeys of Russia" became popular throughout the country—chalked, painted or daubed with tar on fences and walls of towns and villages. In the third phase of this action against the Polish Workers Party, the Government Delegacy, the Council of National Unity and several smaller groups, not associated with the Council, joined in forming the Civic Anticommunist Committee (*Spoleczny Komitet Antykomunistyczny—ANTYK*). Its first proclamation, issued on February 10, 1944, was signed by 24 political parties and groups. Actually, the only groups that did not take part in this action were those who had joined the National Council of the Homeland. The existence of ANTYK served to broaden the scope of anticommunist action and to expand its basis from the Home Army to a far wider political and social scene. The Committee's proclamation unmasked once again the true face of the Polish Workers Party—a Soviet agency, striving behind the smoke screen of patriotic slogans to implement the Soviet's political aims, including the permanent annexation of Poland's eastern territories. The National Council of the Homeland and the Polish Workers Party were branded as traitors to the nation and to the state.

The Civic Anticommunist Committee was headed by Franciszek Bialas of the Polish Socialist Party (WRN fraction), a man whom no one could possibly accuse of "reactionary" affiliations. During its comparatively short existence, ANTYK published a number of leaflets combating the current political and propaganda actions of the Polish Workers Party. At one of the first meetings (attended also by Stefan Korbonski, chief of the Directorate of Civil Resistance), a proposal was advanced to eliminate communist leaders by assassination. It was rejected, with one dissenting vote. This was in sharp contrast to the practice of the Polish Workers Party, whose "disinformation section" supplied the Gestapo with names and addresses of the underground leaders connected with the Delegacy or the Home Army, and whose squads openly liquidated underground leaders in the last months of the underground's existence, in 1944 and 1945, particularly in the provinces.[3]

XVII

UNDERGROUND PRESS AND PUBLICATIONS

In addition to the press organs of the Government Delegacy and the Home Army, there also flourished a wide array of periodicals, published by underground political or military organizations, and sometimes even by small groups of a few people, banded together for the sole purpose of publishing their own paper. One of the chief objectives of practically every underground group was to put out its own publication, which would expound its views, spread them among the clandestine readership and win supporters, and often members, for the organization. This accounts for the extraordinary number of underground publications.

One note was dominant in all underground publications—the imperative to fight against the German occupier until the day of final victory, which no one doubted. With very few exceptions, all underground publications supported the government-in-exile and its representatives in Poland. As the structure of the underground government grew firmer, the underground press began to publish the pronouncements and proclamations of Government Delegates and the underground parliamentary bodies (e.g., the National Political Representation), as well as appeals, warnings, instructions and communiqués of the Directorate of Civil Resistance and the Directorate of Underground Struggle. In time, there appeared polemical articles. Underground publications began to fight among themselves about ideologies, principles, necessary reforms, new constitution, new frontiers, the image of future Poland, a better world organization after victory, and dozens of other more or less important problems. Party publications such as those of the Polish Socialist Party, the Peasant Party or the National Party, represented a wide range of diverse, and often competing, political, social and economic programs. And since the press enjoyed greater freedom in the underground than in prewar Poland, its contents were rich and varied, influencing the readers and forming their views, strengthening the nation's resistance against the German and Soviet occupiers.

Underground papers also carried news from Poland (e.g., about German crimes and terror), news from abroad (e.g., activities of the government-in-exile and international developments) and, most important of all, war news, based on their own radio monitors or supplied by underground news agencies.

The first underground papers appeared as early as October 1939. By the end of 1939, there were already 30 publications in existence; in 1940—200; in 1941—290; in 1942—380; in 1943—500; and in 1944—600. Their number was considerably larger than the number of underground organizations, which decreased, rather than increased, because of consolidation. The growth in the number of underground publications may be explained by the growth of the underground itself: individual organizations began publishing more than one—often several—papers, each different in character and designed for different, and ever growing, circles of readers. Local publications also proliferated in the provinces, which minimized danger involved in distribution of papers originating in such publishing centers as Warsaw or Krakow.[1]

Copies have been preserved to this day of 1,123 periodicals—varying in size from one page to several dozen—published in Poland during the entire period of German occupation. If we were to add to this number publications which have not been preserved or located until now, we would have to raise the total figure to 1,400. Of this number, about 400 had been tracked down by the Gestapo. Only the Netherlands can boast of a higher (by 50 titles) number of underground periodicals, but the Dutch underground press was helped by the printing presses of papers published legally under German censorship—a situation unimaginable in occupied Poland. Other occupied countries—France, Belgium, Denmark, Italy and Norway—are far behind in this respect. Also, the largest number of printed—rather than mimeographed or typewritten—publications appeared in Poland (325). However, the circulation of Polish underground periodicals, although it reached several thousands for some of them, was smaller than that of certain French or Dutch periodicals, which were in a position to use the printing plants of publications that were legal, i.e., printed with the permission of German occupying authorities. Also, the number of periodicals that managed to sustain publication throughout the entire period of occupation was the largest in Poland. There were 17 such publications in Poland, 13 in France, and 8 in Holland.[1] The same names were sometimes used by different publications; thus in Poland there appeared 11 different periodicals all called *Pobudka* (Reveille) and 10 called *Reduta* (The Fort).

With the passing of time, broadly specialized publications began to appear. There were 30 scouting periodicals, 20 literary and cultural magazines, and 14 satirical publications. There were also "professional" periodicals, such as *PP* (Underground Police), or "The Trolleyman"; women's paper *Zywia*, with a children's supplement *Biedronka* (Ladybug); a periodical of the Zamosc district called

"From the Land of the Expelled"; even two trotskyite papers, "The Red Banner" and "The Marxist Review"; finally, there were also two Serbo-Lusatian publications: *Sprawy Luzyckie* in Polish and *Wendischer Bote* in German.

Foreign-language publications—besides the diversionary propaganda materials put out by the psychological warfare Section "N"—included: 25 periodicals in Hebrew and in Yiddish, published mainly in the Warsaw ghetto, as well as one French-language periodical (*L'Information*, published by the Home Army in Krakow), and one published in English for the prisoners of war held in German POW camps in Poland.

Publishing activities were not limited to periodicals only. In occupied Poland, 1075 books and booklets were published by various political parties, by scholarly institutions which carried on their work underground after their dissolution by the Nazis, and even by private persons. These were works devoted to politics, history, journalistic comment, technology, military problems and science. Still another domain was the publication of textbooks and scripts used in underground schools, literary works and music. They often appeared under protective titles, with false names of authors and publishers, and were either printed or mimeographed, or simply typewritten with several copies.[2]

The underground press provided the mortar binding the structure of the Polish Underground State. It was the voice not only of this underground state, but also of the entire Polish nation throughout over five years of its struggle against the German occupier.

XVIII

JEWS UNDER OCCUPATION

1. Organizing a Holocaust

At the outbreak of the war, there were 3.5 million Jews in Poland—about 10 per cent of the total population. This high percentage was the end result of a long historical process. In 1264, Prince Boleslas the Pious of Kalisz granted the Jews a statute guaranteeing their religious freedom and autonomy for Jewish communities. When persecutions of Jews broke out in other European countries, there began a mass migration of Jews to Poland, where subsequent centuries of tolerance favored the growth of the Jewish population and the establishment of centers of Jewish culture in cities such as Lublin and Wilno.

Following Poland's partition into occupation zones in 1939, about 2 million Jews remained in the *General Gouvernement* and in the western territories incorporated into the Reich, while the rest were in the Soviet-occupied zone. When the war broke out between Russia and Germany, with the lightning German occupation of all Polish territories, another million Polish Jews fell under German rule. The rest, i.e., about half a million, had been deported previously, together with the Poles, into the depths of Russia; some Jews also managed to make their way to the Scandinavian countries (through Lithuania, before that country was overrun by the Soviets) and the west, or obtained Japanese visas and, crossing the USSR in transit, reached Japan and went on to, for instance, Australia.

German policy regarding the Polish Jews was formulated in the decree of the Central Security Office of the Reich of September 21, 1939, pertaining to the solution of the Jewish problem by stages. The final goal of complete extermination of the Jews was not spelled out in the decree and remained a state secret. The decree specified, among others, concentrations of Jews in larger cities, in designated districts. The Security Office was headed by Reinhard Heydrich, and it was on his behalf that Adolf Eichmann undertook the implementation of the decree.

To begin with, the Jews were ordered to wear armbands with the Star of David; this was followed by confiscation of all Jewish real estate and partial confiscation of private property. Jews were ousted from all public institutions, but—through a decree of Governor Hans

Frank of October 26, 1939—subject to compulsory labor from the age of 16 to 60; in this connection, special labor camps were established (at the peak of this action, there were 300 such camps). Finally, on January 26, 1940, the Jews were forbidden to move from one place to another and to use public means of transportation.

The most shattering blow, however, came with the establishment of closed ghettos to which Jews from the entire country were driven, though there were also instances of on-the-spot extermination of Jews in small localities, e.g., in Kleczew (Konin county). In Warsaw, the ghetto was established in November 1940; in Lodz, already at the beginning of 1940; in Krakow, only in March 1941. Governor Frank's decree of October 25, 1941, stated that:

"Jews, who leave their designated districts, are liable to penalty of death. The same penalty will be applied to persons, who knowingly provide shelter for such Jews"—that is, to Poles.

The same regulation was reiterated time and again in many decrees issued by local German authorities throughout the years of occupation. The death penalty also threatened the Jews for illegal purchase of food, for using public transportation, for not wearing the prescribed armband. For that matter, the killing of a Jew by a German for whatever reason, or for no reason at all, was not punishable, since Jews and gypsies were removed from under the protection of the law by the decree of March 4, 1941.

According to the letter of the decrees, any person with three grandparents who had been members of a Jewish religious community, was Jewish. As a result, there were many people in the ghettos whose parents had already changed their religious affiliation, and who did not consider themselves Jewish at all.

Both in the labor camps and in the ghettos, the Jewish population was doomed to a slow death of starvation, exhaustion, and illness. The daily food ration in the Warsaw ghetto was the equivalent of 184 calories. In consequence, the mortality rate—particularly among children and older people—was extremely high, several times higher than before the war. One contributing factor was the unbelievable concentration of population, with a dozen people or more living in one room.

Finally, the last stage was reached—extermination of all the Jews gathered behind the walls of the *General Gouvernement* ghettos. It began with mass executions of Jews in eastern Poland and in Russia by the so-called *Einsatzgruppen*, which moved in after the outbreak of the German-Soviet war, following on the heels of swiftly advancing German armies. In the spring of 1942, the Germans began transports of the ghetto populations to the extermination camps of

Auschwitz, Treblinka, Majdanek, Sobibor, Belzec, and Chelm (this last one, for Jews from the territories incorporated into the Reich), as well as a few other, smaller ones. Once in camp, the Jews were killed in the gas chambers and their corpses cremated or stacked outside in big piles and burned. The first transports from the Warsaw ghetto to Treblinka began on July 22, 1942. Within two months, 300,000 Jews (out of the total ghetto population of 400,000) were evacuated from the Warsaw ghetto.

Hundreds of thousands of Jews brought from Italy, Germany, France, Belgium, Holland, Austria, Czechoslovakia, etc. were murdered in German death camps in Poland. According to the calculations of the Institute of Jewish Affairs in New York, of a total of 9,612,000 Jews in Europe, 5,787,000 perished under German occupation; of this number, 1,500,000 were killed in the countries of their habitation, primarily in German-occupied parts of the USSR.

Jewish sources estimate the number of Polish Jews that were saved from the holocaust at between 50,000 and 120,000. According to the estimates of the Directorate of Civil Resistance, there were about 200,000 Jewish survivors in Poland.[1]

2. Liaison with the Ghetto

The underground leadership, and particularly the Government Delegacy and the Home Army (which included a few Jewish officers in its High Command), began to publish daily in their underground press information about the persecutions of Jews, which they denounced in the strongest terms, calling on the Polish population to render the Jews all possible assistance. *Biuletyn Informacyjny*, organ of the Home Army, even had its own correspondent in the ghetto (Jerzy Grasberg). Similarly, Polish underground political parties established contact with their members, or counterpart organizations behind the ghetto walls. Thus, members of the Jewish BUND maintained regular contact with the Polish Socialist Party (WRN) and the Polish Boy Scouts (the Grey Ranks) were in touch with the Jewish *Hashomer Hacair*. The same was also true for the Democratic Party. Among the smaller underground organizations maintaining either contacts or affiliated cells in the ghetto, were: the Corps for Security (responsible for saving about 5,000 Jews during the war), a leftist organization called "Spartakus," a youth organization called "Union of Struggle for Liberation," and the organization of Polish Socialists, which had its chapter in the ghetto. When the Polish Workers Party came into existence in January 1942, it also established a cell in the Warsaw ghetto.

As early as in 1940, the Government Delegate alerted London about the persecution of Jews in Poland. Thereupon, the Polish government-in-exile sent a note on this subject to allied governments (May 3, 1941). Also in 1941, the Polish Ministry of Information in London published a booklet on the persecution of Jews in Poland, entitled *Bestiality Unknown in Any Previous Record of History* and based on information received from occupied Poland. In January 1942, the Ministry issued another publication, *The New German Order in Poland*. Both publications created a stir thoughout the allied world, which after 1941 could no longer plead ignorance of the persecution of Jews in Poland.

3. The Jewish Underground

About that time, the first preparations for armed resistance began in the ghettos. In October 1942, leaders of the incipient Jewish underground joined in forming the Jewish National Committee, composed of representatives of all Jewish organizations, with the exception of BUND. This led to the creation of the Coordination Commission, which logically became in time the central political body of the Jewish underground. Irrespective of this, both BUND and the Jewish National Committee had their separate representatives remaining "on the Aryan side" and maintaining regular contact with the Government Delegate. Dr. Adolf Berman (Borowski) represented the Jewish National Committee, and Dr. Leon Feiner (Berezowski) was the representative of BUND.

On July 28, 1942, the Fighting Organization of the Warsaw ghetto was born. "On the Aryan side," it was represented by Arie Wilner (pseudonym: Jurek). On December 2, 1942, the Fighting Organization, its composition enlarged by that time, took a new name: Jewish Fighting Organization (*Zydowska Organizacja Bojowa*—ZOB). The Jewish Fighting Organization was commanded by Mordecai Anielewicz. At the time of the Ghetto Uprising, it had about 22 combat groups (20-30 men in each), over 700 combat soldiers in all. Liaison with the Home Army was maintained by Arie Wilner, who was in touch with the head of the Jewish Section of the High Command of the Home Army, Henryk Wolinski (pseudonym: Waclaw).

The Jewish representatives—Dr. Adolf Berman for the Jewish National Committee, Dr. Leon Feiner for BUND, and Arie Wilner for the Jewish Fighting Organization—declared their willingness to subordinate the activities of their organizations to the Government Delegate and the High Command of the Home Army. At the same time they asked for arms and ammunition, for financial assistance, and help with the training. The Delegate accepted the declaration and promised to extend help, while the Commander of the Home Army, in his order of November 11, 1942, acknowledged the Jewish Fighting Organization as a paramilitary organization and instructed them to employ the Home Army's organizational methods and fighting tactics. Simultaneously, the High Command assigned Major Stanislaw Weber (pseudonym: Chirurg) and Captain Zbigniew Lewandowski (pseudonym: Szyna) to organize assistance for the Jewish Fighting Organization. Accordingly, the first ten guns and ammunition were passed on to the Jewish Fighting Organization in December 1942, and another ten guns and ammunition in January 1943. For his part, the Government Delegate established the Jewish section of the Delegacy, headed at first by Witold Bienkowski (pseudonym: Kalski) and later by Wladyslaw Bartoszewski (pseudonym: Ludwik), who was decorated after the war with the Israeli medal of Yad Vashem.

Thus the historical joining together of the Polish and the Jewish underground movements was completed. The manner in which it was accomplished testified to the loyalty of the Jewish citizens of Poland to the Polish state.

Also active in the ghetto was another Jewish military organization, which did not merge with the Jewish Fighting Organization. The Jewish Military Union (*Zydowski Zwiazek Wojskowy*—ZZW) consisted of three combat groups, about 400 men in all, mostly former officers and noncommissioned officers of the Polish Army and members of a Zionist organization, BETAR. It was commanded by Pawel Frenkel. The Jewish Military Union established contact with the Government Delegate and the High Command of the Home Army through a Polish underground organization, the Corps for Security.

Within the framework of cooperation between the Polish and the Jewish underground, and at the request of Dr. Feiner, the High Command of the Home Army sent a dispatch to Jewish organizations in London, which responded by forwarding through the Home Army channels the first $5,000 for BUND. This initiated other, more frequent and larger shipments of money, sent to the Jewish organizations via the underground channels of the Government Delegate and the High Command of the Home Army. Contact was also established, by means of the Home Army and the Delegacy transmitters, with Jewish organizations in the United States.

4. The Council of Assistance to the Jews

At the same time, a number of Polish underground organizations came up with a proposal to develop an organizational structure that would channel all assistance to the Jews. With the approval of Government Delegate Piekalkiewicz, the Council of Assistance to the Jews was established on December 4, 1942 (*Rada Pomocy Zydom—* ZEGOTA). It was headed by Julian Grobelny, a socialist, and had its headquarters in Warsaw. Along with the representatives of various political parties operating underground, the Council also included Dr. Leon Feiner (as vice chairman) and Dr. Adolf Berman (as secretary). The Council had branches in Krakow, Lwow, Zamosc and Lublin, and agencies in Radom, Kielce and Piotrkow. It broadened and improved the existing forms of assistance to Jews living in hiding outside the ghettos by providing them with living quarters, documents, food, medical care and financial help, and by facilitating communication between members of the same families living in different localities. In Warsaw alone, the Council was taking care of 4,000 persons (of these—600 children). Financial means were provided by the Government Delegate. At first, they amounted to half a million zlotys per month, but by November and December 1944, the sum grew to 14 million zlotys. All in all, ZEGOTA and the Jewish organizations received over a million dollars, 200 thousand Swiss francs, and 37,400,000 zlotys. In no other German-occupied country was there an organization like ZEGOTA in existence, though the terror directed against the Aryan populations of these countries was nowhere near as extreme as in Poland.[2]

The growing pace of the extermination campaign prompted the Directorate of Civil Resistance to issue the following proclamation, dated September 17, 1942:

> The tragic fate that befell the Polish people, decimated by the foe, is now compounded by the monstrous, planned slaughter of the Jews that has been carried on in our country for nearly a year. These mass murders are without precedent in the history of the world, and all the cruelties known to man pale beside them. Infants, children, young people, men and women, whether of Catholic or of the Hebrew faith, are being mercilessly murdered, poisoned by gas, buried alive, thrown out of windows onto the pavements below—for no other reason but that they are Jewish; even before death, they suffer the tortures of slow agony, the hell of humiliation and torment, the cynical sadism of their executioners. More than a million victims have already been slaughtered, and their number grows with each passing day.
>
> Unable to counteract these crimes, the Directorate of Civil Resistance protests in the name of the entire Polish nation against the atrocities perpetrated on the Jews. All Polish political and civic groups join in this protest. As in the case of Polish victims of German persecution, the executioners and their henchmen will be held directly responsible for these crimes.
>
> The Directorate of Civil Resistance

This proclamation was published by the entire underground press, and transmitted to London, where it was repeated by the BBC, SWIT, and other allied radio stations.

Another proclamation was issued by the Directorate of Civil Resistance on March 18, 1943, to counteract blackmail of Poles who were sheltering Jews:

> The Directorate of Civil Resistance makes the following announcement:
>
> The Polish people, themselves the victims of a horrible reign of terror, are witnessing with horror and compassion the slaughter of the remnants of the Jewish population in Poland. Their protest against this crime has reached the ear of the free world. Their effective assistance to Jews escaping from ghettos or extermination camps prompted the German occupiers to publish a decree, threatening with death all Poles who render help to Jews in hiding. Nevertheless, some individuals, devoid of honor and conscience and recruited from the criminal world, have now discovered a new, impious source of profit in blackmailing the Poles who shelter Jews, and the Jews themselves.
>
> The Directorate of Civil Resistance warns that every instance of such blackmail will be recorded and prosecuted with all the severity of the law—right away, whenever possible, but, in any event, in the future.

In accordance with instructions of the Directorate of Civil Resistance, following the publication of the proclamation the underground courts passed a number of death sentences; underground papers carried the announcement whenever such sentences were carried out (by shooting), and so did the radio. The following Poles were shot for persecuting the Jews: Boguslaw alias Borys Pilnik, Warsaw; Antoni Rozmus, a platoon leader in the criminal police in Warsaw; Jan Grabiec, Krakow; Waclaw Noworol, Lipnica Wielka; Tadeusz Stefan Karcz, Warsaw; Franciszek Sokolowski, Podkowa Lesna; Antoni Pajor, Dobranowice; Janusz Krystek, Grebkow; Jan Lakinski, Warsaw; Boleslaw Szostak, Warsaw; and Antoni Pietrzak, Warsaw.

In urgent cases, when a delay could imperil the safety of Jews who were in hiding, as well as their protectors, the Government Delegate authorized, by his decree of February 7, 1944, immediate liquidation of blackmailers and informers, without court sentence, but on orders of the local underground authorities—usually, the local chief of Civil Resistance. For instance, a local commander, Witold Rudnicki, ordered the shooting without a court sentence, of four blackmailers, threatening to betray Jews hiding in Pustelnik near Warsaw.

Considerably earlier—beginning with July 1942—the Directorate of Civil Resistance began to inform the government in London regularly about each new step-up in the persecution of the Jews. Chiefs of the Jewish sections of the Government Delegacy and the High Command of the Home Army provided the Directorate of Civil Resistance with up-to-date information on the developments.

Unfortunately, the first dispatches—including the information that the liquidation of the Warsaw ghetto was begun on July 22, 1942—were disbelieved in London, where they were taken for exaggerated anti-German propaganda. Only when the British intelligence service confirmed this information some months later, was the proper use made of dispatches of the Directorate of Civil Resistance.

Samples of the more important messages from the chief of the Directorate of Civil Resistance, Stefan Korbonski (pseudonym: Nowak) are given below; the first pertains to the little known incident—the first armed encounter in the Warsaw ghetto, three months before the outbreak of the Ghetto Uprising:

> January 29, 1943. In recent days, Jews in the Warsaw ghetto defended themselves arms in hand and killed a few Germans. The Jewish National Committee requests that this information be passed on to the Histadrut in Palestine.

> March 18, 1943. Remnants of Jews in Radomsk, Ujazd, Sobolew, Radzymin, and Szczerzec near Lwow have been liquidated.

> March 23, 1943. Tests with sterilization of women are being conducted in Auschwitz. New crematoria have a capacity of 3,000 persons per day, mostly Jews.

> March 30, 1943. On March 13, 14 and 15, trucks loaded with Jews left the Krakow ghetto en route to Auschwitz. About 1,000 people were killed in the ghetto. Jews from Lodz are being taken in the direction of Ozorkow and exterminated there.

> June 10, 1943. In Auschwitz, Bloc X scheduled to become experimental station of the Central Institute of Hygiene from Berlin. Castration, sterilization and artificial insemination. At present, there are 200 Jewish men and 25 Jewish women there.

> June 3, 1943. Broadcast repeatedly instructions of the Directorate of Civil Resistance on helping Jews in hiding.

> July 28, 1943. In Lwow, there are still about 4,000 Jews, gathered in the labor camp at Janowskie. During the roll call each morning, two rabbis are forced to fox-trot before the inmates assembled, to the tune of a Jewish band.

> August 31, 1943. Liquidation of Jews in Bedzin started at the beginning of this month. About 7,000 were taken to Auschwitz. The young are liquidated first. As of July 1 of this year, the total number of Jews in Poland—including those in the camps, in the ghettos, and in hiding—is 250-300 thousand. Of these, 15,000 are in Warsaw; 80,000 in Lodz; 30,000 in Bedzin; 12,000 in Wilno; 20,000 in Bialystok; 8,000 in Krakow; 4,000 in Lublin; 5,000 in Lwow.

> September 23, 1943. The Bedzin ghetto has been liquidated. The Germans murdered 30,000 people.

November 19, 1943. Slaughter of Jews in Trawniki goes on. Massacres also in Poniatowa and Lwow.

June 20, 1944. Beginning with May 15, mass murders are carried out in Auschwitz. Jews are taken first, then the Soviet prisoners of war, and the so-called sick. Mass transports of Hungarian Jews arrive. Thirteen trains per day, 40-50 cars each. Victims convinced they'll be exchanged for POWs or resettled in the east. Gas chambers working round the clock. Corpses are burned in crematoria and out in the open. Over 100,000 people gassed up till now.

July 19, 1944. Murder of Jews in Auschwitz is directed by camp's commander Hoess—read: Hess—and his aide, Grabner.

5. *Mission of Emissary Jan Karski*

The Government Delegate also sounded the alarm repeatedly, sending dispatches on the extermination of Jews and transmitting to London messages from Dr. Feiner and Dr. Berman, addressed to Rabbi Stephen Wise and Rabbi Nachum Goldman in the United States, and to the two Jewish members of the National Council in London—Dr. Ignacy Schwartzbart, a Zionist, and Szmul Zygiel-bojm, member of BUND. What was even more important, however, was that an eyewitness, emissary Jan Karski, was sent to London. Dressed as an Estonian guard, Karski bribed his way right into the Belzec death camp for Jews and saw everything with his own eyes. Before leaving Poland, he had lengthy interviews with Dr. Feiner and Dr. Berman, who gave him the following instructions:

"We want you to tell the Polish government, the allied governments and allied leaders that we are helpless against the German criminals. We cannot defend ourselves, and no one in Poland can possibly defend us. The Polish underground authorities can save some of us, but they cannot save the masses. The Germans do not try to enslave us, the way they do other peoples. We are being systematically murdered . . . all Jews in Poland will perish. It is possible that some few will be saved. But three millions of Polish Jews are doomed to extinction.

"There is no power in Poland able to forestall this fact; neither the Polish, nor the Jewish underground can do it. You have to place the responsibility squarely on the shoulders of the Allies. No leader of the United Nations should ever be able to say that he did not know that we were being murdered in Poland and that only outside assistance could help us."

Overcoming tremendous obstacles, Karski reached London in November 1942. He not only informed the Polish government-in-exile and its Premier, General Sikorski, about the genocide in Poland, but also saw personally the following: Foreign Secretary

Anthony Eden; leader of the Labour Party Arthur Greenwood; Lord Selbourne; Lord Cranborne; the chairman of the Board of Trade, Hugh Dalton; member of the House of Commons, Ellen Wilkinson; British Ambassador to the government-in-exile O'Malley; American Ambassador to the government-in-exile, Anthony Drexel Biddle; and Foreign Affairs Undersecretary Richard Law. Karski also testified regarding the extermination of Jews before the UN War Crimes Commission, chaired by Sir Cecil Hurst. Finally, he gave numerous interviews to the British press and also briefed other members of Parliament and organizations of British writers and intellectuals.

Leaving for the United States, Karski then personally told the story of Jews in Poland to the Undersecretary of State, Adolf Berle, Attorney General Biddle, Supreme Court Justice Felix Frankfurter, Archbishops Mooney and Stritch, and American-Jewish leaders such as Stephen Wise, Nachum Goldman and Waldman. Karski was also received by President Franklin D. Roosevelt, who kept on asking specific questions about the extermination of Jews in Poland long past the time allotted for Karski's audience.

The Polish underground emissary accomplished his mission and passed on to allied leaders the message about the fate of Jews in Poland. But, to all practical purposes, his mission produced no results.[3]

6. Demands for Retaliation

As far as the Polish circles were concerned, one result of Karski's mission was the resolution, passed by the National Council on November 27, 1942, appealing to all allied nations to undertake a joint action against the extermination of Jews in Poland. Also, on December 10, 1942, the Polish Minister of Foreign Affairs addressed a note to the allied governments, in which he presented the chronology of specific stages of extermination of Jews in Poland and appealed to allied governments to "devise effective measures likely to restrain the Germans from further mass extermination." Seven days later, on December 17, 1942, twelve allied governments issued a joint communique, announcing that persons responsible for the extermination of Jews would be punished. No other action was taken, however, despite the fact that the Government Delegate in Poland and the High Command of the Home Army demanded retaliatory bombing of German cities, accompanied by an announcement that the bombing raids were carried out in retaliation for the extermination of Jews. Underground leaders reasoned that British bombardment of German cities was already underway to a certain extent, anyway, in accordance with Churchill's statement of 1940, announcing retaliation for the bombardment of British cities. The only difference would have consisted in scattering appropriate leaflets over the target cities and broadcasting announcements of a general nature, i.e., without naming the cities to be bombed. The Polish underground leaders also requested regular bombing missions to destroy all railroad lines leading to extermination camps in order to prevent further transports from the ghettos. The two Jewish representatives, Dr. Feiner and Dr. Berman, made similar demands in their dispatches to London. An anti-Nazi SS officer, Kurt Gerstein, recommended the same course of action in his conversation with Swedish diplomat von Otter, aboard the Berlin express. In his dispatch to the government, dated June 17, 1943, the chief of the Directorate of Civil Resistance Korbonski summed up the demands for retaliation as follows:

"Public opinion here demands that the attention of the Anglo-Saxon world turn to Poland and calls for retaliations against the Reich, in line with the postulate, reiterated over the past year, of listing the crimes responsible for the bombardments of Germany . . . . I beg and urge that appropriate declarations be made simultaneously with bombing raids over the Reich that these are in retaliation for the latest German bestialities."

No such action was undertaken, however, supposedly because of technical impossibility of such long-distance flights. And yet, Sir Arthur Harris, chief of the British Bomber Command, considered the bombing of Auschwitz, for intance, technically feasible, if carried out from bases in Italy. Captain Leonard Cheshire, V.C., held a similar opinion. Moreover, since bombing raids could have been made on factories around Auschwitz, nothing should have prevented the bombardment of railroad lines bringing fodder for the gas chambers of the largest of German death camps.

7. Uprising in the Warsaw Ghetto

Beginning with January 1943, officers of the Home Army and representatives of the Jewish Fighting Organization held meetings to plan for a joint action on both sides of the ghetto walls at the outbreak of the uprising. Three Polish units led by Captain Jozef Pszenny (pseudonym: Chwacki), were to break through the ghetto walls, attacking the Germans on the Aryan side and blowing up the walls with explosives. Since it was assumed from the start that the Ghetto Uprising must inevitably end in disaster, this action was planned only to open the way for the retreat of the Jewish fighters.

At this time the Home Army delivered to the Jewish Fighting Organization 1 light machine gun, 2 submachine guns, 50 handguns (all with magazines and ammunition), 10 rifles, 600 hand grenades with detonators, 30 kilograms of explosives (plastic, received from the air drops), 120 kilograms of explosives of own production 400 detonators for bombs and grenades, 30 kilograms of potassium to make the incendiary "Molotov cocktails" and, finally, great quantities of saltpeter needed to manufacture gun powder. The Jewish Fighting Organization also received instructions on how to manufacture bombs, hand grenades and incendiary bottles, how to build strongholds, and where to get rails and cement for their construction.

On April 19, 1943—the first day of uprising in the Warsaw ghetto—three Home Army units, commanded by Captain Jozef Pszenny, took up their posts near the ghetto walls on Bonifraterska Street and attempted to blow up the wall with mines. Detected prematurely, they attacked the Germans, while four sappers tried to get to the wall. Unfortunately, two of them were killed on the spot—Eugeniusz Morawski and Jozef Wilk—while a third sustained wounds in both legs. Captain Pszenny ordered his men to retreat and withdrew, taking along four wounded men and detonating the mines on the street; the explosion tore to shreds the bodies of Morawski and Wilk. Several Germans were killed during the engagement, but the attempt to blow up the wall ended in failure.

The next day, a unit of the People's Guard of the Polish Workers Party, led by Franciszek Bartoszek, attacked the German machine-gun post near the ghetto wall on Nowiniarska Street. Two SS-men were killed.

On April 22, a detachment of the Home Army, commanded by Wieckowski, routed a unit of the Lithuanian auxiliary police near the ghetto walls.

On Good Friday, April 23, a Home Army unit led by Lt. Jerzy Skupienski, attacked the gate in the ghetto wall at Pawia Street. They had orders to blow up the gate. Two German sentries were killed at the gate, but—under the heavy barrage of fire from Germans converging from all sides—the Home Army soldiers had to withdraw, killing on the way four SS and police officers whose car happened to cross their path of retreat.

In harassing actions, ordered by Colonel Antoni Chrusciel (pseudonym: Monter), the Home Army Commander of Warsaw, German sentries on Leszno and Orla streets were shot by Home Army soldiers, led by Cadet Officer Zbigniew Stalkowski; another unit of the Home Army, led by Tadeusz Kern-Jedrychowski, killed SS sentries on Zakroczymska Street.

There was also fighting in the area of the Powazki Cemetery (under the command of Wladyslaw Andrzejczak) and near the Jewish cemetery (under Leszek Raabe, commander of the Socialist Fighting Organization). Raabe's deputy, Wlodzimierz Kaczanowski, organized the escape of the Jewish members of the Polish Socialist Party from the ghetto.

On Good Friday, April 23, the Jewish Fighting Organization issued an appeal to the Polish population, declaring that the struggle in the ghetto upheld the time-honored Polish motto: "For your freedom and ours," and stressing that the Jews and the Poles had become brothers in arms.

A particularly daring action was undertaken by a unit of the Corps for Security, under the command of Captain Henryk Iwanski. From the very first days of the Warsaw ghetto's existence, Captain Iwanski's brother, Waclaw, and his two sons—Zbigniew and Roman— maintained regular contact with the Jewish Military Union, providing them with arms, ammunition, and instructional materials, smuggled through the sewers or in carts that brought lime and cement into the ghetto. When the uprising began, a unit of the Jewish Military Union occupied positions on Muranowski Square, which was to become the scene of bloodiest fighting. On the first day of the uprising, a Polish and a Jewish flag were raised over this sector. They were clearly visible from the Aryan side, and created a deep impression on the Polish population of Warsaw. The commander of the Jewish unit on Muranowski Square, Dawid Moryc Apfelbaum, sent a message to Captain Iwanski, informing him that he had been wounded, and asking for arms and ammunition. The next day, Iwanski and 18 of his men (among them, his brother Waclaw and his two sons, Roman and Zbigniew) made their way into the ghetto by way of a tunnel dug from the cellar of a house at 6 Muranowska Street to the cellar of a house at 7 Muranowska Street, on the opposite side and behind the ghetto wall which, at this point, ran in the middle of Muranowska Street. They brought with them arms, ammunition and food for Apfelbaum's men and, seeing the utter exhaustion of the Jewish fighters, relieved them at their posts amid the ruins on Muranowski Square and Nalewki Street, repelling repeated German attacks. The same tunnel was used without delay to evacuate the Jewish wounded to the Aryan side. Later on, Iwanski's brother and both his sons were killed during the fighting, and Iwanski himself was seriously wounded. After the collapse of the uprising, Iwanski's men carried their wounded commander back through the tunnel, taking along also 34 Jewish fighters, fully armed.

After the war, Henryk Iwanski and his wife Wiktoria (who provided shelter and hiding places for the Jews throughout the war) were decorated—along with 10 other people—by the Israeli Ambassador in Warsaw Dov Satoath, with the medal of Yad Vashem.[4]

This was not an isolated instance of the Jews and the Poles fighting together. According to the underground paper *Glos Warszawy* (April 23, 1943), when the uprising began "there were Poles in the ghetto, fighting shoulder to shoulder with the Jews in the streets of the ghetto against the Germans."

In his 100-page report, SS and police general Jürgen Stroop, commander of the German forces fighting in the ghetto, confirmed the fact of Polish diversionary operations and Polish participation in the fighting, both within and without the ghetto. He wrote that his soldiers were "constantly under fire from outside of the ghetto, i.e., from the Aryan side"; he described Iwanski's action as follows: "The main Jewish group, with some Polish bandits mixed in, retreated to the so-called Muranowski Square already in the course of the first or the second day of fighting. It was reinforced there by several more Polish bandits."

A little over a year later, during the Warsaw Rising, a detachment of the Jewish Fighting Organization joined the ranks of the Home Army in the struggle against the Germans. The Jewish fighters were commanded by Icek Cukierman, once deputy and contact man on the Aryan side, for Mordecai Anielewicz, commander of the Jewish Fighting Organization.

It was during the Warsaw Uprising, too, that the Grey Ranks—composed of boy scouts and led by Lt. Colonel Jan Mazurkiewicz (pseudonym: Radoslaw)—seized, in what once had been the ghetto, the labor camp still maintained by the Germans for Jews, whose lives had been spared so they could work at tearing down whatever remained of the burned ghetto, but who were also doomed to die. They freed 358 Jews who joined Radoslaw's units enthusiastically. Later, most of them were killed, together with those who had freed them. When Radoslaw was wounded in both legs, but still continued in command, it was the Jews who carried his stretcher, often through the underground passages in the city sewers.

A question arises: should the Home Army have helped the Jews with more than arms, diversionary actions and efforts to open up escape routes for the Jewish fighters? The answer must be negative. Not even the entire strength of the Home Army in Warsaw could have saved the ghetto or brought victory. There was considerable concentration of German army, SS, and gendarmerie forces in Warsaw and vicinity, which would have been sent into action immediately, with but one possible outcome—a crushing defeat of both the Jewish Fighting Organization and the Home Army. An uprising in the ghetto could have been more than a heroic and tragic gesture of protest and self-defense only if the Soviet army could have come to the rescue in time to win victory. The only other alternative would have been a total disarray of the German armies. But in April 1943, the Soviets were hundreds of miles away from Warsaw and the German armies showed no signs of decay, fighting doggedly on all war fronts.

Throughout the Ghetto Uprising, daily reports on the course of the fighting were transmitted by the chief of the Directorate of Civil Resistance Korbonski to the radio station SWIT, which based its broadcasts on their contents. Below are some samples of these messages:

April 20, 1943. Yesterday the Germans began the liquidation of 35,000 in our ghetto. The Jews are defending themselves. We can hear shots and explosions of grenades. The Germans are using tanks and armored cars. They have losses. There are fires in several places. Speak to the ghetto today.

April 21, 1943. The fighting in the ghetto continues. Throughout the night we could hear shots, explosions and fires.

April 28, 1943. Fighting continues in the ghetto. The Germans are burning houses systematically, one after another.

May 7, 1943. *Rzeczpospolita* of May 6 contains a statement of the Government Delegate, denouncing German crimes in the ghetto. He pays homage to the Jewish fighters, voices our solidarity, and calls on all Poles to help those who escape from the ghetto.

May 15, 1943. The horrible massacre of the remnants of the Warsaw ghetto has been going on for three weeks now. Led by the Jewish Fighting Organization, the Jews defended themselves heroically, arms in hand. The Germans used artillery and armored cars. Over 300 Germans have been killed by the Jewish fighters, some 1,000 Germans have been wounded. Tens of thousands of Jews have been deported, murdered or burned alive by the Germans.

May 22, 1943. A rumor circulates among the Germans that the Gestapo chief in Warsaw, Dr. von Sammern, who had been recalled, was sentenced to death for the disgrace suffered by the Germans because of the armed resistance in the ghetto.

June 9, 1943. The underground Economic Bulletin reports on May 15 that 100,000 living units, 2,000 industrial locations, 3,000 commercial establishments and several factories have been burned or blown up in the Warsaw ghetto. In September 1939 only 78,000 living units were destroyed in the entire city of Warsaw.

June 29, 1943. All inhabitants of the ghettos in Stanislawow, Lukow, Wegrow and Zolkiew have been murdered. In Warsaw, some 2,000 Jews are breathing their last in cellars and ruins. There is still some fighting during the nights. At Sobibor, German bands playing at the station greet Jews arriving from abroad.

In his letter to Cukierman, dated April 23, 1943, Mordecai Anielewicz refers to the first of the above dispatches, on which the SWIT broadcast was based:

The fact that . . . . the radio station SWIT broadcast a beautiful program about our struggle (which we heard on our set here), was the source of great satisfaction. It gives us courage in our fight to know that we are not forgotten on the other side of the ghetto wall.[5]

Government Delegate Jankowski also sent urgent dispatches to the Polish government in London, beginning with April 21, 1943.

Meanwhile in London, Szmul Zygielbojm, a member of the Polish National Council, committed suicide on May 13, 1943, in protest of the indifference of the Allies to the sufferings of the Warsaw ghetto; he explained the reason for his action in letters addressed to the President of the Polish Republic, Wladyslaw Raczkiewicz, and to the Premier of the government-in-exile, General Wladyslaw Sikorski.

8. Jewish Partisan Units

Towards the end of the Ghetto Uprising, there began an organized evacuation of the Jewish fighters. It was not free from tragic mistakes, such as the suicide of Mordecai Anielewicz and his staff in the bunker at 18 Mila Street, despite the fact that there was a way for them to escape, which was discovered later by others. Jewish fighters escaped through tunnels dug from cellar to cellar and through the city sewers. Members of friendly Polish organizations, such as the Socialist Fighting Organization, awaited them on the Aryan side with trucks, which transported the rescued Jews to the woods near Warsaw. On April 29, for instance, soldiers of the People's Guard, led by Lieutenant Wladyslaw Gaik, organized the escape of 40 men of the Jewish Fighting Organization, fully armed, and took them to the woods in the vicinity of Wyszkow. The same operation was repeated again on May 10, when another 30 Jewish fighters were rescued, joining the others and forming a partisan group named after Mordecai Anielewicz. Other Jewish partisan units were formed, often named after Polish national heroes. In the Lublin district, for instance, there were Jewish partisan groups, commanded by Samuel Jegier and named after Emilia Plater (a heroine of the Insurrection of 1831) and Jan Kozietulski (a hero of the Napoleonic wars). One of the partisan groups, led by Chil Grynszpan, was named after Berek

Joselewicz, a Jew and a colonel in the Polish armies during the Insurrection of 1794. Another partisan group was composed of Polish peasants from the village of Polichno, but had a Jewish commanding officer, using the pseudonym of "Szymek;" when he was killed in action, the peasants buried him in a Catholic cemetery as a sign of their respect. Among still other partisan groups, there was a Jewish unit commanded by Mieczyslaw Gruber, a mixed Polish-Jewish unit under the command of a Jewish veterinarian, Dr. Mieczyslaw Skotnicki, operating in the woods near Parczew, and in the Radom district, a group led by Julian Ajzenman-Kaniewski (pseudonym: Chytry). Small bands of stragglers usually joined the first partisan unit they met and many of them fought together with the Home Army partisans.

Other Jews, who managed to survive the uprising in the ghetto and to escape through tunnels and sewers to the Aryan side, fared much worse. The most fortunate among them made their way to the forests and either joined the partisans hiding there, or set up camps under the partisans' protection. The rest were swept into the nets of special manhunts, conducted by the Germans, or blended with the Polish population, which—spurred on by three successive appeals of the Council of Assistance to the Jews (ZEGOTA), an appeal from General Sikorski (May 5, 1943), and an appeal from the Government Delegate Jankowski (May 6, 1943)—was doing all it could to save the tragic remnants. At the same time, ZEGOTA requested that the Polish government-in-exile take steps to initiate an international agreement in an effort to save the remaining Jews through exchange or some other means. However, no such agreement was ever concluded.

Also at that time, three publications printed by the underground presses, reached London: *Before the Eyes of the World*, a book by Maria Kann, presented the story of the Warsaw ghetto and the Ghetto Uprising; *One Year in Treblinka*, a booklet written by Jankiel Wiernik, an escapee from the death camp; and a volume of poems, entitled *From the Abyss*, the work of eleven Jewish poets. These books created a deep impression in the west—and that was the end of it.

This state of affairs lasted until the German armies, defeated by the Soviets, began their retreat.

9. Polish Losses Due to Helping Jews

There are no complete data as to the number of Poles murdered by the Germans for giving shelter to the Jews or helping them in other ways. There are, however, many fragmentary reports pertaining to specific instances, e.g., an announcement of the SS and police commander in the district of Galicja (January 28, 1944), listing the names of five Poles sentenced to death for helping the Jews. Widely known was the case of a gardener, Ludomir Marczak and his family, who were shot in the Pawiak Prison on March 7, 1944, for hiding in a dugout in their garden about 30 Jews—among them, Dr. Emanuel Ringelblum, the chronicler of the Ghetto Uprising, who perished with the others. Between September 13, 1942 and May 25, 1944, about 200 peasants were shot or burned alive in the Kielce district in reprisal for helping the Jews. The same fate befell 17 persons in the Krakow district. In the cemetery of the town of Nowy Sacz, 300-500 Jews and Poles were shot between 1939 and August 1942—the Poles for sheltering the Jews. The same reason accounted for the execution of 40 Poles in the Lublin district, 47—in the Rzeszow district and 19 in the Warsaw district. In the Lwow district, nearly a thousand inhabitants of the city of Lwow were punished with death in the Belsen camp for having helped the Jews. Witnesses during the Eichmann trial also referred to several individual cases (e.g., Dr. Jozef Barzminski).

A dispatch from the chief of the Directorate of Civil Resistance Korbonski illustrates one case:

"May 3, 1943. In Mszana Dolna, on March 22, *Volksdeutsch* Gelb hanged a peasant by his feet and tormented him to death for having sold potatoes to a Jew. Threaten him."

Still, most of the Poles who had been helping the Jews survived the war and the German persecutions. Today, they are frequently in touch with the Jewish families they have helped, visiting them in Israel, in the United States and in other countries, and even settling in Israel at the invitation of the Jewish families living there. In the Avenue of the Righteous in Jerusalem, most of the plaques commemorating those who were saving Jews bear Polish names.*

Among the Polish masses, which tried to save as many Jews as possible, there were also exceptions other than the blackmailers and the informers, whom the Polish underground punished with death. Partisan units of the fascist fraction of the National Armed Forces hunted down the Jews hiding in the forests. They were also responsible for the killing in Warsaw of two officers of the High Command of the Home Army, who were of Jewish origin—Jerzy Makowiecki, an engineer, and Professor Ludwik Widerszal.

On the other hand, some prominent and outspoken prewar anti-semites—such as the leader of the radical right ONR, Jan Mosdorf, editor of the weekly *Prosto z mostu*, Stanislaw Piasecki, or the well

---

*See page 253 for the List of the Righteous Among the Nations. According to the brochure entitled "Las Sprawiedliwych" ["The Forest of Righteous"] published by Szymon Datner, director of the Jewish Historical Institute in Warsaw, The Institute listed up to April 1968 the names of 343 Poles murdered for helping the Jews. However, the names of 101 additional victims the Institute was unable to identify.

known journalist Adolf Nowaczynski—changed completely: Mosdorf did everything in his power to help the Jews in the Auschwitz camp, and he died together with the Jews; Piasecki and Nowaczynski became the champions of the persecuted Jews.

A surviving leading representative of the Jews, Dr. Adolf Berman, now living in Tel Aviv, appraised the role played by the Poles as follows:

> Descriptions of the Jewish martyrdom in Poland often dwell on sufferings inflicted upon the hunted Jews by Polish black-mailers and informers, by the "blue" police, by fascist hooligans and other scum of the society. Far less is being written about the fact that thousands of Poles put their own lives in jeopardy to help the Jews. It is much easier to see the foul scum and flotsam on a river than to discern the deep, clear current under its surface. But the current was there . . . .
>
> Time will come when we will have a great Golden Book of Poles who, in that hideous 'time of contempt' held out a brother's hand to the Jews, saved Jews from death, and became a symbol of humanitarianism and the brotherhood of peoples to the Jewish underground movement.

10. Why Was Poland Chosen the Site of Extermination?

Antisemitism of the local population certainly was not the reason for the Nazis' choice of Poland as the main extermination site for the Jews (who were also being murdered in the Reich, e.g., in Dachau, Sachsenhausen, and other camps). Certain segments of the Polish population were, indeed, antisemitic, but this had changed when the Poles saw the persecution of Jews with their own eyes and when they themselves became subject to deportations, mass arrests, concentration camps and mass executions. Historians of Jewish persecutions are unanimous in their agreement that, next to the Jews, the Poles were the most oppressed of all nations and were doomed to gradual extermination, in accordance with the General Eastern Plan. Among charges listed in the indictment presented by Gideon Hausner, prosecutor at the Eichmann trial, one (no. 9) was that Eichmann was responsible for the deportation of 500,000 Poles. Eichmann was convicted on this count, too, and the sentence assumed he had been motivated by his intention to destroy the intelligentsia class of Polish society.

The real reason why Poland had been chosen was the fact that of all the European Jews marked for extermination, three and a half million were already in Poland. German railroad transportation lines were overburdened because of the war. It was much simpler to build the extermination camps in Poland and to bring in the Polish Jews from nearby areas, rather than to transport them by rail to Hungary or France. The largest of these camps, Auschwitz, was established near the German border to shorten the distance for the transports of Jews from Hungary, France, and Italy. After the outbreak of the Soviet-German war, when the transportation problems became even more acute, one and a half million of Polish and Russian Jews were murdered by special units, the so-called *Einsatzgruppen*—not in the extermination camps, but on the spot, in front of the mass graves they had been forced to dig for themselves.

Transport problems played a role not only in the extermination of the Jews, but also in considerations of ways to save them. In 1942, British Foreign Secretary Anthony Eden told President Franklin D. Roosevelt:

"The whole problem of the Jews in Europe is very difficult and we should move very cautiously about offering to take all Jews out of a country. If we do so, then the Jews of the world will be wanting us to make similar offers in Poland and Germany. Hitler might take us up on any such offer, and there simply are not enough ships and means of transportation in the world to handle them . . . ."[6]

The Germans also undoubtedly reasoned that this greatest crime in the history of the world might be easier to hide in eastern Europe, cut off from the world by German occupation, than in the west, which—although also under German occupation—could never be isolated effectively from neutral countries, like Switzerland or Spain, or even from England.

One cannot end an account of the extermination of the Jews without stating that the guilt of genocide will rest forever on the entire German nation, which—from the first anti-Jewish excesses in prewar Germany and as long as Hitler was winning the war—supported the Führer and identified fully with him and with the Nazi party. Nothing but words—protesting or threatening—came from the Allies, but their responsibility is of an entirely different kind and can in no way be compared to that of the Germans. The sin of commission cannot be compared to the sin of omission.

XIX

COLLABORATION

Collaboration was defined as voluntary cooperation with the enemy to the detriment of the country or fellow citizens. This accusation was never made lightly—pressure of circumstances and conditions of life under occupation were always taken into account. One could, for instance, recognize that workers in munitions plants or farmers delivering their contingents were actually harming the country by strengthening the German war potential. Still, this did not make them collaborators, because, first, they and their families had to live somehow, and, second, the evasion of compulsory labor and of deliveries was punishable by concentration camp or even death. Hundreds of peasants have been shot by the special punitive expeditions for the so-called "sabotage of contingents." In the two examples cited above, the voluntary aspect was absent. On the other hand, even voluntary cooperation with the enemy was not enough by itself to be considered collaboration if it brought no harm to the country or to fellow citizens. Functionaries of the Central Welfare Council, or its chairman Adam Ronikier, were not regarded as collaborators, even though by the very nature of their work they had to cooperate with the occupying authorities. Their cooperation, however, brought no harm either to the country or to their fellow citizens. On the contrary, the welfare work of the Council, which provided clothing, food and financial assistance to the poor, benefited the country. In any event, the Central Welfare Council did not hesitate to lodge protests with the occupying authorities against terror, executions, pacification actions, and deportations, and thus became to a degree the only official spokesman and defender of the Polish population.[1]

For similar reasons, the underground authorities did not regard as collaboration the cooperation with the Germans of the Polish Red Cross, headed by Wladyslaw Lachert, the Bank of Poland, renamed the Bank of Issue GG and headed by Feliks Mlynarski, or the Polish officials in city administrations. In Warsaw, for instance, the highest Polish official, deputy to the German mayor of Warsaw Leist, was Julian Kulski, who served with the permission of the underground authorities. The Association of Cooperatives "Spolem," headed by Marian Rapacki, and other similar institutions, operating in the interests of the country and the population, also were not regarded as collaborators.

Finally, the underground authorities did not regard as punishable collaboration contacts maintained with the Germans by various groups of Russian, Ukrainian, Georgian and other emigrés; they took into consideration the fact that in such cooperation the emigrés saw their only chance to regain the freedom of their countries, or—where the Russians were concerned—a chance to bring about the downfall of the communist rule.

The political activities of Wladyslaw Studnicki, on the other hand, approached the borderline of collaboration. Studnicki was a lifelong proponent of close cooperation between Poland and Germany and a fervent opponent of "Poland's involvement in a war waged by France and England against Germany." In his letter to Poland's Minister of Foreign Affairs Jozef Beck (April 13, 1939) Studnicki had warned against such an involvement and advocated neutrality; among other, he foresaw that Germany's defeat would constitute a threat to Poland's sovereignty. He failed to foresee, however, that Germany would attack Poland first. With the help of the last prewar German Ambassador in Poland, von Moltke, and other like-minded officials of the *Auswärtiges Amt*, Studnicki traveled to Berlin in January 1940. He took with him a memorandum, sharply critical of German policies in occupied Poland, particularly of expropriations, deportations, executions and arrests, the closing of schools and the destruction of Polish culture. In conclusion, he demanded the reestablishment of the Polish State and the transfer of governmental powers to a Polish Central Committee. For the chairman of such a committee, Studnicki had chosen Wincenty Witos (leader of the Peasant Party), but when he approached Witos with this proposal, his letter of October 19, 1939, was not even answered.[2]

Studnicki had intended to see Minister von Ribbentrop, but before he could do so, he was arrested on orders of Goebbels, who had read Studnicki's memorandum and wanted to prevent its dissemination. However, Studnicki's positive attitude toward Germany was taken into account and, following an intervention of the Security Police chief Heydrich, he was placed in a sanitarium; released after the fall of France, he was permitted to return to the *General Gouvernement*. His Berlin experiences failed to deter Studnicki from further contacts with the occupying authorities and further sharp critique of their rule in Poland, or from interventions on behalf of Poles arrested by the Germans. As a result, he was arrested again and spent 14 months in the Pawiak Prison.

The underground leadership followed closely Studnicki's activities, but decided not to regard them as collaboration, because Studnicki acted in good faith and in the best interests of the country and the nation, as he saw them. Also, nothing came of his plans of collaboration with the Germans. On the contrary, his proposals were rejected, and he, himself, was put in prison, not once but twice.[3]

Such cautious interpretation of what constituted collaboration with the enemy, was responsible for the fact that only very few people have been charged with collaboration. The most important of such cases was that of Waclaw Krzeptowski, former Peasant Party representative in the prewar Polish *Sejm*. On instigation of the German Governor Hans Frank, greatly impressed by the Polish mountaineers' bearing and colorful costumes, Krzeptowski—together with the renegade Szatkowski and a group of befuddled mountaineers—undertook to establish a separate "mountaineer nation." Krzeptowski's activities ended in a complete failure. The vast majority of the mountaineers refused to accept the *Goralenvolk* identity cards and jeered at the "mountaineer prince" (as Krzeptowski was called by the Germans) and his comrades, regarding them as traitors.

In an epilogue to this abortive venture, the underground court sentenced Krzeptowski to death. Carrying out the court's sentence without delay, the mountaineers hanged Krzeptowski on Krupowki, the main street of Zakopane, which was to become the capital of the "new nation." After the war, Krzeptowski's collaborators were sentenced to a few years in prison.

The first celebrated case of individual collaboration was that of a well known film actor, Igo Sym, who registered as a *Volksdeutsch* and worked for the propaganda office of the Warsaw district. He was shot on March 7, 1941, before the establishment of the underground courts of justice. Another case, which created a considerable stir, was that of a well known writer, Ferdynand Goetel, who also worked for the same propaganda office and tried to persuade other writers to register there and to submit to the directives of German propaganda. However, Goetel ceased his activities even before the establishment of the underground courts. Whether out of patriotic motives or out of his desire for rehabilitation, he joined the underground movement and worked for a publication of the Committee for the Defense of Poland (a national-radical organization), *Polska zyje* (Poland Lives On).[4] By the decision of the Directorate of Civil Resistance, Goetel's case was postponed until after the war.

The most renowned case of collaboration in Krakow was that of journalist Feliks Burdecki and writer Jan Emil Skiwski, who in 1944-1945 published a Polish-language periodical *Przelom* (The Turning

Point), which served the German propaganda objectives. The underground press denounced their activities. After the war, both men managed to escape from Poland.

In Wilno, the most serious case of collaboration was that of Czeslaw Ancerewicz and Jozef Mackiewicz, who worked in the editorial offices of *Goniec Codzienny*, the German "reptile daily," published in Polish. The organ of the Wilno Home Army *Niepodleglosc* denounced both men for their activities in its issue of December 1-15, 1942. Because of Mackiewicz's prominence in local circles, the commander of the Wilno district of the Home Army, Colonel Aleksander Krzyzanowski (pseudonym: Wilk), first brought his case before the Wilno District Council, a body composed of representatives of the local underground political parties (with the exception of communists), and the representative of Archbishop Jalbrzykowski, the Reverend Romuald Swierkowski. Among the members of the Wilno District Council were: Dr. Jerzy Dobrzanski, representative of the Polish Socialist Party and, subsequently, Government Delegate for the Wilno district, and Adam Galinski who later became the last Government Delegate for the Wilno District. Having heard the statement of the District Commander and after consideration of the evidence presented, the Council confirmed that the charges of treason brought against Mackiewicz and Ancerewicz were valid, and referred the case to the District Commander for further action in full observance of binding legal procedures and executive instructions. Accordingly, Colonel Krzyzanowski brought the case before an underground court which sentenced both defendants to death. Ancerewicz was shot in March 1943. Mackiewicz's sentence was suspended because of various interventions and pressures brought upon Colonel Krzyzanowski, to postpone the execution of the sentence until the end of the war and to give Mackiewicz a chance to rehabilitate himself in the meanwhile.[5] *

In brief, collaboration in Poland was never widespread and involved only isolated cases. The statement that "there was no Quisling in Poland" was fully borne out by actual events in Poland under the German occupation.

---

* After the war, Jozef Mackiewicz denied categorically that he had ever collaborated with the Germans, and particularly that he had ever worked for *Goniec Codzienny*, a Polish-language paper published by the Germans—the crux of charges leveled against him. On the contrary, Mackiewicz claims that he maintained regular contact with the underground and that he lodged a complaint with the underground prosecutor's office against his calumniator, Wronski, the author of the article in the underground paper *Niepodleglosc* (December 1–15, 1942), in which he accused Mackiewicz of collaboration. Mackiewicz states that *Goniec Codzienny* has published only one interview with him—an account of his travel to the mass graves in the Katyn Forest—but with the knowledge, or on the initiative, of the underground authorities in Wilno.

KATYN

1. The Shocking Discovery

At the beginning of 1940, letters from Polish officers interned by the Soviets in the Kozelsk, Starobelsk and Ostashkov camps, began reaching their families in Poland. Simultaneously, the Germans advised the Polish Red Cross that these officers would be transferred to the *General Gouvernement*, in accordance with the German-Soviet agreement, and that camps for them should be set up in Poland. Working fast, the Polish Red Cross reported within a short time that they were ready to receive the repatriated officers. A few months of fruitless wait followed. Then the Germans announced that the camps prepared by the Polish Red Cross should be liquidated, because the Polish officers would remain in the USSR. At the same time, letters from Kozelski, Starobelsk and Ostashkov ceased, and letters mailed by the officers' families in Poland were returned undelivered. This created an understandable anxiety, but all questions—either from the families or from the Polish Red Cross—remained unanswered by the Soviet authorities.

On April 9, 1943, the Germans called a conference in the Brühl Palace in Warsaw, the seat of the German authorities for the Warsaw district. The conference was attended by representatives of the Polish Red Cross, the Central Welfare Council, the administration of the city of Warsaw, and a few other prewar civic organizations. They were informed by a representative of Minister Goebbels, arrived from Berlin, that mass graves of Polish officers murdered by the Soviets had been found near Smolensk.

The next day, i.e., on April 10, 1943, a Polish commission flew to Smolensk on a plane provided by the German authorities. The group included: Edmund Seyfryd, director of the Central Welfare Council; writers—Jan Emil Skiwski and Ferdynand Goetel; Dr. Konrad Orzechowski, director of the city hospitals in Warsaw; Dr. Edward Grodzicki, from the Warsaw office of the Central Welfare Council; Wladyslaw Kawecki, a reporter from the "reptile press;" Kazimierz Didur, a photoreporter from the "reptile press;" and Kazimierz Prochownik, a worker from the Zieleniewski factory in Krakow. The group spent the day of April 11 viewing the mass graves and the bodies in the Katyn Forest, and late that same day they returned to Warsaw.

On April 13, the German radio broadcast the news of the horrifying discovery throughout the world. The "reptile press" carried the same information on April 14, 1943.

On April 14, another German plane left Krakow for Warsaw and then Smolensk. It carried a second group of Poles, including: the Reverend Stanislaw Jasinski, representing Cardinal Adam Sapieha; representatives of the Polish Red Cross: Dr. Adam Szebesta, Dr. Tadeusz Susz, Dr. Praglowski, and Stanislaw Klapert; and a reporter from the "reptile press," Marian Martens. In Warsaw, the plane also picked up other representatives of the Polish Red Cross: Kazimierz Jerzy Skarzynski, Captain Ludwik Rojkiewicz, Jerzy Wodzinowski, Dr. Hieronim Bartoszewski and Roman Banach; also aboard were Stefan Kolodziejski and Zygmunt Pohorski. On April 16, this second group was already back in Warsaw, leaving behind a few of its members to assist with the exhumation and identification of the bodies. Later on, this group was increased to twelve persons, who stayed in Katyn for five weeks.

Immediately upon their return, members of both groups reported to the institutions they represented and also to the underground authorities. Beginning with April 13, the dispatches of the Government Delegate, the High Command of the Home Army, and the Directorate of Civil Resistance kept the government in London abreast of every new development.

Meeting for several hours with the chief of the Directorate of Civil Resistance Korbonski, the Red Cross representative Skarzynski gave an account of what he had seen in the Katyn Forest. In his dispatch of April 19, 1943, Korbonski passed on this information to the government in London:

"I talked today with a member of the delegation. He confirmed everything the Germans are saying, except for numbers. He saw one huge mass grave; bodies were also exhumed in seven other places. He estimates that up to now 2-3 thousand bodies have been found. Notes and diaries break off in March 1940."

Members of both groups reported that in the Katyn Forest there were eight huge mass graves, containing well preserved corpses of 4–6 thousand Polish officers, dressed in Polish uniforms and military coats. The bodies were laid in layers, one on top of the other. There was one bullet hole in the back of each skull; with the exception of those who must have defended themselves, each officer was killed with one shot. Military decorations were also well preserved, and—most important—in the pockets of uniforms were found cigarette cases, wallets, personal papers, letters, family pictures and diaries. In time, 22 diaries were found in the graves. They all ended in March-

April 1940. This—in conjunction with the testimony of the local people, the state of decay of bodies examined by medical experts, and the size of the pine trees planted to camouflage the graves—indicated that the massacre must have occurred in March-April 1940. At that time, the murdered officers were held in the Soviet POW camp in Kozelsk. Obviously, there could be no doubt whatsoever that the Soviets were responsible for the crime.

Both during their stay in Smolensk and in the Katyn Forest and upon their return to Poland, the more prominent representatives of the Polish Red Cross and the Central Welfare Council were urged by the Germans to give interviews to the German press, to broadcast over the German radio, and to send letters to the German authorities, denouncing in each statement the murder perpetrated by the Soviets on Polish officers. They were given to understand that to acquiesce to these pressures could mean a new era in Polish-German relations. All German proposals of this kind were rejected categorically, even though such refusal could have dangerous consequences. Aware that the Germans wanted to exploit the "Katyn affair" for their own propaganda purposes, the Poles steadfastly refused to make any statements whatever. Only Dr. Heinrich, the German overseer of the Polish Red Cross, succeeded in obtaining, because of his position, a record of the board meeting at which Kazimierz Skarzynski was giving his report on Katyn.

On the other hand, Jozef Mackiewicz—who went to Katyn after May 20 at the invitation of the German authorities—on his return to Wilno published an interview in the "reptile daily" *Goniec Codzienny*, denouncing the mass murder of the Polish officers as a Soviet crime.

The news of the gruesome discovery in the Katyn Forest spread like wildfire throughout the country, arousing horror and despair. In addition, as the identification of the bodies proceeded, the "reptile press" began to publish the names of the murdered officers. Each day new families learned about the death of someone they loved, and there were thousands of such families. There was also the gnawing question: What happened to the 10,000 officers from POW camps in Starobelsk and Ostashkov, from whom there was no news? The answer was hard to evade—they, too, had been murdered, though their graves had not yet been found. Gloom spread throughout the country; shortly it turned into national mourning. It was reflected in the underground press. All headings that included the word "Katyn" were printed with black borders.

On April 15, the Soviet news agency TASS published a communique denying German accusations and stating that the Polish prisoners of war were working west of Smolensk and, following the outbreak of the German-Soviet war, fell into Nazi hands and were shot by the Germans in the fall of 1941.

In view of the conflicting statements of the Germans and the Soviets, the representative of the Polish Red Cross in Geneva, Stanislaw Radziwill, turned to the International Red Cross on April 17, 1943, with the official request that the Katyn crime be investigated on the spot. Alerted by a Reuters communiqué, the Germans made an identical request through their own representative, and on the same day. This convergence was exploited by the Soviets as proof of the Polish-German collaboration against the USSR, and a pretext for breaking off diplomatic relations with the Polish government-in-exile on April 26, 1943.

The news of the break served to intensify the gloomy mood prevailing in Poland. It demonstrated that physical destruction of Poland's leading classes was the aim of the Soviets, as much as the Nazis. The Katyn murder and the disappearance of 10,000 Polish officers was proof enough of that. But, in addition, there was also the new fear that, by breaking off diplomatic relations with the Polish government, the Soviet Union wanted to gain a free hand in shaping future developments in Poland, whose territories the Soviet armies were about to enter in their drive toward Berlin. People in Poland realized that the future was bleak and there was no leeway for hope.[1]

The underground authorities reacted to the news of the break by issuing two statements. In his declaration of April 30, 1943, Government Delegate Jankowski affirmed that the Russians were responsible for the infamous mass murder in Katyn; he went on to list the even more numerous and shocking German crimes and bestialities, and appealed to all Poles to denounce and repudiate the hypocritical German propaganda, exploiting the Katyn murders in order to show the Germans as defenders of Christian morality and civilization. A few days later, on May 9, 1943, the National Political Representation issued a statement rejecting Soviet allegations that the Polish government's request for an investigation of the Katyn murders had been made in conjunction with the Germans. The Katyn affair provided the Russians with a pretext for breaking off relations with the Polish government, in preparation for the Soviet takeover of Poland's eastern territories. Recalling the German-Soviet alliance in 1939, the NPR declared that the Polish people were united in supporting their government's position, based on the principle of Poland's territorial integrity, and that they expected full understanding and support from other allied nations.

Subsequently, news reached Poland that the bodies of murdered Polish officers had been examined by members of an International Commission, composed of distinguished scholars and specialists in forensic medicine from twelve countries (not including Germany), who arrived in Katyn on April 28, 1943, at the invitation of the German government. Among the Commission's members were Professor François Naville from the University of Geneva and Professor Dr. Marko Antonov-Markov from the University of Sofia. The Commission concluded unanimously that the Polish officers had been murdered in the spring of 1940, that is, more than a year before the outbreak of the German-Soviet war; at that time, the Polish POWs from the Kozelsk camp were held by the Russians, and the area around Katyn was, of course, under Soviet control.

Factual findings confirmed the conviction universally held in Poland. It was not shaken by the findings of a Soviet Commission, called to Katyn after the area had been recaptured from the Germans. The Soviet Commission concluded, on the basis of testimonies and the examination of the bodies, that the Polish officers had been murdered by the Germans in the fall of 1941, i.e., after the outbreak of the Soviet-German war; working in the region of Smolensk, they were caught in the rapid advance of German armies. According to the Soviet Commission, German officers from the 537th Battalion of Engineers—Lt. Col. Arnes, Lt. Rekst and 2nd Lt. Hott—were responsible for the crime.

When the Soviet armies entered Poland and the specter of a new occupation loomed ahead, the Katyn murders were overshadowed by bleak reality. But the memory of the crime—rekindled occasionally by its reappearance on the international forum—remains fresh and lives on.

2. Katyn at the Nuremberg Trial

After the war, the Katyn murders were brought up for the first time during the Nuremberg trials. The Soviet prosecutor, Colonel Pokrovsky, demanded that Hermann Goering and his associates be punished for the Katyn massacre. As the only, and supposedly sufficient, evidence, he presented the report of the Soviet Commission. The Nuremberg tribunal, however, did not share this view; it admitted three witnesses for each side, i.e., for the prosecution and for the defense. The Soviet witnesses—Professor Dr. V. I. Prozorovsky and Professor Boris Basilevsky—confirmed in their testimony the Soviet version of events, i.e., that the crime had been perpetrated by the Germans in the fall of 1941; the third witness, Dr. Marko Antonov-Markov from the University of Sofia, former member of the International

Commission investigating the Katyn murders, refuted the findings of the International Commission and claimed that he had signed the Commission's report under duress. Neither the tribunal nor the defense were much surprised by Dr. Markov's statement. Everybody knew that shortly after the Soviet armies had entered Bulgaria, Dr. Markov was tried for his participation in the International Commission; he testified at the time that he had been compelled to do so, and was released to be used as a witness in Nuremberg.

The real surprise came when Colonel Friedrich Ahrens appeared as a witness for the defense. Colonel Ahrens (mistakenly referred to as "Arnes" in the Soviet report) was the commanding officer of a communication unit designated as the 537th Signal Regiment (not a Battalion of Engineers). The Russians claimed that he was responsible for the Katyn crime. Colonel Ahrens testified that in the fall of 1941 he was not commanding the 537th Signal Regiment and could not possibly have been in the Katyn area. Another witness, Lt. Reinhard von Eichborn of the 537th Signal Regiment, testified that the discovery of the graves was made in August 1941, when some 20 soldiers from the communication unit occupied the NKVD villa in the Katyn Forest to install a communications center for the German Fifth Army. These testimonies were confirmed by the two witnesses' commanding officer, General Eugen Oberhäuser. They undermined the testimony of the Soviet witnesses to such an extent that the Soviet prosecutors simply dropped the whole thing and never again returned to the Katyn affair. When the final verdict was rendered by the Nuremberg tribunal on September 30, 1946—not a word was said about Katyn.[2]

The tribunal, however, sentenced to death the German Governor General in Poland, Hans Frank, basing its decision on testimony provided, among others, by the chief of the Directorate of Civil Resistance Korbonski, whose account of street executions (filed with the Ministry of Justice in Warsaw) was admitted as evidence.[3]

XXI

BEFORE "TEMPEST"

As the underground military organization evolved from the Service for Poland's Victory through the Union for Armed Struggle into the Home Army, its goal remained the same: a universal rising in Poland. In the early years—1939 and 1940—this concept was simple: an armed action against the Germans, carried out by organized underground forces with the support of the entire population, the Polish armed forces operating in the west, and the western allies. Complications set in as it became clear that, instead of the western allies entering Poland from the south or from the west, it would be the Soviet forces that would come from the east. The defeat of German armies at Stalingrad in 1942 signaled the beginning of the German retreat. Its gathering momentum forced the Polish government in London and the Polish underground leadership to formulate precisely their position in regard to Soviet authorities and Soviet armies about to enter Poland, as well as Soviet claims to Poland's eastern territories.

With this in mind, the National Political Representation issued its declaration of March 14, 1943, asserting that "the Polish people stand steadfast and united in their support of the inviolability of Poland's frontiers as of September 1939."

On November 15, 1943, the Government Delegate Jankowski warned the inhabitants of the eastern borderlands of the impending Soviet arrival in Poland; he advised them to stay where they were and to maintain a correct attitude toward the Russian troops.

Finally, on January 20, 1944, the Council of National Unity issued a statement, rejecting again all Soviet claims to Poland's eastern territories. In its resolution of February 15, 1944 (transmitted to London on that same day), the Council also registered its opposition to any discussions by the government-in-exile pertaining to the revision of Poland's eastern frontiers.

The situation was made much more difficult by the fact that the Soviet government had broken off diplomatic relations with the Polish government on April 26, 1943. As a result, there was no communication whatsoever between the two governments. In addition, the activities of the Polish Workers Party in occupied Poland, the hostility of the Soviet partisans toward the Polish partisans in eastern territories and the anti-Polish propaganda they spread, the Soviet government's declarations claiming all Polish territories east of the Curzon line as Russian—indicated that the Russians were about to enter Poland not as her formal ally, but as an enemy.

The dangers inherent in this situation were clearly understood both in London and in Poland. In his dispatch to General Bor-Komorowski (Commander of the Home Army after General Rowecki's arrest on June 30, 1943), General Kazimierz Sosnkowski (Polish Supreme Commander after General Sikorski's death on July 4, 1943, in an air crash at Gibraltar), defined the Soviet aims as follows:

"In my opinion, the real object of the Soviet game is to transform Poland into a vassal communist republic or even into the seventeenth Soviet republic . . . ."

These fears were shared by General Bor-Komorowski, who stated in his report to the Supreme Commander (July 14, 1944) that it would be harmful if the Home Army remained inactive in the territories gradually taken over by the Soviet armies, because then "nothing would stand in the way of simulating the will of the Polish people to establish the seventeenth Soviet republic."[1]

Such sober evaluation contrasted with the compelling political and practical realities in Poland. The underground leadership thought that, in view of the approaching Soviet armies, a policy should be devised and followed that would strengthen Poland's rightful claims to independence. An exchange of several dispatches between the government in London and the underground authorities in Poland brought to light differences of opinion, with the government and the Supreme Commander on one side, and the Government Delegacy, the National Political Representation and the High Command of the Home Army on the other.

In the event it proved impossible to reestablish official Polish-Soviet relations, the government instruction of October 27, 1943, prescribed intensified sabotage-diversionary operations against the Germans, but only of a protective and political-manifestative character; on the other hand, it prohibited all attempts to establish cooperation with the Soviets and ordered the underground authorities and the Home Army to remain under cover, and to defend themselves in the event of arrests and repressions—a clear command to resort to the use of arms.

Government Delegate Jankowski, the National Political Representation and General Komorowski disagreed with that part of the instruction which prohibited their disclosure to the Russians. They felt that, unless the Russians were confronted with those who represented the Republic and its lawful authorities, a dangerous void would be created, and would be promptly filled by organizations subservient to the Russians. Besides, it was clearly impossible to maintain a secret underground army which, in addition, was supposed to step up its sabotage-diversionary operations against the Germans. To cover all probabilities, it was determined that a new underground organizational network should be established, separate from the Home Army and the existing underground movement; it was to carry on the struggle for Poland's independence under the changed conditions of a foreseen Soviet occupation of Poland. General Bor-Komorowski's dispatch of November 26, 1943, informed the Supreme Commander, General Sosnkowski, of this position of the underground leadership in Poland.

Though equally pessimistic in their evaluation of the Soviet plans, the government and the underground leadership were obviously poles apart on the question of whether the underground should or should not be revealed to the Russians. This difference of opinion was caused primarily by the formal, bureaucratic approach of the Poles in London to the problem of disclosure. They were thousands of miles away from the daily reality of life in occupied Poland; they knew this reality from reports, but could not feel it in their bones. As a point of departure for their policy, they accepted the fact of broken diplomatic relations and concluded—logically but impractically—that the entire country should repudiate those who did not recognize the Polish government and should refuse to accept the new reality in the making. Just how theoretical was such an approach could be seen readily in the government's directives to intensify the sabotage-diversion operations against the Germans without, however, revealing to the Russians the Home Army units that were to carry them out. These two directives were contradictory. Polish units, striking from the rear at the communications lines of the retreating German armies, could not but come in contact with the Russians, attacking from the front. This was tantamount to disclosure, inevitable in any case since Soviet partisan units were operating in the same areas as the Polish units.

The underground leadership, on the other hand, took as a point of departure in formulating their policy the existing conditions in Poland, i.e., the imminent entrance into Poland of the Soviet armies, and everything their arrival implied. The underground leaders thought that the Home Army, disregarding the risks involved, should take part in fighting the Germans, which would necessarily result in their disclosure, but would also thwart communist claims that the Russians alone had liberated Poland. Also, they thought it necessary for the Polish underground authorities to reveal themselves to the Russians as rightful hosts in Poland, lest this role be usurped by communist organizations, especially by the Polish Workers Party. To remain underground—even if it were possible—would mean creating a void facilitating the realization of the most daring Soviet schemes, including making out of Poland the seventeenth Soviet republic. The underground leadership had no illusions about the Soviet intentions, but felt they should be counteracted by the disclosure of the underground government and the underground army—two attributes of Poland's sovereignty.

Following a further exchange of dispatches, the government finally conceded and confirmed the underground's position in resolutions of February 2-18, 1944. These resolutions represented a compromise between the Supreme Commander, General Sosnkowski, and Stanislaw Mikolajczyk, who replaced General Sikorski as premier of the Polish government-in-exile. General Sosnkowski foresaw the loss of Poland's independence, Mikolajczyk thought that Poland would lose her eastern territories, but would be able to save her independence within the new borders.

Finally, General Sosnkowski yielded, though unwillingly. In his dispatch of February 12, 1944, he wrote:

". . . the government and I are of the opinion that the will of the homeland cannot possibly be ignored."

Once the policy was coordinated, the Government Delegacy and the High Command of the Home Army passed on the following directives to their local representatives throughout the country:

1. Sabotage-diversion activities behind the German lines should be intensified under the new code name: Operation "Tempest," consisting of destruction of German communication lines and attacks on the German rear guard.

2. In view of the nature of "Tempest," Warsaw and all other larger cities will not be included.

3. Instructions preparatory to general rising will remain in force, but the timing of the uprising will be subject to proper military and political conditions.

4. The Home Army units which, in the course of fighting, will come in contact with the Soviet army, will maintain their autonomy and refuse to be incorporated into Berling's army. Their commanders will make the following declaration to the Soviet commanding officers:

"On orders of the government of the Republic of Poland, I come to propose coordinating our operations with the armed forces of the USSR, upon their entrance on the territory of the Polish Republic, in a joint military action against our common enemy."

5. Representatives of the civil authorities (delegates) will present themselves to the Soviet authorities as functionaries of the Government of the Republic of Poland, and will make an identical declaration.

6. Inhabitants of the territories that fall under the control of the advancing Soviet armies should be prevented from fleeing their homes; abandonment would facilitate the seizure of these lands.

Meanwhile, mobilization for Operation "Tempest" was carried out. In central Poland, particularly in the *General Gouvernement*, small partisan groups were merged into larger units. In eastern Poland, where "Tempest" was to begin, all Home Army soldiers were called in. All units were provided—to the extent possible—with arms, ammunition, clothing and medical supplies. Also, the process of designating the Home Army units, giving each the name or the number of a prewar regiment or division of the regular Polish army was completed at that time.

On the night of January 3, 1944, Soviet armies crossed the prewar frontier of Poland near the town of Sarny. Three months later, Government Delegate Jankowski and the Council of National Unity stated once more, in their declaration of April 3, 1944, their position regarding this development. They reiterated that in crossing the line near Sarny, the Soviet armies crossed Poland's eastern frontier, established in agreement with the USSR by the Treaty of Riga, and entered territories that are and will be Polish, since the Polish nation will never give up the lands west of the Curzon Line; that Poland is governed by Polish constitutional authorities, currently discharging their functions partly abroad and partly in Poland; that the people of Poland, while maintaining a correct behavior with regard to the Soviet armies, are bound to obey the directives of their government, functioning throughout the entire country, and not those issued by other, self-styled bodies, particularly when those bodies initiate a draft into the Soviet army, or the army commanded by General Berling, or when they arrange a plebiscite. The declaration appealed again to the population not to leave their homes and to maintain their national dignity and their faith that the territories now occupied by the Soviet armies will remain forever an integral part of Poland.

At the time this declaration was issued, both the principles it set forth and the instructions contained in the resolutions of the government-in-exile of February 2-18, 1944, were undergoing a trial by fire, because it was in February 1944 that units of the Home Army in the Wolyn region first came face to face with the regular Soviet army.

XXII

"TEMPEST"

1. "Tempest" in the Wolyn Province

Mobilized for Operation "Tempest" in the province of Wolyn, seasoned partisan units of the Home Army, commanded by Major Jan Wojciech Kiwerski (pseudonym: Oliwa), were designated as the 27th Infantry Division, consisting of 6,000 soldiers, all local men. The Division carried out a number of strikes against German communication lines, i.e., railroad lines and highways, connecting the Reich with the eastern front. Their operations were all the more difficult because of the raids, conducted by the Ukrainians living in the Wolyn region, against Polish villages and settlements, which the raiders burned to the ground, killing off all Polish inhabitants. These raids, which began in the spring of 1943, affected the areas near the towns of Dubno, Kowel and Luck. German police units, composed of the Ukrainians, but armed and trained by the Germans, also took part in the raids. This prompted the area commander of the Home Army to undertake the defense of the local Polish population. People were assembled in specified localities, called "bases," protected by specially assigned units of the Home Army, which, however, were not too well armed at that time and only in the process of completing their equipment with arms and ammunition captured from the Germans.

The news of the murders perpetrated on the Polish population caused Delegate Jankowski to issue in May 1943 a statement, warning the Ukrainians against joining the SS Division *Galizien*. The National Political Representation also appealed to the Ukrainians on July 30, 1943, denouncing the killings and calling for their cessation; it expressed its support for the Ukrainian aspirations to national independence, but stated that the territories with mixed Polish-Ukrainian population could not be included in an Independent Ukraine.

Under the prevailing circumstances, it seems doubtful that the appeal ever reached wide masses of the Ukrainian population. It did, however, reach its leaders—with the effect opposite to that intended: the killings of Poles increased, in order to clear out the Polish elements in areas of mixed population, and to make them wholly Ukrainian.

In February 1944, a Soviet cavalry reconnaissance patrol crossed the Stochod River and ran into a partisan unit of the Home Army. The meeting between the Polish and the Soviet commanders prepared the ground for the first joint combat action of the 27th Infantry Division and the Soviet army. It took place on March 20, 1944, when the 27th Division, in an operation coordinated by the two commands, seized the small town of Turzyska and took part in fighting in the area of Kowel and Wlodzimierz.

On March 26, 1944, Major Jan Wojciech Kiwerski (pseudonym: Oliwa), the commanding officer of the 27th Infantry Division, met with the Soviet army's commander, General Sergeyev and with Colonel Kharitonov. It was established at that meeting that the 27th Division was a unit of the Polish armed forces, subject to the government in London and Warsaw; that the Division's communication with these authorities would not be hindered in any way; that the Division would receive from the Russians full equipment and provisions, including artillery and motor vehicles. In operational matters, however, the Division was to be subject to the orders of the Soviet command.

Informed of this agreement, Government Delegate Jankowski approved it, as did the Council of National Unity in its resolution of May 29, 1944.

From that time on, the 27th Division fought the Germans shoulder to shoulder with the Soviet army. During the dogged fighting with German forces, augmented by the armored division Viking, the Russians were repulsed eastward, while the 27th Division stubbornly defended their positions, in accordance with the orders received. They were surrounded near the Turia River, and the Division's commander, Major Kiwerski, was killed in battle on April 18, 1944. His place was taken by Major Tadeusz Sztumberg-Rychter (pseudonym: Zegota) who managed to break through the encircling German ring and, after heavy fighting, led his men to the Szack Forest. It was there that he met the commanding officer of some Soviet partisan units, a colonel of the NKVD, who refused to honor the agreement made with General Sergeyev and demanded that the 27th Division be merged with General Berling's army. Since word had reached the Poles that the Russians were disarming smaller units of the Home Army, and were shooting their commanding officers, Major Rychter decided to escape from the danger zone. They fought their way through German lines again, and eventually one part of the 27th Division reached the woods near Parczew. But Rychter's orders failed to reach the other part of the 27th Division, which proceeded to the rear of the Soviet armies and was disarmed by the Russians. The soldiers were incorporated into General Berling's army. The officers were deported to parts unknown.

2. *"Tempest" in the Wilno District*

The second contact with the Soviet army occurred in the Wilno district. Soviet partisan units operating in that area had long been hostile to the Home Army; occasional agreements on mutual toleration were consistently broken by the Russians. In spite of this, the Home Army units, mobilized for Operation "Tempest" in the Wilno and Nowogrodek districts, fought about 30 battles and engagements with the Germans and captured Turgiele, Rudomino, Troki, Bieniakonie, Juraciszki, Radun; for a time, they even held the prison in Lida, where they released 77 prisoners. A few hundred Germans were killed during these encounters and a great deal of equipment, automatic weapons, ammunition and matériel fell into Polish hands.

The Home Army units in the two districts, combined for "Tempest" into several brigades and regiments (but not a division), numbered 5,500 men and were under the command of Colonel Aleksander Krzyzanowski (pseudonym: Wilk). On the night of July 6, 1944, after the Soviet armies had captured Smorgonie, the Home Army launched its attack on Wilno; within the city, other Home Army units attacked the Germans simultaneously. On July 7, 1944, at 16:00 hours, the Soviet armies joined in the battle. Heavy fighting went on until July 13, when the city was captured. Amid indescribable enthusiasm of its population, Wilno became Polish once again. Polish organizations and committees sprang up spontaneously to take over the administration of the city.

Immediately upon the capture of the city, the Soviet Command ordered the Home Army units to leave Wilno. Accordingly, Colonel Krzyzanowski ordered his men to leave the city and to reassemble on the outskirts of the Rudnicka Forest. He then went to General Chernyakhovsky, the Soviet commander of the Third Byelorussian Front, to clarify the situation. An agreement was reached during the meeting, whereby General Chernyakhovsky promised to provide arms and equipment for one division of infantry and one brigade of cavalry. He attached no political conditions to his offer.

On July 16, 1944, the Russians invited Colonel Krzyzanowski— this time, together with his staff—for another meeting with General Chernyakhovsky. Neither the Colonel, nor any of his staff officers ever returned from that meeting. Simultaneously, other Polish officers, assembled in the village of Bogusze, where they were to meet with the Russians to discuss the needs of the division (or brigade), were surrounded by Soviet army units, arrested, and taken to Wilnó, where they were put in prison.

Also at the same time, the Russians arrested and deported the Government Delegate for the Wilno district, as well as other members of the Wilno Delegacy.

Alarmed at this turn of events, the new district commanders of the Home Army (Lt. Col. Strychanski for the Wilno area, and Lt. Col. Janusz Prawdzic-Szlaski, pseudonym: Prawdzic, for the Nowogrodek area), led their men, under strafing from about 30 Soviet aircraft, into the depths of the Rudnicka Forest. Once there, they told their men to break into small groups and either to disperse throughout the area or to fight their way westward, toward Grodno and Bialystok. It was then that the great Soviet manhunt began. Hungry and totally exhausted, most of the small bands of Home Army soldiers fell into the Soviet hands. They were placed in a detention camp at Miedniki, where—at the end of the sweep-up operations—the Russians assembled about 5,700 Home Army soldiers from the Wilno and the Nowogrodek districts. They did not yield. To all propaganda, calling them to join Berling's army, they had one answer: "We want Wilk!" (their commander, Col. Krzyzanowski). Shortly, they were all deported to concentration camps in the USSR. The fate of the Home Army officers, imprisoned at first in Wilno by the NKVD, was the same.

The battle of Surkonty was the epilogue to the struggle for Wilno. But this time it was not against the Germans that the Home Army had to fight. It was against the Russians. Although they had two hours in which to retreat and disperse, a detachment of the Home Army chose instead to make a stand against the overwhelming Russian odds. Their commanding officer, Lt. Col. Maciej Kalenkiewicz (pseudonym: Kotwicz), three other officers and 32 soldiers were killed during the battle. On the Soviet side, 132 officers and men were killed.

3. "Tempest" in Southeastern Poland

The Home Army units in the Lwow district were designated as the 5th Infantry Division and the 14th Regiment of Uhlans. In March 1944, when the Soviet-German front stabilized along the Tarnopol-Kolomyja line, they joined in Operation "Tempest," stepping up their sabotage-diversion operations. Forty-six trains were derailed, 28 locomotives and 177 railroad cars were destroyed, 17 tanks were damaged in transport; railroad tracks were torn up in 55 places; 24 Germans were killed and 160 wounded.

Ukrainian raids on Polish villages, burnings and killings that began in 1943-44, here, too—as in the Wolyn province—hampered the Home Army's operations. The number of victims as of April 1944, was estimated at 5,000 men, women and children. To protect and defend the Polish population, assembled in bases, the district commander of the Home Army was obliged to detach a number of small partisan units which, therefore, could not take part in Operation "Tempest."

In the summer of 1944, two Home Army formations joined in the Soviet offensive—the 5th Infantry Division, with 3,000 men, led by Colonel Wladyslaw Filipkowski (pseudonym: Janka), and the 14th Regiment of Uhlans, under the command of "Draza," a major of the Yugoslav army, who had escaped from a German POW camp. Supported by Soviet armored units, they captured Lwow after four days of heavy fighting (July 23-27, 1944). The commandant of the Soviet First Army (First Ukrainian Front) cited the 14th Regiment of Uhlans for bravery in action and the fraternal cooperation with the Soviet armies. The citation was delivered to "Draza" by Colonel Yevtimov.

Both the Government Delegate Professor Adam Ostrowski and the Home Army region commander, Colonel Wladyslaw Filipkowski, revealed themselves to the Russians. At the meeting held with Colonel Filipkowski on July 29, 1944, the Soviet Command was represented by General Grushko, the NKVD chief of the First Ukrainian Front, and by General Ivanov. The Soviet representatives demanded that the Home Army formations be disbanded and that they lay down their arms within two hours; they left the Home Army soldiers one option: to join the ranks of either the Soviet army or the army of General Berling. Colonel Filipkowski saw no other solution, but to accept the Soviet conditions. He informed his officers and men accordingly, and the news was received with dismay.

Still, Colonel Filipkowski decided to go to Zhitomir on July 31, 1944, together with five officers of his staff, in order to intercede with General Michal Zymierski. Learning of the plan, the Soviet authorities first forbade the Colonel to leave and then put all officers under arrest. Government Delegate Ostrowski was also arrested. On the same day, about 30 Home Army staff officers, gathered at the headquarters at 14 Kochanowski Street, were surrounded by the NKVD and taken to the prison at Lacki Street. Shortly, the prison began to overflow with officers and men of those Home Army units, which had refused to heed Colonel Filipkowski's order to lay down their arms and disband; they crossed the San River, but, once on the other side, they were surrounded and disarmed by the Russians.

The last note of Operation "Tempest" and the struggle for Lwow was sounded in the dispatch sent by the District Government Delegacy, the local political representation and the Home Army regional command to the Polish government in London:

"We call for an allied commission. We implore you to intercede for imprisoned members of the Home Army and the Delegacy, who are being cruelly maltreated."

4. "Tempest" in the Lublin District

The Home Army area commander for the Lublin district, Colonel Kazimierz Tumidajski (pseudonyms: Edward, Marcin) brought three infantry divisions to Operation "Tempest:" the 3rd Division, commanded by Colonel Adam Switalski (pseudonym: Dabrowa); the 9th Division, commanded by Major General Ludwik Bittner (pseudonym: Halka); and the 27th Division, comprising those soldiers who had crossed the Bug River and fought their way to the Parczew Forest, as well as supplements from the Lublin district. Colonel Jan Kotowicz (pseudonym: Twardy) assumed the command of the 27th Division. The three divisions began a series of vast sabotage-diversion operations. On their own, they seized the following localities: Belzec, Wawolnica, Urzedow, Konskowola, Lubartow, Poniatow and Kock; and in cooperation with the Soviet armies: Biala Podlaska, Chelm, Miedzyrzec Podlaski, Radzyn, Lukow, Krasnystaw, Szczebrzeszyn, Pulawy, Deblin, Zamosc, and Lublin. In a few instances, in the heat of the battle, the command over the Soviet troops was assumed by Polish officers. On some occasions, units of the Home Army, fighting together with the Russians, won laudatory citations in orders of the day of the Soviet commanders.

In liberated cities and towns, local underground authorities— among others, the Government Delegate for the Lublin district, Wladyslaw Cholewa—stepped forward, revealed themselves and took over the administration. Various functionaries moved into government buildings, underground police assumed their duties. After the Germans had left the town of Zamosc, about a week elapsed before the arrival of the Russians. It was time enough for the local underground authorities to assume control of all sectors of life. Zamosc began to return to normal.

When the front line moved on toward the Vistula, a meeting was held between Colonel Tumidajski and the commander of the Soviet Sixth Army, General Kolpachev. The Soviet General offered the Home Army divisions a choice: to merge with the Red Army or General Berling's army—or to be disarmed and dissolved. When Colonel Tumidajski chose the second alternative, he was arrested, together with Government Delegate Cholewa, another member of the Delegacy, Judge Jozef Dolina, and others.

Government Delegate Cholewa was taken under guard, first to Lublin, to General Byelfyev, and then—also under guard—to Chelm, to General Zhukov, who represented the Red Army with the Polish Committee of National Liberation. Finally, after a temporary stay in two swampy camps (one of them in Kraskow, county of Wlodawa), all the arrested underground leaders were deported to Russia.

The disarmament of the three divisions was meanwhile carried out gradually and by subterfuge. Together with the Soviet armies, they took part in the Russian offensive, rolling toward Warsaw. In the course of the offensive, the Soviet troops surrounded and disarmed one Polish division after another. Officers and soldiers of the Home Army were then shipped off to the infamous German concentration camp at Majdanek. Within a short time, there were 200 officers and 2,500 soldiers of the Home Army in the camp. In time, they were all deported to Russia.

5. *"Tempest"* in the Bialystok District

The Home Army district of Bialystok was commanded by Colonel Wladyslaw Liniarski (pseudonym: Mscislaw), whose name appeared more than once in the Soviet command's orders of the day, cited for his outstanding cooperation with the Soviet partisans. Two infantry divisions—the 18th and the 29th—were mobilized for Operation "Tempest"; there were also two smaller formations: the Suwalki and the Podlasie cavalry brigades. Colonel Liniarski did not reveal himself to the Russians in the course of Operation "Tempest," but a Home Army inspector and a few sector commanders did and were arrested. The local Soviet commandant, General Zakharov, demanded the disbandment and disarmament of Home Army units. Soldiers from those Home Army units that had not cached their weapons and withdrawn into hiding were now arrested and disarmed. Among them, there were many Byelorussians, soldiers of the Home Army, who had taken part in partisan operations.

6. *"Tempest"* in the Polesie Province

On establishing contact with the Soviet armies, the nucleus of the 30th Infantry Division—under the command of Colonel Henryk Krajewski (pseudonym: Trzaska)—was ordered to the vicinity of Hajnowka, where its soldiers were to be merged with General Berling's army. Refusing to carry out these orders, they moved on westward, crossed the Bug River, and reached Biala Podlaska, where one part of the division was dissolved. The rest—8 companies, about 1,000 men—marched on toward Warsaw. Only five companies reached Deby Wielkie, where they were surrounded by the Soviets, and disarmed. Officers and soldiers were arrested and deported to Russia.

7. *"Tempest" in the Capital Region*

The Home Army units mobilized for Operation "Tempest" in the Warsaw region (commanded by Major General Albin Skroczynski, (pseudonym: Laszcz), were designated at the 8th Infantry Division. Led by Colonel Hieronim Susczynski (pseudonym: Szeliga), the 8th Division carried out diversionary actions in the rear of the German armies. The town of Siedlce was taken after three days of heavy fighting (July 27-30, 1944), and on August 9, Wegrow was captured. On the following day, Soviet units entered Wegrow. They disarmed the Home Army men, and arrested the officers and the county Government Delegate. The same happened to Colonel Susczynski, who—following the capture of Minsk Mazowiecki—established cooperation with the Soviet command, as a result of which the 8th Division fought shoulder to shoulder with the Russians, taking, among other, the small town of Tluszcz on July 30, 1944. On August 6 Colonel Susczynski called his officers together in order to present them formally to the Soviet command. This act of military courtesy never came off: the officers were arrested by the Soviets, and the Home Army units were surrounded, disarmed, and interned.

8. *"Tempest" in the Lodz District*

Since nearly the entire Lodz District had been incorporated into the Reich, only the Piotrkow inspectorate participated in Operation "Tempest." Partisan units of the Home Army were mobilized as the 25th Infantry Regiment (about 1,200 men) and augmented by four reserve county units of 80-100 men each. They conducted diversionary operations near Opoczno (September 16-27, 1944), inflicting heavy losses on the Germans. No contact with the Soviet armies was established.

9. *"Tempest "in the Radom District*

Under the command of Colonel Mieczyslaw Zietarski-Lizinski (pseudonym: Mieczyslaw), the Radom district was among the most active, similarly to the Lublin district. A considerable number of partisan units were operating in this area and, as a result of their partial mobilization for Operation "Tempest," they were combined into the 2nd Infantry Division (4,000 men) and the 7th Infantry Division (2,000 men). At their peak, the two divisions numbered 9,700 men. In addition, in each of the thirteen counties of the district, a small partisan force of about 50 men was left for special tasks, such as protecting the air drops. Altogether, the Radom district of the Home Army numbered 30,000 men.

Within the framework of Operation "Tempest," the two divisions engaged the Germans more than a dozen times, inflicting heavy losses in killed and wounded (running into several hundreds), and capturing substantive quantities of arms and war matériel. Of these engagements, the battle of Dmosice and Niedzwice (July 31-August 1, 1944) was the most important, because it covered the Soviet crossing of the Vistula and allowed the Soviet armies to establish on the western bank the so-called Sandomierz bridgehead, which later served as a springboard for the decisive Soviet offensive in the winter of 1944-1945. The Home Army also joined the Soviet forces in capturing Staszow and fought together with the Russians to establish bridgeheads at Magnuszew and Baranow.

Within a short time, orders began to arrive from the Soviet commanders for the Home Army to dissolve, lay down their arms, and join the ranks of Berling's army. Forewarned about Soviet tactics in eastern Poland, Colonel Zietarski followed in principle his instructions on disclosure, but limited the practice to large units. However, he prohibited his officers from participating in meetings and banquets with the Soviet officers, and from engaging in political debates with the Russians. He also forbade joining General Berling's army. In case of the imminent threat of disarmament, he ordered his men to hide their weapons, disperse throughout the area, stay in hiding, and remain in contact with their commanding officers.

Colonel Zietarski's orders prevented in the Radom district the repetition of the pattern of encirclement and disarmament of the Home Army by the Soviets. But it was not long before individual arrests of Home Army soldiers by the communist security police began, and before the NKVD and the Internal Security Corps (*Korpus Bezpieczenstwa Wewnetrznego*—KBW) embarked on liquidating the partisan units of the Home Army.

10. "Tempest" in the Krakow District

The scope of Operation "Tempest" was considerable in the Krakow district, despite the fact that three district commanders of the Home Army had been successively arrested there by the Germans: Colonel Jozef Spychalski (pseudonym: Jurand), brother of the future communist "marshal of Poland" Marian Spychalski; Major General Stanislaw Rostworowski (pseudonym: Odra); and Colonel Edward Godlewski (pseudonyms: Izabelka, Garda). Home Army units mobilized for Operation "Tempest" formed: the 6th Infantry Division and the 21st Infantry Division in the Krakow area, the 24th Infantry Division in the Rzeszow area, and the 22nd Infantry Division in the Przemysl-Jaroslaw area; in addition, there was also the Krakow Cavalry Brigade.

The units that comprised these divisions fought scores of battles and engagements against the Germans. The most important of these was the 7-hour battle on September 12-13, 1944, in the area of Poreba, Robczyce and Wisniowa, in which a 358-man unit of the 22nd Division fought against a battalion of German police. Eighty-three Germans were killed and six vehicles captured.

In the subdistrict of Rzeszow, the Germans lost several hundred men, 3 tanks, 20 heavy machine guns, 8 light machine guns, several hundred rifles, 40 field telephone sets, and 2 radio stations.

During the final phase of "Tempest," in September 1944, 68 armed actions were undertaken, in the course of which 70 prisoners were freed, 315 Germans disarmed, 582 Germans killed, 6 cannons and 4 heavy howitzers captured, 5 aircraft burned, 56 motor vehicles burned or captured, 3 heavy machine guns, 61 submachine guns and 102 antitank mortars captured, and railroad communication disrupted 84 times.

The first contact with the Soviet army was established by the 17th Infantry Regiment which captured Rzeszow together with the Russians on August 2, 1944. The Polish underground mayor of Rzeszow disclosed himself to the Russians immediately, as did one unit of the Home Army, whose men put on red-and-white armbands and assumed the duties of official Polish police. On August 6, Colonel Kazimierz Putek (pseudonym: Zworny), commander of the 24th Infantry Division, disclosed his identity to the Soviet authorities, who demanded an immediate surrender of all arms by the Home Army. Colonel Putek ordered the Home Army unit that had assumed police duties in town, to do so. Then he lodged a formal protest against the Soviet demands, broke off all contacts with the Soviet authorities, and thus managed to escape arrest. The underground mayor of the town, who had revealed his identity, was removed from the office. Town administration was taken over by Polish communist authorities. The situation in Jaroslaw was similar: both the underground mayor and the Home Army commander of the town were arrested.

When the hostile attitude of the Soviet authorities toward the Home Army became obvious, only some Home Army units decided to risk disclosure, while the rest remained underground. The process of disclosure ended with the order of the Commander of the Home Army to disband those Home Army units that were active in the territories occupied by the Soviets. The Home Army soldiers were to return to their homes and their families.

11. Operation "Jula"

The cryptonym "Jula" was given to a special operation, carried out within the overall framework of "Tempest." It consisted of the simultaneous, coordinated disruption of rail communication on a few railroad lines at once. Operation "Jula" had been suggested originally by the allies, but the Supreme Commander, General Sosnkowski, agreed readily, since it presented an opportunity to demonstrate the proficiency of the Home Army and, at the same time, to refute Soviet charges that the Home Army was incapable of undertaking an organized, directed action.

The signal from London was received on April 3, 1944. Three days later, on April 6, 1944, the following actions of great military importance were carried out: a 155-foot span of the railroad bridge over the Wisloka River was blown up, disrupting the Przeworsk-Rozwadow line for 48 hours; a 27-foot iron culvert near the Rogozno station was blown up under a passing train, disrupting the line for 34 hours; a 247-foot iron culvert was blown up under a train carrying war matériel near the Nowosielce station, on the Jaslo-Sanok line, disrupting the rail communication for 33 hours.

A letter from the British Minister of Economic Warfare, Lord Selborne, to General Sosnkowski, dated May 13, 1944, confirmed that Operation "Jula" had achieved its objectives. It expressed admiration for the precise and effective execution of this important mission. The letter also urged that the world be informed of "the unreserved support which the Soviet troops are receiving from the Polish Secret Army." The letter showed that the British Minister either did not know, or did not want to know, that the Home Army officers were being shot by the Soviets, and the Home Army soldiers were being disarmed and put in internment camps, even though this had been going on since March 1944 and the first contacts in the Wolyn province.

12. A Balance Sheet for "Tempest"

To sum up: Operation "Tempest," together with Operation "Jula," inflicted heavy losses on the Germans, both in men and in war materiel. Systematic disruption of German communication lines in many places, delayed and rendered more difficult transports to the eastern front. Finally, it tied up several large German units, which otherwise would have been used at the front.

Operation "Tempest" went beyond its original scope; despite the exclusion of larger cities, Kowel, Wilno, Lublin, Lwow and Rzeszow were all wrested from the Germans in the course of the "Tempest." This happened because the basic directives for Operation "Tempest" were subsequently broadened by General Sosnkowski's instruction of July 7, 1944, to seize—circumstances permitting—Lwow, Wilno, and other large cities, and even small regions, before the arrival of the Soviet armies.

The purely military objectives of Operation "Tempest" were achieved; it also proved a successful test of mobilization of the Home Army. Combining the mobilized units of the Home Army into Divisions and Regiments designated after their prewar predecessor formations, which had fought in September 1939, served to emphasize the unbroken continuity of the Polish Armed Forces. The importance of this was more than symbolic. It established the Home Army officially as one of the allied armies in the war theater, and this status was officially recognized in August 1944.

On the other hand, the establishment of cooperation with the Soviet armies and the disclosure of the underground to the Soviet authorities, did not bring about the expected political results, because of the failure to create *faits accomplis* that could force the Soviets to modify their policies. Anyway, the pattern of military collaboration with the Soviets differed from the pattern of disclosure, even though the time and place were often the same. As a rule, the first joint actions against the common enemy brought highest praise for the Home Army from the Soviet commanders of a given front or army. Home Army units were often cited in the orders of the day; provisions and equipment were promised readily; conditions of cooperation, as stated by the Home Army officers, were accepted willingly. The Soviet commanders advanced no political demands. They insisted only on military subordination of Home Army units to the operational orders of the Soviet command. Officers of the Home Army were invited to banquets, where fraternization and frankness—fueled with vodka—were the order of the day. Not infrequently, a Soviet officer would take a Home Army officer to the side and warn him that everything would change once the NKVD got there. Then, the front line units, comrades-in-arms of the Home Army, would move on, the NKVD units would replace them, and the curtain would rise on the second act of the drama—the disclosure. The behavior of the NKVD officers was always the same, which indicated the existence of a general directive. They refused to recognize the agreements made with Soviet front line commanders; they demanded that the Home Army units lay down their arms and join the army of General Berling; if refused, they threatened internment and deportations to the Soviet Union. A great majority of Home Army soldiers refused, anyway, regardless of dire consequences. As a result, at the end of the war, there were 50,000 Home Army soldiers in Soviet detention camps.

In 1946, when the former chief of the Directorate of Civil Resistance Korbonski tried to intercede at the Ministry of Security in Warsaw for the soldiers of the Home Army and the Peasant Battalions, held in Soviet camps, Colonel Jozef Mrozek, at that time chief of cabinet of the Minister of Security, General Stanislaw Radkiewicz, leaned over confidentially and said: "Don't bother us with this thing and get it out of your head, too. Neither you nor we have anything to say in this matter. This is the business of the NKVD exclusively."

In Home Army circles, in 1946, an account was making the rounds of a conversation between the super-communist Jakob Berman (brother of Adolf, member of the Council of Assistance to the Jews) and the legendary NKVD General Malinov (pseudonym of the future NKVD chief, General Ivan Serov). Berman tried to convince the NKVD general that in the interest of calming the country it would be better to transfer the interned Home Army soldiers from the Soviet Union to Poland, even if they were still to be held in camps. The Russian stopped Berman short: "I am surprised, Comrade Berman, that you are interceding for people who certainly would not help in building a people's democracy in Poland, but on the contrary, would hinder it. Anyway, the camp conditions in which they live are very satisfactory, and you can check it for yourself, on the spot, if you want to." Berman could take a hint. He never broached the subject again. With the passing of years, however, most of the soldiers from the Home Army and the Peasant Battalions returned to Poland from the Soviet Union, only to suffer further harassments and persecutions there.

These two interventions, however, were still a long way to come at the time when the "Tempest" rolled to the gates of Warsaw.[1]

XXIII

THE WARSAW RISING

1. Making the Decision

The concept of a general rising against the Germans originated, like the underground movement, in the days preceding the capitulation of Warsaw in 1939, and was elaborated in the course of the following four years. On September 26, 1939, General Tokarzewski approached General Rommel (appointed by Marshal Rydz-Smigly as the supreme military commander in Poland) with the proposal that Rommel transfer his command to Tokarzewski—since he himself had no chance to evade capture by the Germans—and thus enable Tokarzewski to organize the underground armed resistance in Poland, and to prepare the country "to engage in an open struggle at a time when the war situation would make it feasible," i.e., to prepare for a general rising. The statute of the Union for Armed Struggle called this "open struggle" by name, when it referred to "preparing behind the lines of the occupying forces an armed uprising that will go into effect at the moment when the regular Polish armed forces will enter the country." General Sikorski's plan for a general rising (October 10, 1940) detailed some of these preparations, e.g., flying to Poland the largest possible contingents of land forces in support of the rising.[1] Three years later, the military and political situation dictated a more realistic conception of a general rising in Poland. In specifying the conditions under which Operation "Tempest" would go into effect, the government instruction of October 7, 1943 (modified by resolutions of February 2-18, 1944) also spelled out in detail the conditions for the outbreak of a general rising, and defined its aims. The instruction anticipated the entry of the Soviet armies into Poland and the need to coordinate further military operations with the Soviets (through allied channels). However, it admitted the possibility of a rising regardless of conditions specified, in the event of a collapse of the German eastern front and a breakdown in the morale of the German army. The sole stipulation was that the government would have the final decision and the choice of the proper moment for the uprising.

In accordance with these directives, General Bor issued on November 20, 1943, an instruction which was transmitted to the government in London together with the Home Army Commander's report of November 26, 1943. General Bor's instruction confirmed his previous directives pertaining to the general rising; it emphasized that the actual outbreak of the uprising would be preceded by three successive orders: first—intensified monitoring; second—a state of alert; third—a state of readiness, evolving automatically into an open armed struggle.

On July 21, 1944, General Bor met with General Pelczynski, chief of staff of the Home Army, and with Major General Leopold Okulicki (pseudonyms: Kobra, Niedzwiadek), deputy chief of staff for operations. They all agreed that the rout of the German army and the collapse of the German front combined to create a propitious moment for striking against the Germans in Warsaw. They felt that the capital had to be liberated by the Poles themselves, without waiting for the approaching Soviet armies. This was tantamount to the inclusion of Warsaw into Operation "Tempest," since they were to attack a German garrison located behind the front lines and guarding communication lines across the Vistula, which were of crucial importance. They thought that the rising would lead to the liberation of the capital, just as Wilno, Lwow, Lublin and other cities had been liberated, even though originally they, too, were not included in Operation "Tempest." Their decision was also based on General Sosnkowski's instruction of July 7, 1944, extending the basic directives of October 27, 1943.

Having arrived at this decision, General Bor ordered the state of alert, beginning with July 25, 1944, and informed the Supreme Commander, General Sosnkowski, accordingly in his dispatch of July 21, which was received in London on July 23, 1944.

Meeting with Government Delegate Jankowski (July 22-24, 1944), General Bor informed him of the decision and obtained the Delegate's approval in principle. Plans for the Warsaw Rising were also discussed in detail by General Bor in daily sessions with his staff. These plans were based on the assumption that, once the rising began, it would take 5 to 7 days for the Soviet armies to occupy Warsaw.

This assumption coincided with the Soviet expectations. Meeting with Mikolajczyk at the Kremlin on August 9, Stalin told the Polish Premier that the Soviet armies had been expected to occupy Warsaw on the 5th or 6th of August. The general assumption at a conference in Stalin's headquarters was that Prague would be taken between the 5th and the 8th of August.[2]

In his dispatch of July 25, General Bor informed the Supreme Commander, General Sosnkowski that everything was ready to begin the struggle for Warsaw at any time and that he would report on the exact timing of the outbreak of fighting. This dispatch arrived in London on July 26, but it was not until July 28 that it reached General Sosnkowski, who was in Italy at the time, on an inspection tour of the Polish Second Corps of General Anders. Despite his addendum to the basic directives pertaining to Operation "Tempest" (July 7, 1944), General Sosnkowski opposed the uprising in Warsaw and frequently voiced his misgivings at the Cabinet meetings and in his dispatches to General Bor. While in Italy, he sent a telegram to the Chief of Staff, General Stanislaw Kopanski, with instructions that were to be transmitted to General Bor. In the event of Soviet occupation of Warsaw—these instructions said—General Bor should not disclose his identity, but should assume the leadership, together with the Delegacy, in resisting the Soviet policy of *faits accomplis*. Its inconsistency aside—if the Home Army were to hold Warsaw even for a short time, the disclosure to the Soviets was a foregone conclusion—the instruction did not contain approval for the rising. This, however, was immaterial, anyway, because on July 25, 1944, the following resolution was passed by the Cabinet in London:

"The Council of Ministers resolved on July 25, 1944, to authorize the Government Delegate to undertake all decisions required because of the pace of Soviet offensive, without a prior communication with the government, if necessary."

Premier Mikolajczyk, who had presided at the meeting of the Cabinet on July 25, was about to leave for Moscow for a meeting with Stalin. But before leaving, he sent a dispatch to the Government Delegate, interpreting authoritatively the resolution of the Cabinet (July 26, 1944):

"The Government of the Republic resolved unanimously to empower you to announce the uprising at a time determined by you. If possible, advise us beforehand. Copy through army channels to the Commander of the Home Army."

On July 30, 1944, at noon, an emissary from the government, Jan Nowak, arrived to see General Bor. Meeting with the High Command of the Home Army, Nowak declared that "in terms of its effect on allied governments and public opinion," an uprising would be literally "a tempest in a teacup." One year later General Bor told Nowak that his information "would have been taken into account had it been received a week earlier."[3]

On the following day, July 31, 1944, General Bor met with the General Commission of the Council of National Unity. He briefed the Commission members on the situation on the Soviet front, and then posed the following questions: In the opinion of the Commission, should the Home Army take over the city before the Soviet troops entered Warsaw? How much time was needed between the seizure of the city by the Home Army and the arrival of the Soviets for the civil authorities to assume their functions before they disclosed themselves to the Russians? To the first question, all members of the Commission gave an affirmative answer. As for the second, they declare that 12 hours would be enough.[4]

On the same day, July 31, 1944, the Home Army General Staff was to meet at 18:00 hours in an apartment at 67 Panska Street. Colonel Antoni Chrusciel (pseudonym: Monter) arrived one hour early, but found General Bor, General Pelczynski, and General Okulicki already there. He informed them that the Soviet tanks were already approaching the suburb of Praga, and that a number of localities in the immediate vicinity of the capital—Radosc, Milosna, Okuniew, Wolomin and Radzymin—were already in Soviet hands. On the basis of this information, they concluded that a Soviet attack on Warsaw might be launched at any time and that they should take up arms without delay, or else it would be too late to achieve the main object of the uprising: liberation of Warsaw by the Poles themselves. Government Delegate Jankowski was brought in hurriedly. He was briefed by General Bor, asked a few questions concerning the preparations for the struggle, and then said: "All right. Go ahead." General Bor then gave his orders to Colonel Chrusciel: "Tomorrow, at 17:00 hours, you will go into action."

The decision to start the uprising in Warsaw was made for the very same reasons that had prompted Operation "Tempest" with the disclosure of the Polish underground authorities and the Home Army to the Soviets. They were twice as valid in the case of Warsaw, the capital of Poland, the city that had never lost its crown, despite German efforts to downgrade it by making Krakow the capital of the *General Gouvernement*. It was Warsaw that sheltered within its walls the Home Cabinet, headed by vice premier Jankowski—i.e., the underground government; the departments of the Delegacy—i.e., the underground ministries; the Council of National Unity—i.e., the underground parliament; and the High Command of the Home Army which numbered 40,000 men in Warsaw alone. The entire country looked up to Warsaw and followed its lead in the struggle against the invaders. Warsaw also had a long tradition of insurrections: in 1794, in 1831, and in 1863. During the Insurrection of 1863, it had been the seat of the national government, while partisan groups were waging guerilla warfare throughout the country, much as the Home Army units were doing. It was unthinkable for Warsaw to be liberated by the Soviet armies, not by the Home Army. It would run counter to the national sense of honor and dignity. Also, it would confirm Soviet claims that the Polish Underground State and the Home

Army were a fiction, and would allow the Polish Committee of National Liberation, created by the Soviets on July 21, 1944, to parade in Warsaw as *the* Polish government, uncontested and unquestioned. Establishing control over the city by the Home Army, and taking the reins of government by the underground authorities was to forestall this and to create a *fait accompli*, which the Soviets were bound to take into account. What had happened in Wilno and Lwow was known in Warsaw. But it was felt that, should the Russians follow the same policy in Warsaw and arrest the underground authorities following their disclosure, even this risk had to be taken in the name of a historical exigency to manifest Poland's right to independence.

Fears that the Polish Committee of National Liberation might usurp for itself the place of the rightful authorities, should these remain in hiding, were not unfounded. The Polish Workers Party and the command of the People's Army had their own plans for an uprising and a takeover of the capital. This was not surprising in view of the fact that their radio stations, Kosciuszko and Moskwa, as well as the proclamation of the Polish People's Army of July 29, 1944, called on the people of Warsaw to rise immediately. Also, the High Command of the People's Army ordered its units to seize certain important objectives in the city, in the event the Soviet armies or Berling's army launched an attack on the city; this meant that the People's Army received assignments identical with those of the Home Army. In addition, the communist Warsaw National Council issued on July 30, 1944, a proclamation calling for the rising:

"We shall not permit the Germans to make out of Warsaw a bulwark of their resistance. The enemy in our capital should be defeated and annihilated with the speed of lightning. Thus we have to bend all our efforts to help the allied Soviet armies in liberating our city.

"People of Warsaw! To arms! Let there be armed Polish soldiers in every sector of the city. Let the entire population of Warsaw rally round the Warsaw National Council, the People's Army, the soldiers of underground Poland. Let them attack the enemy together. Let us oust them from the streets of our city, smoke them out of the buildings. Let us transform our houses into unconquerable fortresses. . . ."

Finally, at the meeting of the Central Committee of the Polish Workers Party on July 31, the question of welcoming General Berling and the Soviet troops was discussed, as well as the problem of assuming power in Warsaw by the National Council of the Homeland.

These plans of the Polish Workers Party were synchronized with Stalin's plans, as described by Molotov to the American Ambassador in Moscow, Averell Harriman, on July 5, 1944. According to Molotov, Warsaw was to be liberated jointly by the People's Army and the army of General Berling.

On July 23, 1944, the Moscow radio announced the formation of the Polish Committee of National Liberation in Chelm. On that same day, Stalin sent a telegram to Churchill, which contained the following passage:

"We do not want to, and will not, establish our own administration on the territories of Poland, because we do not want to interfere in Poland's internal affairs. The Poles should do it themselves. For this reason, we deem it appropriate to establish contact with the Polish Committee of National Liberation, created recently by the National Council of the Homeland, which had been established in Warsaw at the end of last year with the participation of representatives of democratic parties and groups. We could find no other forces in Poland, capable of establishing a Polish administration. The so-called underground organizations, directed by the Polish government in London, turned out to be ephemeral and of no consequence at all."

Briefly, the outbreak of the Warsaw Rising on August 1, 1944, anticipated the implementation of the plans laid out by the Polish Workers Party to start the uprising and gain control of the city on their own.[5]

Since the Polish Workers Party and the command of the People's Army were in close contact and coordinated their plans with the Soviet command, it would be correct to state that there were two plans for an uprising in Warsaw: the Polish plan and the Soviet plan. The realization of the Polish plan forestalled the realization of the Soviet plan.

Neither could the underground leadership disregard the mood in the capital. The flame of hate burned bright in Warsaw, whose inhabitants had yearned for revenge during five years of unspeakable German terror. From the very beginning, the Home Army men had been preparing for this one great moment, and now they could not wait for the action to begin. A restraining order could conceivably bring on some spontaneous actions, which would be easily drowned in blood.

Finally, the Warsaw Rising began also in self-defense. On July 28, 1944, the Germans had posted notices, ordering 100,000 men to report at specified assembly points for work on fortifications. This presented a clear threat that the Germans would apprehend the youth of the capital, which—according to rumors, long circulated in Warsaw by the Germans themselves—was marked for liquidation on Hitler's orders in any event.

On the other hand, the decision to begin the rising in Warsaw did not take into account Poland's position among the Allies, and particularly the agreement concluded more than half a year before between

Roosevelt, Churchill and Stalin in Teheran (November 28-December 1, 1943). The Teheran Agreement placed Poland within the Soviet sphere of influence, which in practice meant: within Russia's power. The negative attitude of the combined Chiefs of Staff in Washington toward the inclusion of the Warsaw Rising in allied operations plans (June-July 1944) was not taken into account, either. The Chiefs of Staff listened to the Home Army emissary, General Stanislaw Tatar (pseudonym: Tabor), but the Polish representative with the Combined Chiefs of Staff, Colonel Leon Mitkiewicz, was told repeatedly that Poland belonged to the Soviet operations theater, and that all Home Army actions, such as the rising, should be co-ordinated with the Soviet command.[6]

The reason for not taking into consideration the attitude of the allies toward Poland and the uprising was simple: the underground leaders did not know anything about the developments cited above. The position taken by the Combined Chiefs of Staff was consequent in terms of the Teheran decisions and the military situation in Poland. The terms of the Teheran Agreement were undoubtedly known to the Polish government in London; if not, it meant one thing only: a gross neglect of trustworthy sources through which confidential information has never been difficult to obtain in Washington. Certainly, General Sosnkowski was thoroughly familiar with the position of the Combined Chiefs of Staff from the many reports sent by Colonel Mitkiewicz. There was no doubt that he passed these reports on to the government. But did he also pass them on to General Bor, who could have easily been deluded by the air drops made by allied aircraft in Poland—i.e., in the Soviet operations theater—within the framework of the Special Operations Executive, directed by General Colin Gubbins? In any event, General Bor had never mentioned any such thing at the meetings of, for instance, the Directorate of Underground Struggle. In any event, these factors were not known to the underground civil leaders, and thus could not have been taken into consideration by them before they approved the decision on the Warsaw Rising.

The manner in which this decision had been made, also indicated the primacy of the military over the political leadership. The decision to be made was twofold: political and military. The first was undoubtedly the more important of the two. To decide whether or not the uprising should begin, required a careful prior assessment of the international situation, allied interrelationships, Poland's position in the hierarchy of problems that were being debated and solved in the west, the Soviet policy, the Polish reasons of state, the national exigencies, and many other complicated, important matters of a non-military character. There were two bodies in Poland, qualified to make such an assessment: the Home Cabinet and the Council of National Unity. On the other hand, the assessment of purely military factors governing the uprising decision lay within the exclusive competence of the High Command of the Home Army. However, the process of decision-making in the case of the Warsaw Rising shows that it was the High Command of the Home Army that passed judgments on both the military and the political aspects of the situation, while the Government Delegate played only a secondary and subordinate role, although the Premier's dispatch of July 26 had empowered him to make the final decision about the uprising. All problems related to the uprising were debated in the Headquarters of the Home Army and not—where political matters were concerned—in the Home Cabinet or the Council of National Unity. The Government Delegate was merely informed about the outcome of the deliberations and asked to approve them. Such requests had all the earmarks of a formality. General Bor met with the General Commission of the Council of National Unity only on the eve of the uprising, on July 31, 1944; even then, instead of a debate on the political aspects of the decision, only two questions were put to the Commission. Kazimierz Puzak, the most prominent of the underground political leaders and chairman of the Council of National Unity and its General Commission, was not present at that meeting; and yet, he was known to have misgivings about the Soviet armies' coming to the aid of the insurgents.[7]

The proclamation of August 3, 1944, signed by Government Delegate Jankowski, chairman of the Council of National Unity Puzak and the Commander of the Home Army General Bor—was not entirely accurate when it stated that "the Government Delegate in Poland, vice premier of the Government of the Republic and the chairman of the Council of National Unity have decided, in agreement with the Commander of the Home Army, to launch the open armed struggle on August 1, 1944." Actually, it was the other way around. The Commander of the Home Army, in agreement with the Government Delegate, and without the participation of the chairman of the Council of National Unity, decided to take up arms on August 1, 1944. In spite of this, however, Puzak later approved of the decision.

As far as the Home Cabinet was concerned, they had no part in making the decision. No one either asked or consulted them about anything. This unhealthy reversal of roles of the political and the military leadership cannot be explained by the requirements of underground secrecy. Whatever was known to every platoon leader of the

Home Army, could certainly be entrusted to a member of the Council of National Unity, especially since the Germans knew very well about the brewing insurrection. Log entries in the German *Kriegstagebuch* No. 11 of the 9th Army (which defended the approaches to Warsaw and took part in suppressing the Warsaw Rising), include the following:

1. July 25, 1944: "It is known that preparations for an uprising are being made; details are lacking as to the degree of preparedness and the timing."

2. July 26, 1944: "The Polish nationalist underground movement ordered a state of alert for its military units."

3. July 29, 1944: "Polish insurgents are expected to begin armed action in Warsaw about 23:00 hours. . . . However, nothing happened."

4. August 1, 1944: "The expected Polish uprising in Warsaw (the Home Army) began at 17:00 hours. Fighting goes on throughout the entire city."[8]

Premier Mikolajczyk's dispatch of July 26, 1944, played an important part in the decision to proceed with the uprising; based on the Cabinet's resolution of July 25, it authorized the Government Delegate to "announce the uprising", which, in effect, meant that the government approved of the action. It was easy to conclude from the resolution and the dispatch that the premier and members of the government in London agreed with the position taken by the underground leaders in Poland. Mikolajczyk's memoirs confirm this view. In precise detail, he repeats there the arguments presented by the underground leaders, regarding the necessity of Operation "Tempest," the disclosure, and the uprising; he adds no word of reservation or comment from himself. His trip to Moscow, for a meeting with Stalin, was timed to coincide with the supposed date of the outbreak. Since Mikolajczyk wanted to reinstate diplomatic relations between Poland and the USSR, and to discuss the overall problem of Polish-Soviet relations, he obviously considered the outbreak of the Warsaw Rising, the takeover of the city by the Home Army, and the disclosure of the underground authorities as a trump card in discussions that were to obtain the Soviet recognition of Poland's sovereignty—if possible, within the prewar frontiers.[9]

This approval for the uprising did not accord with the position of the Supreme Commander, General Sosnkowski. However, General Sosnkowski was in Italy during the last critical ten days of July, though he was aware that crucial decisions might be made in London during his absence.

Under the circumstances, the main responsibility for the outbreak of the uprising belonged to the government in London, which—despite everything—was in the best position to evaluate the international situation and the importance of the Warsaw Rising in terms of Polish policy aims. If the government thought that the rising would have no bearing on the future fate of Poland—as emissary Nowak said—it could forbid it categorically. Had the Government Delegate Jankowski received such a prohibition, he could not have given his approval for the uprising to begin.

The underground leaders in Poland, and particularly Government Delegate Jankowski and the Commander of the Home Army, General Bor, who made the final decision, were also responsible. It was true that at the General Staff councils a sort of vote was taken, or rather that everyone present stated his opinion. But an army Staff is not a parliament. All these votes, or opinions, could do was to assist the Commander of the Home Army in arriving at the proper decision, for which he, and he alone, bore the full responsibility, regardless of whether it had, or had not been forced upon him.

Neither was General Sosnkowski free from his share of responsibility for the Warsaw Rising. He could have tipped the scales by issuing an order to forego all plans for the uprising. And, if the government failed to go along with him, he could have resigned his post of Supreme Commander.

Briefly, the government in London, the underground authorities, and the Supreme Commander were all responsible for the Warsaw Rising.

To say that they were responsible for the Warsaw Rising, does not at all mean that they were guilty of it, as might be the case if an assertion were made that the Warsaw Rising had caused an enduring and irrevocable harm to Poland. Such an assertion could be true if there were any proof that had it not been for the uprising, Warsaw and its inhabitants could have survived till the end of the war just as they were on July 31, 1944, on the eve of the Warsaw Rising. But all evidence is to the contrary. It shows that Warsaw was to be defended by the Germans and turned into a fortress, which automatically would expose the city to protracted bombardment from the air and to artillery shelling from the land, i.e., to destruction. The evidence comes from German sources, particularly from the *Kriegstagebuch* No. 11 of the German 9th Army, which notes the following:

1. July 25: "The task of the [9th] Army is to stop the enemy before Warsaw, on the other side of the Vistula, and to defend positions and bridge approaches in Warsaw, Deblin and Pulawy."

2. September 13: The line to which the German forces have withdrawn "still charges the 9th Army with the responsibility to defend Warsaw on the west bank of the Vistula."

3. October 1: " . . . the fortress command (lacking at present) will be responsible for the expansion and the provisioning of the fortress Warsaw."

4. October 2: " . . . in view of the suppression of the uprising in Warsaw, the Army Group Center is implementing the directives pertaining to the expansion and outfitting of Warsaw as a fortress."

5. October 6: "The work of expanding Warsaw into a fortress is in full swing. . . it will be officially designated as a fortress when a degree of defense capability will be reached."[10]

Briefly speaking, the German plans for Warsaw were to turn it into a German Stalingrad, with all the consequences of such a decision.

Once Warsaw was turned into a fortress, everything that was not needed for its defense was to be destroyed on Hitler's orders. The German Log No. 11 of the 9th Army, contains the following monstrous entry under October 9, 1944:

"Reichsführer SS delivered the Führer's command to carry out total destruction of Warsaw. In this operation, all military exigencies will be taken into account. Technical auxiliary units from the Reich will be used in carrying out the demolition work."

What makes this even more monstrous is that, according to existing evidence, the order to annihilate Warsaw—carried out after the rising with a truly Teutonic precision—was not a spontaneous act of revenge for the uprising, but an implementation of one part of the General Eastern Plan, hatched in the perverted minds of the Nazi leaders as far back as 1939, and aimed at colonizing Poland and destroying the Polish population. This is indicated by a notation in the diary of Governor Hans Frank, dated October 4, 1939., i.e., immediately after the September campaign. Frank noted that he had won Hitler's approval for his decision not to rebuild Warsaw from the destruction of war, and to downgrade the city—as he thought—by making Krakow the capital of the *General Gouvernement*, instead of Warsaw. The order of the *Reichsführer SS* Himmler, issued on February 16, 1943—more than a year before the Warsaw Rising—was equally indicative " . . . houses of the subhumans [i.e., Poles] should disappear from the surface of the earth, and Warsaw, now a city of one million inhabitants, should be cut down in size."[11]

Finally, the underground authorities came into possession of plans for a future, German Warsaw, prepared by German urbanists; according to these plans, Warsaw was to be the size of its prewar downtown district, wedged in, on the Vistula side, between the Kierbedz Bridge and the Poniatowski Bridge. The demolition—in fulfillment of Hitler's command—of all buildings and streets in Warsaw that did not form part of the German fortress, was in complete agreement with the urbanists' plans and was not necessarily connected with the Warsaw Rising. Whether razed by bombs and artillery fire as a fortress, or sketched on the drafting boards of Nazi planners, Warsaw was doomed

to extinction—that was the crux of the plan to change the capital into a small provincial town. The thought behind it was a far-reaching
one: no matter what the outcome of the war, the destruction of a city
that was the heart and brain of Poland was certainly in the German
interest.

In this situation, Warsaw could be saved only if General von
Vorman, the commander of the 9th Army, failed to carry out his
orders to destroy the city (just as General Dietrich von Choltitz did
in the case of Paris), or if the Red Army encircled and entered the
city promptly—rather than in January 1945.

According to plans, the inhabitants of Warsaw were to be evacuated.
A notation of October 3, 1944 in the *Kriegstagebuch* No. 11 of the
German 9th Army, stated that, in view of the ongoing evacuation of
the Warsaw population following the surrender of the insurgents,
there was a need to issue "regulations that would prevent the return
of the civilian population to the city." Even if there were no Warsaw
Rising, the population of Warsaw was to be driven out of the city.
From this mass exodus of one million people, flowing through the
streets of the capital, it would not have been difficult for the Germans
to pick out 100,000 young men for work on the fortifications of the
"Warsaw fortress," and even more for labor in the Reich, or for concentration camps, where a good part of the Warsaw population wound
up after the capitulation, anyway.

For these reasons one may speak of the responsibility for the
Warsaw Rising, but not of the guilt for it, even though the refusal to
condemn those who were responsible for the uprising is based only
on the hypotheses cited above.

As regards the military aspects of the decision, the order to take up
arms on August 1, 1944, was prompted by the information brought
to generals Bor, Pelczynski and Okulicki by Colonel Chrusciel on the
afternoon of July 31, 1944, that the Soviet tanks were approaching
the suburb of Praga, and that the Soviet armies had already occupied
the neighboring localities of Radosc, Milosna, Okuniew, Wolomin and
Radzymin. A notation of July 30, 1944, in the *Kriegstagebuch* No. 11
of the German 9th Army reported the Soviet presence in Radzymin
and stated that the 19th German Armored Division was attempting
to recapture Radzymin and that the Warsaw suburb of Praga was
"open and almost defenseless." On July 31, the log noted that little
progress was made by the attacking 19th Armored Division and the
Herman Göring Armored Division, and that the 9th Army would endeavor to open up the Warsaw-Radzymin communication line.[12] This
would indicate the presence of the Soviet tanks on the highway Praga-
Radzymin at that time.

This picture is not at variance with the Soviet sources. Soviet Marshal Konstantin Rokossovsky recalled in his memoirs that at that time the Soviet "Second Armored Army was fighting on the approaches to Praga, repulsing the attacks of the panzer units . . . . Yes, Warsaw was right before us—we were involved in heavy fighting in the forefront of Praga."[13]

Thus it may be accepted as a fact that at the time the final decision on the uprising was being made, on the afternoon of July 31, 1944, the Soviet armies were already in Wolomin and in Radzymin, while a tank battle was in progress on the highway linking Praga with Radzymin. Over the preceding months, the Soviets invariably emerged victorious in this type of engagement, due to their tremendous superiority in terms of matériel and numbers. The three generals—Bor, Pelczynski and Okulicki—had every reason to believe that the Soviet armies would enter Praga, a suburb of Warsaw, within a very short time, perhaps even within a few hours. Further delay would only imperil the entire political and military concept of the uprising. Thus the order was given to begin fighting on August 1, at 17:00 hours. This historic decision should not be viewed today with the benefit of hindsight, in the context of events unfolding over the intervening 30 years, but in the context of the military situation and the known circumstances prevailing on the day the decision was made—July 31, 1944.

On one and the the same page of his memoirs, Marshal Rokossovsky voiced in 1968 two divergent opinions regarding the timing of the uprising. According to one, the time would have been well chosen, had the Home Army succeeded in seizing the bridges on the Vistula, capturing the suburb of Praga, and attacking from the rear the German forces engaged in fighting the Soviet Second Armored Army. According to the other, the time was ill chosen and—since the objectives cited above had not been achieved—should have been deferred until the Soviet armies occupied the suburb of Praga, i.e., until September 14. Soviet Army General Shtemenko voiced an identical opinion.[14] Neither Rokossovsky nor Shtemenko explained one thing: How was it possible to seize the bridges and the suburb of Praga without taking up arms openly in an uprising? Anyway, the uprising did break out in the Praga suburb, too, but, unfortunately, was quickly suppressed.

From the military point of view, the decision of July 31, 1944, to begin the uprising on the following day, was justified. The Home Army generals could not have known that on that very day, when fierce fighting was already going on in the streets of Warsaw, the SS IV Panzer Corps would fight its way to a point 5 km. east of Okuniew and would begin to encircle the Soviet III Armored Corps, extended toward Wolomin and Radzymin. By August 3, the encirclement was completed near Wolomin, and 76 Soviet tanks were destroyed. The Soviet advance on Praga was halted.

2. The Course of the Struggle

On August 1, 1944, at 5 p.m., when the Home Army soldiers, distinguished by their red-and-white armbands, first attacked the German garrison in Warsaw, the relative strength of the two adversaries appeared as follows:

The Home Army sent into action, under the command of Colonel Antoni Chrusciel (pseudonym: Monter), 32,500 men in Warsaw and 4,000 men in the suburban sector. These were joined by 800 men from the National Armed Forces, 500 men from the Communist People's Army, and 100 men from the Polish People's Army. In the course of the uprising, they were also joined by a Jewish formation (which came from outside of the city through sewers), a platoon of Slovaks, some Georgians, an unspecified number of Soviet soldiers, freed from German captivity by the uprising, a few Frenchmen, and a British airman, John Ward.

The armament of the Home Army in Warsaw was as follows: 20 heavy machine guns and 35,000 rounds of ammunition; 98 light machine guns and 15,800 rounds; 844 submachine guns and 121,000 rounds; 1,386 rifles and 234,000 rounds; 2,665 handguns and 52,000 rounds; 2 anti-tank small caliber guns and 100 shells; 12 anti-tank rifles and 1,170 rounds; 10 flame throwers (in the course of the uprising, the number increased to 150); 6 6-inch mortars; several British anti-tank guns (PIAT); 50,100 hand grenades; 5,000 "Molotov cocktails"; and 700 kg. of explosives.

These figures grew larger in the course of the uprising, due to 73 air drops made by Polish and allied planes and received by the Home Army. From these air drops the Home Army obtained: 13 mortars and 325 rounds; 150 light machine guns and 1,400,000 rounds; 300 submachine guns and 1,000,000 rounds; 230 PIATs (anti-tank) and 3,450 projectiles; 130 rifles and 280,000 rounds; 950 handguns and 36,000 rounds; 10,300 hand grenades; and 3,000 anti-tank grenades.

Towards the end of the uprising, on the night of September 13, low-flying Soviet planes also began to drop arms and ammunition for the Home Army fighting in Warsaw: 5 heavy machine guns and 10,000 rounds; 700 submachine guns and 60,000 rounds; 143 anti-tank rifles and 4,290 rounds; 48 mortars and 1,726 anti-tank grenades; 160 rifles and 10,000 rounds; and 4,000 hand grenades.

On the other hand, figures quoted above decreased in the course of fighting due to losses. In any event, according to the *Kriegstage-buch* No. 11 of the German 9th Army, after the capitulation on October 2, 1944, the following weapons were surrendered by the 11,668 Home Army soldiers taken prisoner by the Germans: 1,087 rifles, 633 hand guns, 54 anti-tank rifles, 467 submachine guns, 33 grenade throwers, 49 light machine guns, and 7 heavy machine guns. The data cited above confirm the general impression that only one out of every four Home Army soldiers actually had some weapons at the beginning of the uprising.[15] The rest were to capture their arms from the Germans or to receive them from the air drops.

According to *Obergruppenführer* SS Erich von dem Bach-Zelewski, the commander of the German armies combating the insurgents—against these Polish forces, during the 63 days of the Warsaw Rising, were ranged German forces numbering 50,000 men, and commanded by 14 officers with the rank of general. This figure does not include the German air force under the command of General Colonel Ritter von Greim, which bombarded Warsaw daily, nor the men from the two SS panzer divisions (Herman Göring and Viking), the 73rd Infantry Division, and the armored train, who were also involved for a time in the fighting in Warsaw.[16] The Germans had at their disposal the most up-to-date weapons and the support of their artillery (188 cannon), 600 mm. mortars (mounted on railroad platforms), and small tanks, guided by remote control, the so-called "Goliaths."

Unmindful of this tremendous superiority of the Germans, the Home Army soldiers attacked furiously. Fighting bravely and with total disregard for personal safety, they seized control of most of the city during the first four days of the uprising. The downtown and the city sections of Zoliborz, the Old Town, Wola, Ochota, Mokotow, Powisle and Czerniakow were all in Polish hands. However, the Germans managed to hold the fortified strongholds into which they had turned the army barracks and command posts, office buildings and institutions guarded by special units. These were surrounded by the Home Army and isolated. But, repeated attempts to seize them, brought heavy losses to the Home Army.

Although the Germans knew about the preparations for the uprising, on August 1 some motorized columns, marching troops, and individual soldiers were still caught unawares in the streets of Warsaw by the insurgents, and soon the streets of the capital was strewn with their bodies. The same happened to tanks, sent into action by the German command. Those that had not been destroyed by the all too scanty anti-tank weapons, were burned down with flame throwers and incendiary bottles. Some teenage boys distinguished themselves particularly in this action.

At nightfall, the elated inhabitants of Warsaw swarmed out onto the streets and crisscrossed them—as instructed—with a network of barricades. They broke through the cellar walls of adjacent buildings and created a vast underground labyrinth from one end of the city to the other. Warsaw blossomed with red-and-white Polish flags. German loudspeakers in the streets were promptly put to use and blared patriotic songs, appeals and instructions for the population of Warsaw. Throughout the city, underground authorities, courts and police came forth and began to function. At long last, there was a feeling of freedom in Warsaw.

On August 5, the Germans began their attack. Its object was to reopen two communication lines, running over the Kierbedz Bridge and the Poniatowski Bridge and linking the Reich with the German armies on the eastern bank of the Vistula. From behind the barricades and building walls, the insurgents defended their positions doggedly. The German attack, advancing toward the Kierbedz Bridge, was supported by a tank company of the SS Division "Herman Göring," an armored train, and the air force. It moved along Wolska Street, Chlodna Street, the Saxon Gardens, and the Pilsudski Square. Along the way, in accordance with the orders received, the German soldiers were evacuating all the houses, shooting their inhabitants— men, women and children—on the spot, and setting fire to the buildings. In the Wola section of Warsaw, they killed 38,000 people. The attack was halted for a time by the crack "Kedyw" units, commanded by Lt. Colonel Jan Mazurkiewicz (pseudonym: Radoslaw). But, launched again in twice the strength and without any reprieve, it finally succeeded—but only toward the end of the uprising—in opening up the approaches to the Kierbedz Bridge. Before that happened, the German attack cut off from the rest of the city the Zoliborz section and the Old Town, where the Government Delegate, the High Command of the Home Army, and the chairman of the Council of National Unity remained.

However, the second German attack, advancing along the main thoroughfare of Aleje Jerozolimskie toward the Poniatowski Bridge, never succeeded in reaching its objective. Although the German tanks and troops progressed as far as the intersection of Marszalkowska Street and Aleje Jerozolimskie, they failed to gain control of the sector between Marszalkowska Street and Nowy Swiat, which remained in Polish hands throughout the uprising. Thus the Germans lost once and forever the second, and most important communication artery.

Long-drawn and ferocious battles began in the city. The Home Army units attacked and captured isolated German strongholds, such as the Police Headquarters and the neighboring church of the Holy Cross on Krakowskie Przedmiescie, the Telephone Exchange at Zielna Street, the building at the corner of Aleje Jerozolimskie and Bracka Street (which guarded the approach to the Poniatowski Bridge), or the building of PASTA (Polish Telephone Company, Inc.) on Pius XI Street. In these actions, the Poles used flame throwers of their own production. During the siege of the telephone exchange, the Home Army units had to fight on two fronts at once; not only did they have to contend against a strong and well armed garrison within, but also against attacks from the direction of the Saxon Gardens, barely 200 yards away, aimed at breaking through the Polish ring around the Telephone Exchange and freeing the besieged Germans. All these attacks were beaten back, and the Telephone Exchange was captured after grim fighting, with submachine guns and hand grenades, on every stairway and for every floor of the building.

The struggle for the similarly besieged PASTA building was also waged on two fronts. Within the building, there was a large German contingent, including sharpshooters. Without, German tanks from the Gestapo Headquarters on Szuch Street hurried to the rescue, proceeding along Aleje Ujazdowskie to Pius XI Street. On Pius XI Street, between Aleje Ujazdowskie and Mokotowska Street, they were greeted with a hail of Molotov cocktails. German crews, fleeing their flaming tanks, were mowed down with submachine gun fire, and the remaining tanks withdrew hastily.

In this way, the Poles succeeded in liquidating most of the German strongholds in the city.

Meanwhile, the Germans reorganized their forces and proceeded with a systematic attack against one section of the city after another, according to a prearranged pattern. The section under attack was first bombarded from the air, from early morning until late in the afternoon. The German Stukas could fly low over the section, because the Home Army had no antiaircraft. In the course of the entire Warsaw Rising, only one German plane was downed (in the Old Town). Thus building after building, and street after street were razed by the German bombers. Whatever remained after the bombing and the resulting conflagration, was finished off by the artillery. This was followed with an attack by tank and infantry units. They expected no further opposition from the ruins, but were greeted instead with machine gun fire, rifle fire, and grenades. More than one tank would be destroyed by PIATs from the British air drops, by flame throwers and the Molotov cocktails; more than one German infantry column would be annihilated. Those eager to save their lives would throw down their arms, raise their hands, and surrender to the Poles—often only to die later from German bombs. The log of the German 9th Army (No. 11) provides the best testimony on the fierceness of fighting:

1. August 5, 1944: "We are up against a stubborn resistance from the insurgents.

2. August 6: "The Kaminski group is still fighting in the Ochota section, where the insurgent resistance is very stubborn."

3. August 8: "The resistance from the insurgents stiffens."

4. August 9: "No special progress in Warsaw may be noted. The initial, improvised disturbances gave way gradually to a militarily well organized resistance movement.

5. August 11: "The insurgents' defense of their positions is extremely stubborn."

6. August 12: "The fighting against the insurgents in Warsaw continues equally intense . . . . The Poles fight with an extreme doggedness . . . . On the German side, all manner of technical equipment is being brought into the fighting. Besides the "Goliaths" and the "Taifuns", used by the sapper storm units, the *Funklenpanzer* were also introduced [armored cars, directed by remote control] ."

7. August 15: "No conspicuous progress in Warsaw can be noted. A new piece of equipment will arrive shortly in Warsaw 040, 60 cm. mortar 'Karl',"

8. August 28: "Our losses up to August 28 amount to 91 officers and 3,770 enlisted men. In fighting in the Old Town we are losing an average of 150 men each day."

9. September 5: "The fighting in Warsaw continues with unabated stubborness."

10. September 24: "The defense [of Mokotow] is very fierce."

Still, it was an unequal struggle. The Old Town, first subjected to a concentrated attack and turned into rubble, could no longer be defended. On the night of September 1, the last Home Army units, led by Colonel Karol Ziemski (pseudonym: Wachnowski), took to the sewers, making their way—often neck-deep in sewage—to the center of the city. It was only then that the Germans could begin to use their communication line over the Kierbedz Bridge without any interruption. The Government Delegate, the chairman of the Council of National Unity and the Commander of the Home Army also left the Old Town by way of the sewers, and reached the center of the city. In the ruins of the Old Town, a few thousand wounded and the civilian population were left. The Germans savaged the Old Town, similarly to Wola, killing off some 35,000 inhabitants and wounded Home Army men.

The German attack now turned to Powisle, a riverside section of Warsaw, situated between the Kierbedz Bridge and the Poniatowski Bridge. Captain Cyprian Odorkiewicz (pseudonym: Krybar) was in command of the Home Army forces in this section. After heavy fighting, Powisle fell on September 6, giving the Germans the control over the western bank of the Vistula between the two bridges.

On September 13, the Germans pushed on southward, attacking the section of Czerniakow Gorny. After prolonged heavy fighting, Czerniakow was captured on September 24. The entire bank of the Vistula on the Warsaw side was now in German hands.

On September 24, the German attack on the Mokotow section began. The Home Army units there, combined into the 10th Infantry Division named after Maciej Rataj, were commanded by Lt. Col. Jozef Rokicki (pseudonym: Karol). After three days of furious fighting, Mokotow fell on September 27.

On September 28, the German panzer division moved against the Zoliborz section. Led by their wounded commander, Lt. Col.Mieczyslaw Niedzielski (pseudonym: Zywiciel), the Home Army units in Zoliborz—combined into the 8th Infantry Division named after Romuald Traugutt—fought gallantly for two days, surrendering on September 30 on General Bor's orders.

In downtown Warsaw, defended by the 28th Infantry Division, under the command of Colonel Edward Pfeiffer (pseudonym: Radwan), it was another story. By the end of September, all underground leaders—both civil and military—were gathered in the center of the city. It withstood concentrated German attacks from September 6 to September 20. Shortly thereafter negotiations began with the German commanding officer, von dem Bach-Zelewski, regarding the capitulation, and thus the central section of the city remained in Polish hands throughout the uprising. Its capture by the Germans was forestalled by the signing of the act of capitulation on October 2, 1944, which, among other, accorded the Home Army soldiers all the privileges specified in the Geneva Convention of July 27, 1929.

Closely connected with the Warsaw Rising were the Home Army operations in the region of Kampinos Forest, where a base had been established to provision the uprising and to receive allied air drops. Arms, ammunition and men flowed to Warsaw from the Kampinos Forest, where some 1,500 Home Army soldiers were concentrated under the command of Major Alfons Kotowski (pseudonym: Okon). As part of the overall German operations against the Warsaw insurgents, large German forces launched an attack on the Kampinos Forest on September 27, forcing Major Kotowski to lead his men out of the forest in the hope of getting to the Holy Cross Mountains. However, on September 29, superior German forces, supported by three armored trains, the air force, panzer units and artillery, succeeded in surrounding the Home Army forces near Jaktorow, and crushing them completely. In this unequal battle, Major Kotowski was killed. But part of the infantrymen fought their way back to the Kampinos Forest, and some 250 cavalrymen managed to get to the Opoczno region. Polish losses were: 110 killed, 180 wounded and 100 captured by the Germans. German losses: 200 killed, 1 plane shot down, and several tanks and armored cars destroyed.

Polish losses in the course of the Warsaw Rising were considerable. Including the Kampinos operation, they were: 10,200 killed, 7,000 badly wounded, and 5,000 missing—altogether about 22,000 casualties.

German losses, according to the report of von dem Bach-Zelewski, were: 10,000 killed, 7,000 missing, and 9,000 wounded—altogether about 26,000 casualties.[17]

Thus casualties on both sides were tremendously high in relation to the total numbers engaged, i.e., about 40,000 men on the Polish side, and about 50,000 men on the German side. There was a discrepancy between the Polish and German sources as to the number of Home Army soldiers captured by the Germans. According to Polish sources, 20,000 Home Army soldiers were taken prisoner by the Germans, while the *Kriegstagebuch* No. 11 of the 9th Army cites the figure of 11,668. This may be explained by the fact that a few thousand Home Army soldiers, rather than going into captivity, mixed with the civilian population of Warsaw and left the city together with them.

General Bor (appointed during the Warsaw Rising as Supreme Commander of Polish Armed Forces, following General Sosnkowski's resignation) joined his soldiers in captivity, and so did the Chief of Staff, General Pelczynski, the Home Army commander in Warsaw Chrusciel (advanced meanwhile to the rank of Major General), and several other officers from the High Command of the Home Army and from General Chrusciel's staff. However, General Leopold Okulicki (pseudonyms: Kobra, Niedzwiadek), named by General Bor as his successor after the capitulation, left Warsaw with the civilian population in order to carry on his command of the Home Army in the continued struggle against the Germans.

3. The Soviet "Help"

There was no question but that the Soviet Second Armored Army suffered a defeat on August 3, on the approaches to the suburb of

Praga, which thwarted its advance on Warsaw. The Soviet offensive was renewed only a month later, on September 10, and resulted in the taking of Praga on September 14. Two days later, on September 16 (and the following days), a few battalions from the Polish army of General Berling crossed the Vistula and landed on the western bank, in Warsaw; the First Battalion was commanded by Soviet Major Latishonek.

The question arises whether the Soviets delayed the renewal of their offensive on purpose, in order to have Warsaw and the Home Army destroyed by German hands, or whether they were actually unable to advance before September 10. In considering this question, we should examine the evidence as presented by the three parties involved: the statements of the Soviet marshals Rokossovsky and Zhukov, and of the General of the Army S. Shtemenko; the Log No. 11 of the German 9th Army; and the many Polish publications and statements, of which the most important are certainly the pronouncements of General Bor.

The three Soviet generals agree that a dangerous and complicated situation had developed at the front, following the successful attack against the Soviet Second Armored Army (and the destruction of its Third Corps) by the German 19th Panzer Division, two SS panzer divisions (Death's-head and Viking), the Herman Göring airborne and panzer division, and infantry units from the German Second Army. To liquidate this situation required a long time and heavy fighting against large German forces. It was not until the beginning of September that the Soviet reconnaissance discovered that one German panzer division and other units, previously in the forefront of Praga, had been transferred elsewhere. Taking advantage of the weakened front line, the Soviet 47th Armored Army launched an attack on September 10 and captured Praga. Even so, in his telephone conversation with Stalin on September 13, Marshal Rokossovsky, in answer to Stalin's query, replied that his armies "would not be able at the present time to liberate Warsaw." The Soviets, therefore, limited themselves to ferrying an infantry battalion from General Berling's army across the Vistula, to the Czerniakow section of Warsaw, which at that time was in the hands of the Home Army. The landing party—according to one statement of General Shtemenko—asserted that "there were no insurgents there"; but in another statement Shtemenko claimed that the landing party found some "insurgent subunits" in Czerniakow, and that they hindered the fighting by withdrawing toward the center of the city. Throughout the Warsaw Rising, according to General Shtemenko, Stalin returned time and again to the problem of the Warsaw Rising in his conversations with various Soviet commanders; it was obvious that he was greatly concerned with the fate of Warsaw and its inhabitants.

Stalin's supposed concern is in no way confirmed by German accounts or by the facts cited in the Polish sources. Quite the contrary, in the *Kriegstagebuch* No. 11 of the German 9th Army this period is described as follows: " . . . Moscow could have only a seeming interest in the success of the rising. Still, as long as the fighting in Warsaw went on, it constituted a harassment of the Germans that could not but be welcomed by the Soviet command. A successful outcome of the uprising was not in the interest of Moscow, because it was bound to bring demands totally incompatible with Moscow's intended course of action. In order to deflect the charges of passivity and intentional withdrawal of assistance to Warsaw, the Kremlin adopted a special tactic of claiming that a strong German assault east of Warsaw forced the Soviets to limit their operations to defensive."

" . . . For days after the German operations, aimed at destroying the Soviet Third Armored Corps, had ended in this region, the Moscow broadcasting station continued to report strong German attacks east of Praga and dressed up this news with detailed descriptions of battles that were completely fictitious."[18]

The bad faith of Stalin and the Soviets is documented by the facts cited in the Polish sources:

On August 14, General Bor ordered the Home Army units outside of Warsaw to come to the rescue of the fighting capital; these units were intercepted by the Soviets on their way to Warsaw, disarmed and interned (e.g., detachments of the 3rd, the 9th, the 10th, and the 30th infantry divisions). The High Command of the Home Army was informed of these developments through dispatches and by the commander of the Lublin district on August 26, September 3 and September 21, 1944.

When the western allies approached the Soviet command with a request that the planes bringing arms for the fighting Warsaw be permitted to land behind Soviet lines after completing the air drops—they met with a refusal. The Soviet command warned that the crew of any plane that would, for any reason whatever, land behind the Soviet lines, would be interned until the end of the war. This prohibition was removed only on September 10th, when the Soviet armies began their attack on Praga—and when Warsaw was already doomed.

The planes that did bring aid to Warsaw—both Polish and those of the western allies—suffered tremendous losses. Taking off from a base in Italy, near Brindisi, they had to fly some 1,200 miles over enemy territory, wending their way through antiaircraft fire, and pursued by German fighter planes. At the same time, the Soviet planes were no more than threescore of miles away from Warsaw and their flight would have taken them over the Soviet-held territories. According to the log of the German 9th Army, the Soviets had about 100 airfields at their disposal in the area between the front line and the Brest-Chelm line. Flying time to Warsaw from any one of these airfields would have been, at the most, one hour. Technically speaking, this would have been an easy operation in view of the tremendous Soviet air supremacy, and involving practically no losses.

There seemed to be no way to reverse the Soviet decision. Mikolajczyk asked for help in the course of his meetings with Stalin on August 3 and 9; General Bor sent a dispatch to Marshal Rokossovsky via London on August 8, and sought in vain to establish direct contact with Rokossovsky; the Polish government in London appealed to Stalin repeatedly through the intermediary of the British government; Prime Minister Churchill and President Roosevelt interceded for the embattled Polish capital. But all this was to no avail. Not only did Stalin refuse all Soviet aid, when it could still have made all the difference in the outcome, but he also did not admit aid from other quarters.

Landing of a few battalions from General Berling's army on the Warsaw side of the Vistula on September 16 (in the Czerniakow section and between the Kierbedz Bridge and the Poniatowski Bridge), and of a small infantry detachment in the Zoliborz section on the following night, was an improvised gesture rather than the beginning of a large-scale military operation along the entire western bank of the Vistula. It should be mentioned here that, contrary to General Shtemenko's statement, the landing party found in Czerniakow one of the best formations of the Home Army, commanded, despite his wounds, by Lt. Colonel Jan Mazurkiewicz (pseudonym: Radoslaw). Berling's men fought under the Home Army commander, too, until heavy casualties and the lack of support by larger landing parties, forced them to withdraw back to the eastern bank of the Vistula. At the same time, an entry in the log of the German 9th Army noted that the Germans were "not strong enough to repel a mass-landing by the enemy" and that "in the event of a large-scale drive, the effectiveness of our counteraction cannot be fully assured." In other words, the Soviet command had dispatched forces that were too small to ensure the success of the landing operation.

In addition to facts cited above, one should also take into account the fact that Stalin viewed the Warsaw Rising as an act of hostility toward Russia. Throughout the uprising, the official Soviet TASS agency and other organs of Soviet propaganda deluged the world with mendacious information about the uprising, starting with claims that there was no rising in Warsaw at all, and ending with assertions that the High Command of the Home Army wanted no Soviet help whatsoever.

Everything points to the conclusion that the Soviet decision not to undertake the kind of military effort that was needed to render real assistance to the Home Army in Warsaw was intentional. This was in accordance with Stalin's statement that "under the existing circumstances, the Soviet command concluded that it should cut itself off from the Warsaw adventure, since it could not assume either direct or indirect responsibility for the operations in Warsaw."[19]

In this situation, Soviet permission to land (granted to allied planes after September 10), Soviet air drops after September 13, the landing of a Polish battalion on September 16, and of a few small units later, must be viewed as propaganda moves, calculated to appease and delude the alarmed public opinion in the west, and not as a serious effort to help the Warsaw insurgents. The Soviet "help" did come, but only a few months after the collapse of the uprising, when the Soviet armies began their winter offensive in 1945, advancing from bridgeheads on the Vistula, which the Home Army units from the Radom district had helped to establish. The Soviet encirclement of Warsaw forced the Germans to beat a hasty retreat from the city. On January 17, 1945, after a brief battle with the German rear guard, units of the First Polish Army, under the command of a Soviet general, S. Poplavsky, captured Warsaw—or rather, the ruins of Warsaw.

An analysis of the Soviet policy with regard to the Warsaw Rising invites comparison with the Nazi policy—with one difference: the Soviet policy was more sophisticated. According to the German plans, Warsaw was to be destroyed and replaced with a small, provincial town. According to the Soviet plans from the time of the uprising, Warsaw was to be destroyed, too, but with German hands, which is precisely how it happened. This, however, is not the only similarity. In 1939/40 both the Germans and the Russians initiated their rule with mass expulsions and deportations of the Polish population, and with depolonization of the territories incorporated into the Reich or into the USSR. The Nazis embarked on extermination of the Polish intelligentsia class, and the Soviets followed suit by arresting and deporting thousands, crowning their actions with the murder of 15,000 Polish army officers—mostly from the reserves—whose mass graves, containing 4,253 bodies, were found in the Katyn Forest. The Germans destroyed all traces of Polish culture and history in the western part of Poland; the Soviets did exactly the same thing in the eastern Polish territories. A seemingly endless list of such examples could be compiled. *Vae victis!*

4. Civil Authorities During the Warsaw Rising

The outbreak of the Warsaw Rising found Government Delegate Jankowski and the chairman of the Council of National Unity Puzak at General Bor's headquarters in the Wola section. Members of the Home Cabinet—Adam Bien (pseudonym: Walkowicz), Stanislaw Jasiukowicz (pseudonym: Opolski), and Antoni Pajdak (pseudonym: Traugutt)—members of the Council of National Unity, most of the departments of the Government Delegacy, and the delegacy for the capital city of Warsaw—were all downtown. Within a short time, however, both Wola and Ochota fell to the Germans, and consequently the High Command of the Home Army, General Bor, Delegate Jankowski and Chairman Puzak moved to the Old Town, where they remained until August 26.

The second dispatch, sent by the Government Delegate and General Bor to the government in London on August 1, already contained a request for Soviet help in terms of military matériel and an immediate attack against the Germans. This was the first of a long string of dispatches, frequently signed also by the chairman of the Council of National Unity Puzak. Addressed to the Polish authorities in London, to the allies, to Prime Minister Churchill and President Roosevelt, these dispatches described the situation in Warsaw—tragic from the onset—and appealed endlessly for any kind of help from the allies and from the Soviets for the fighting, but perishing, Polish capital.

On August 3, Government Delegate Jankowski, chairman of the Council of National Unity Puzak and General Bor issued a joint proclamation to the Polish people, informing the country about the outbreak of the Warsaw Rising and the achievements of the first three days of fighting. The proclamation stressed the cooperation of the inhabitants of Warsaw with the Home Army, and expressed the hope that the struggle would bring the complete liberation of Poland. On August 8, the Government Delegate issued a proclamation to the people of Warsaw, united in the struggle against the enemy, in which he described the situation within the city and denounced German atrocities—the shootings of the civilian population and the burning of the city sections seized by the Germans. The proclamation ended with an appeal to the people of Warsaw, spurring them on to even greater efforts in fighting ranks, in auxiliary services, and in caring for the hungry and the homeless.

On August 15, the Army Day, Government Delegate Jankowski, chairman of the NCU Puzak and General Bor issued a joint proclamation to the Polish Nation, calling, among other, all Home Army units to come promptly to the aid of Warsaw, and all young men to join the ranks of the Home Army.

On September 1, the anniversary of the outbreak of the war, Government Delegate Jankowski broadcast over the Polish Radio, reinstated by the insurgents in Warsaw. He spoke mainly to the inhabitants of Warsaw, reviewing the five years of struggle and suffering, and expressing his hope that the tremendous efforts and sacrifices of the entire nation would win back the freedom and independence of a democratic Poland.

After the Old Town became cut off from the center of the city (except for the precarious liaison through the city sewers), the Deputy Government Delegate, Minister Adam Bien, took over Jankowski's functions, presiding at the Cabinet meetings and sending to London dispatches that described the catastrophic situation in Warsaw and begging for help. Other ministers did the same on their own.

Meeting almost daily under the chairmanship of Minister Bien, the Home Cabinet set for itself the task of taking the reins of authority in the entire country at the propitious moment, and returning Poland to the rule of law. The Home Cabinet ordered the dissolution of the state police and its replacement with the State Security Corps, established during the occupation years. On August 20, the Home Cabinet issued a proclamation to the people of Poland, stating that, until the return of the President of the Republic and the government, the Home Cabinet would remain the only constitutional authority in Poland.

Due to the Home Cabinet's exertions, two issues of the official *Journal of Laws* were published during the uprising. Identical in format and appearance with its prewar predecessor, the publication contained decrees and orders defining the legal basis for the functioning of the underground civil authorities. The first of these issues, antedated July 20, 1944, appeared on August 17. It contained the decree of the President of the Republic of Poland of April 26, 1944, regarding the temporary governmental organization on the territories of the Republic; the decree of the Government Delegate of May 3, 1944, on the establishment of the Home Cabinet; and four provisional Home Cabinet decrees pertaining to: the resumption of functions by governmental institutions and authorities, calling the government employees into service, restoration of the local territorial self-government, and criminal and special courts of justice.

The second issue of the *Journal of Laws* appeared on August 28 and contained 12 decrees of the Home Cabinet, among other: on Polish citizenship, on agrarian reform, on safeguarding the property of the state and of absent owners, on the establishment of district offices for the liquidation of the effects of war, on activating the courts and the Bar, and the workers councils in factories and plants.

Towards the end of the uprising, a significant difference of opinion arose within the Home Cabinet. The rift was caused by the request from the Polish Cabinet in London that the Home Cabinet render its opinion on a proposal regarding the further course of Polish-Soviet relations, as drafted by Premier Mikolajczyk on his return from Moscow. Mikolajczyk's proposal included, among other, the following: the participation of the Polish Workers Party in the future Polish government; a Polish-Soviet alliance that would give the Soviets some influence in Poland's internal and external affairs and foreign policy; it left open the question of Poland's frontiers in the east. With certain corrections, the Premier's proposal was approved by Minister Bien, a member of Mikolajczyk's own political party. But it was rejected categorically by Government Delegate Jankowski, while the other two ministers from the Home Cabinet—Jasiukowicz and Pajdak—reacted with some highly critical comments. In his dispatch to the government in London, dated August 29, 1944, General Bor supported the position of the Government Delegate and rejected Premier Mikolajczyk's proposal as tantamount to capitulation.

The first activity of the Council of National Unity during the Warsaw Rising was its appeal of August 12, 1944. Addressed to the Allied Nations, it stated that the uprising so far had not received any significant assistance from the Allies, and none from the Soviets; on the contrary, the Red Army had halted its advance on Warsaw, and would not give the capital any assistance from the air. In view of this, the Council of National Unity renewed its appeal for help.

On August 15, 1944, the Council of National Unity issued a proclamation to the Polish Nation, emphasizing the bonds that united all Poles in the struggle against the enemy during the uprising. As the underground parliament of Poland, the Council of National Unity set forth the essentials of the future form of government in Poland:

a) Future constitution, ensuring efficient government in accordance with the will of the people.

b) Democratic electoral law that would reflect faithfully the public opinion within the country, both in the legislative and in local governments.

c) An agrarian reform to be carried out by parceling designated German estates and all land holding of over 123 acres, and by directing the surplus rural population to work in industries and crafts.

d)Public ownership of key industries.

e) Worker and employee participation in the direction and control of industrial production.

f) Guaranteed work and adequate living conditions for all citizens.

g) Equitable division of social income.

h) Dissemination of popular learning and culture.

The proclamation constituted an elaboration of the program issued on March 15, 1944, under the title "What the Poles Are Fighting For." The two declarations testified to the reformative tendencies animating the Polish society and its underground representation. The trend was to establish in Poland a democratic form of government in every sector of national life, including a radical agrarian reform and public ownership of heavy industries.

On August 28, 1944, the Council of National Unity was faced with a difficult task. Similarly to the Home Cabinet, it had been asked by the government in London to give its opinion regarding Premier Mikolajczyk's proposal, charting the future course of Polish-Soviet relations. After highly charged debates, the Council of National Unity approved the Premier's proposal, with nine corrections (August 28 and August 30, 1944).

However, on August 29, before the Council's amendments of August 30 had reached London, the Polish government-in-exile sent a memorandum to Moscow, based on the amendments of August 28. Claiming it was not competent to consider it, the Soviet government passed the memorandum on to the Polish Committee of National Liberation, as its proper addressee. This was tantamount to rejection.

On September 29, toward the end of the Warsaw Rising, the Council of National Unity—alarmed at the evidence of German preparations for mass shipments of Poles to concentration camps, and particularly to Auschwitz—appealed once more to all allied and neutral governments and nations, and to the International Red Cross, begging them to undertake an effort to prevent the annihilation of the Poles. On that same day, with pardonable bitterness, the chairman of the Council of National Unity sent a message to General Charles de Gaulle, congratulating him on the liberation of Paris. Paris was free, while Warsaw was fast becoming one huge cemetery.

When Government Delegate Jankowski and chairman of the Council of National Unity Puzak made their way through the city sewers from the Old Town to the center of the capital on August 26, all the underground authorities were assembled in one section of Warsaw. Government Delegate and vice-premier Jankowski resumed the leadership of the Home Cabinet, while Puzak once again began to preside over the debates of the Council of National Unity. The two bodies began to meet daily in joint sessions. These meetings were also attended by the director of the Information and Press Department of the Government Delegacy, Kauzik, and by the chief of the Directorate of Civil Resistance, Korbonski. (During the uprising Korbonski was also appointed as director of the Department of Internal Affairs, succeeding Kazimierz Baginski, who had joined the Council of National Unity as its vice-chairman.) It was becoming more and more difficult to find a place to hold such meetings. Systematic German bombardment was turning the heart of the city into a monstrous pile of rubble, and the shortage of living quarters was becoming acute, as noted in the Government Delegate's dispatch to London on September 20, 1944. According to the Government Delegate's decision, made at the beginning of the Warsaw Rising, in the event of Soviet occupation of the capital and the disclosure of the Polish underground authorities, Korbonski—with a small staff and a radio station—was to move westward ahead of the retreating German armies, and carry out the functions of the Government Delegate in the territories still held by the Germans. This plan, however, was never realized because of the unforeseen turn of events.

Of all the departments of the Government Delegacy, the most active during the uprising were the departments of Information and Press, Labor and Social Welfare, and Internal Affairs. Other departments, working mainly on future projects, were of necessity largely inactive during the Warsaw Rising. On the other hand, heavy demands were made on the energies of the Department of Information and Press because of the flourishing underground press, the establishment of the broadcasting station "Blyskawica", and the introduction of programs aired over the Polish Radio.

For its part, the Department of Labor and Social Welfare tried to alleviate the lot of those who needed public assistance. Its activities were stymied by the death of the department's director, Judge Stefan Mateja, who had been shot by the Germans while putting out a fire on the roof of the house at 60 Wawelska Street. He was succeeded by Franciszek Bialas (Polish Socialist Party), previously the head of ANTYK (Civic Anticommunist Committee).

The most important job fell to the Department of Internal Affairs, which collaborated closely with General Chrusciel, the Home Army commander of the Warsaw Rising, and with Marceli Porowski, the Government Delegate for the Capital, i.e., the underground mayor of Warsaw; since Porowski (pseudonym: Sowa) remained in the Old Town until August 26, the delegate for the Warsaw district, Jozef Kwasiborski, substituted for him in the central part of the city. As far as the Home Army was concerned, all decisions of the civilian authorities, pertaining to problems that were also of immediate interest to the army, were coordinated with General Chrusciel or his staff; the Department's relations with the Capital Delegacy, which coped with all city problems connected with the uprising, was more of a supervisory and inspiratory character.

Following the prewar organizational pattern of administration in the city, there were section delegacies, headed by section delegates, and subordinated to the Capital Delegacy. They operated in the areas occupied by the Home Army—four in the central part of the city, and one each in Mokotow, Zoliborz, and Powisle. Next in order of importance were the bloc commanders and, finally, the building commanders, who were often, but not always, assisted by the building committees. This network of city administration performed very effectively, maintaining regular contact and close cooperation with the military authorities at corresponding levels.

During the uprising, it became an established practice that the director of the Department of Internal Affairs participated in the frequent meetings held by the Capital Delegate with the section delegates. The insight and knowledge gained at these meetings served him in good stead in making his daily reports to Government Delegate Jankowski and the CNU Chairman Puzak on the situation within the city.

Among the more important decrees issued by the Department of Internal Affairs were those pertaining to: requisitioning of necessities; safeguarding of government property and property left behind by the Germans; functioning of the city administration (August 13); providing obligatory services for the defense required of men and women 17-60 years of age (August 16); sharing the remnants of food provisions with those who were hungry (September 28).

Among the more important decrees issued by the Capital Delegacy were those pertaining to: opening up the stores; maintaining round-the-clock watches in the buildings; organizing teams for defense against bombardment and fire; rescuing people buried beneath the rubble; burying the dead in the city squares and in the courtyards; observing sanitary regulations, whenever feasible.

All these and similar regulations and instructions were printed for the information of the inhabitants of Warsaw in the City Announcements Journal.[20]

The last act of the underground authorities during the Warsaw Rising was the joint proclamation, issued on October 3, 1944, by Government Delegate Jankowski, the Home Cabinet, the Council of National Unity and the Commander of the Home Army, General Bor. It informed the nation about the causes of the Warsaw Rising, the lack of outside help and the resulting collapse, which by then had already become a fact. It expressed the conviction that the sacrifice of the uprising would not be in vain, but would one day become the binding mortar of national unity and the source of future strength of the nation.

5. Life in Embattled Warsaw

One of the most crucial tasks in Warsaw during the rising was to fight fires, especially in those sections of the city that were under a systematic, day-long bombardment which usually began with incendiary bombs. The Home Army had no antiaircraft. German planes flew low over the rooftops, not worried in the least about the fire from the few machine guns that were trying to economize on their ammunition, anyway. The streets of the city were so crisscrossed with barricades that the few firemen's units still left in Warsaw by the Germans were unable to get to the fires. Every building or apartment house was therefore on its own, counting on little else for its defense but its inhabitants, sandbags and axes. It was in fighting the fires that the people of Warsaw showed an unbelievable courage and stamina. Stationed on housetops, in broad daylight, they braved the strafing from the German planes that had just dropped their incendiary bombs. Almost as many civilians were killed fighting the fires as the Home Army soldiers repelling the German attacks, and yet they would not give up defending their city against conflagration. Toward the end of the rising, when it became clear that no help was forthcoming and that the capital was doomed to total destruction, this fighting spirit waned and people began to abandon their burning houses resignedly.

The problem of water was no less important, because the Germans eventually seized the waterworks and cut off the supply from the city. However, human resourcefulness and the know-how of the Polish employees of the municipal waterworks carried the day. Old plans were studied, probes made, and finally, after strenuous, round-the-clock work, 92 old wells were located and put to use. Hand pumps were installed and armed guards posted at the wells. Priorities were established for drawing the water: first, the hospitals; then, the Home Army; finally, the civilian population. Armed with kettles, buckets and pitchers, hundreds of people queued up at the wells. Shortly the Germans noticed the long lines and began flying over, strafing the queues. At the sound of an approaching plane, people would disperse, hiding as best they could, but there were always many killed. Then the queue would form up again, moving past the bodies laid near a wall. This went on all day long. A lively trade developed, with water bartered for cigarettes and food.

The problem of food provisions was of decisive importance for the uprising. The few German food warehouses had been sequestered by the Home Army, so that the soldiers were fairly well supplied. But this was not true for the civilian population of Warsaw. The secrecy of preparations for the uprising, strict rationing imposed by the Germans, and the general impoverishment left no leeway for laying in food supplies. Hunger came after the first few days of the rising. From the very beginning, bread and potatoes were scarce, and there was a lack of vegetables in the central city; there were some small stocks of fats, and considerably larger of groats, coffee substitutes, and sugar. In the first weeks of the rising, all horses were eaten; next came the turn of dogs and cats. The half a million people in the liberated sections of the city were saved from death by starvation when large stores of raw wheat and barley were found in Haberbusch's brewery. Toward the end there was nothing to eat, except boiled grain and black coffee with sugar. Communal kitchens were set up in each apartment house and they fed not only the inhabitants of the house, but also large numbers of people who had been caught away from their homes by the outbreak of the uprising, and sought shelter elsewhere.

There was electricity in the city for a relatively long time (a few weeks), due to the heroic exertions of the Warsaw Power Plant employees. Not only did the power plant provide electricity for the liberated sections of the city, but also it was a stronghold in its own Powisle section and as such, it was under constant German fire. Teams of workers labored day and night repairing the lines, disrupted by grenades and bombs, and many of them were killed. Finally, after heavy bombardments, the plant ceased its operations. Shortly afterwards, Powisle fell, and the Germans seized the power plant. All that remained from then on were some accumulators that were being charged in insurgent workshops, using automobile engines. This provided lighting for the operating rooms in the hospitals, for the most important offices, and for some passageways, such as the tunnel dug under Aleje Jerozolimskie toward the end of the uprising.

Surprisingly, health conditions in Warsaw were good. There was no outbreak of any serious epidemic, despite the hot summer, the lack of water and soap, despite the makeshift open latrines, dug in the streets and never emptied, despite the shallow graves in courtyard cemeteries, despite thousands of decaying bodies beneath the rubble of destroyed houses. The doctors in charge of the insurgent health services were amazed and pleased, because they had anticipated the worst. Medical service during the uprising functioned exceedingly well. The insurgent health service had several hundred doctors and more than a dozen hospitals, set up in the cellars for the most part. After every air raid or artillery bombardment, long caravans of stretchers moved through the rubble, bringing the wounded to the hospitals. Operating rooms were working round the clock, with changing shifts of surgeons.

The state of public safety was also good, largely due to generally self-imposed discipline, which was not equally impressive, however, where other people's property was concerned. Abandoned or destroyed houses were thoroughly searched, primarily for food. Both the State Security Corps and the Home Army gendarmerie failed the test. They busied themselves mostly with unlawful requisitions, instead of tending to their job.

A different problem was posed by the need to bury the bodies of those killed in the fighting, in air raids, through artillery fire or mines. Corpses lying in the street were a sight as common as the sight of children playing in the courtyards an excitingly new and popular game—the uprising. Casualties among the civilian population far outnumbered those of the front line Home Army soldiers. Although precise data are lacking, it is estimated that between 150 thousand and 200 thousand people were killed during the Warsaw Rising, as compared to 10,200 Home Army soldiers killed (a very high percentage—every fourth soldier was killed).

Since Warsaw cemeteries were situated in outlying sections that were held by the Germans, the dead had to be buried in the courtyard flower beds, in private backyards, on city squares, even on the sidewalks, beneath the torn flagstones. Every patch of land was thus used, and Warsaw—already reduced to mounds of rubble piled high over thousands of decaying bodies—now turned into one huge cemetery, dotted with makeshift crosses marking the graves. Warsaw descended underground, its inhabitants herded in the cellars to escape the bombs and artillery fire, devastating everything above the surface.

Death, hunger and thirst did not prevent the people of Warsaw from creeping out of their cellars at night, when the German bombardment halted, to pray and sing religious hymns before the provisional altars set up in every courtyard, lighted with a candle or two, and adorned with flowers. From nearby quarters of Home Army units, relieved by replacements, there would come other sounds of music, dancing, and singing of insurgent songs, born between battles. The uprising uncovered a rich lode of poetry which was to win a prominent place in Polish literature and came to be honored in anthologies published in postwar Poland. Unfortunately, most of these talented young poets, writing during the Warsaw Rising, were killed in battle. It was a good time for love, too. Often one would see in the street a young man, gun in hand, walking to church with his fiancée, only to go back to the front line right after the wedding. Front line theatres, featuring the best Polish actors, played for the soldiers. Cinemas opened and showed films from the uprising. Loudspeakers on street corners played light music, interspersed with the allied and insurgent communiqués. People visited from cellar to cellar, played chess or cards by the light of a single precious candle. In the center of the city there were even two or three small coffee shops, where ersatz coffee was served.

The city was flooded with publications, put out without any control or restriction by every political grouping (including the Polish Workers Party) and by the editorial staffs of prewar Polish publications. Printing presses were running round the clock and people reveled in the free press, replacing the "reptile press" of the occupation years. Postal service was organized by the Boy Scouts, who delivered letters, often at the risk of their lives. The morale was splendid. There were a few exceptions, of course—people who could not bear bombardments and artillery fire and who took shelter in the cellars at the very beginning of the uprising never to emerge until the very end; but these were few. Everybody helped everybody else, and there was a spirit of brotherhood everywhere. No one complained that the city was being turned into a heap of rubble, that thousands of men, women and children died, that everyone went hungry, that there was a lack of absolutely everything. Everybody reasoned that, since the uprising did break out, one had to take part in it and to stick it out to the very end. This feeling prevailed even when it became clear to everybody that the Soviet offensive had been halted intentionally. People of Warsaw realized then that the rising must collapse, still they persisted. On the front line—i.e., streets, where one side was held by the Germans and the other by the Poles—all distinctions between the Home Army soldiers and the civilians were quickly forgotten; inhabitants of the houses where battles were being fought, joined in the fighting and often died in the ruins of their own houses.

Three dispatches, sent to the government in London by Korbonski, best illustrate the situation in Warsaw at that time:

Warsaw, September 22, 1944. In my capacity as director of the Department of Internal Affairs I hold regular meetings with local delegates. The report on yesterday's meeting follows. It does not include Mokotow and Zoliborz, because these sections are completely cut off from us; military liaison is maintained only by radio and through occasional couriers. In the downtown section of the city, about half of the total population of some 260,000 are refugees from other sections. The store of supplies, both military and civilian, consists of about 100 tons of barley and 50 tons of wheat. The supply of fats will be exhausted tomorrow. We have enough sugar for another four days. We are requisitioning food from abandoned houses and from the merchants, but with insignificant results. We have been without electricity, gas, or city water for a long time. We are using 92 wells, and about 80 more are being drilled. There is a mild epidemic of dysentery, but nothing else. Medical service is provided by four doctors in every precinct, one doctor for each block. Six hospitals are being used for both the army and the civilians; twelve hospitals are for the civilian population only. They are all located in cellars.

Warsaw, September 23, 1944. Supplementing yesterday's dispatch. Things look better in Mokotow and Zoliborz. They are less overcrowded there and they have some vegetables. A trade in water has developed downtown. The wells become exhausted quickly and cannot be used. Starting with today our diet is limited to boiled wheat and coffee with sugar. We're under heavy mortar fire today.

Warsaw, September 26, 1944. Yesterday's meeting with the local delegates brought out the fact that hunger is rampant. Our entire store of wheat has been distributed, and we are distributing now the remainder of the 60 tons of barley. There are no other reserves. People are eating dogs. We are again facing the specter of capitulation or having to send the civilians over to the German side—this time because of starvation. Unless large quantities of food are provided daily by air drops, we cannot last longer than one week, ten days at the most. We've had twelve confirmed cases of scarlet fever.

Since there was no longer any doubt that the uprising was doomed, the High Command of the Home Army and the Home Cabinet decided to capitulate, and truce negotiators were sent to the German commander, General von dem Bach-Zelewski. As a result of negotiations, a capitulation agreement was signed on October 2, 1944. By its terms, the Home Army was to go into German captivity, and the civilian population was to leave Warsaw.

Even before the capitulation, an agreement had been concluded between the German command and the Polish Red Cross, permitting the old people, the sick, women and children to leave Warsaw on September 7 and 8. According to the log of the German 9th Army, 15,000 people left Warsaw on September 7, and 30,000 on September 8; after Mokotow fell on September 27, another 5,000 were evacuated, and 15,000 more after Zoliborz was captured by the Germans on September 30.

Following subsequent initiatives of the Polish Red Cross and the beginning of surrender negotiations on September 29, the civilian population of she city could actually leave Warsaw as of September

29. An entry of October 1 in the log of the German 9th Army cited above states that "instead of the expected mass outpouring of the civilian population, only small numbers are leaving the midtown section of the city. . . ." It notes "an unwillingness of the people to leave the encirclement." The reason for this reluctance was the general determination of the inhabitants of Warsaw to share the lot of the Home Army. At that time it was not known yet that the surrender negotiations were in progress. The civilian population began to leave Warsaw when it was announced that the capitulation agreement had been signed on October 2. Polish data on the number of people leaving Warsaw at that time are lacking. But the log of the German 9th Army recorded on October 8 that 153,519 persons had been evacuated since October 1.

This tragic finale brought to an end the epic of the Warsaw Rising.

XXIV

UNDERGROUND AUTHORITIES
AFTER THE WARSAW RISING

1. Civil Authorities

Article 9 of the capitulation agreement of October 2, 1944, stipu-
lated that no one in Warsaw would be prosecuted "for his involvement during the uprising in the activities of the organs of administration, justice, security, social welfare, civic and philanthropic organizations, or for his participation in the fighting or in war propaganda.
Neither will members of the above mentioned institutions and organizations be prosecuted for their political activities preceding the
uprising." This meant that the Government Delegate, the Cabinet,
the Council of National Unity and the Delegacy departments need
not disclose themselves to the Germans, as was the case with the
military authorities, and could blend with the civilian population
evacuated from Warsaw. Accordingly, some underground leaders left
Warsaw as employees of the Central Welfare Council or the Polish
Red Cross, while others left with the civilian population and thus
could see for themselves German nonobservance of Article 10 of the
capitulation agreement which stated: "The evacuation of the civilian
population from Warsaw, demanded by the German command, shall
be carried out at a rate and in a manner calculated to spare the inhabitants undue hardships." Contrary to this commitment, the civilian population of Warsaw was first subjected to the hellish conditions of the segregation camp at Pruszkow and then was either transported to other parts of the *General Gouvernement* (the old, the sick,
and children) or deported to forced labor camps in the Reich (men
up to 50 years of age and women up to 45 years of age). On leaving the
Pruszkow camp (or the hospital, as was the case, for instance, with Government Delegate Jankowski), the underground leaders found themselves dispersed in various localities along the railroad line Warsaw-
Koluszki-Krakow. Anticipating some such situation, the Department
of Internal Affairs had worked out during the last days of the Warsaw
Rising a system for reestablishing contact, which now helped to locate
Government Delegate Jankowski, members of the Home Cabinet
and the chairman of the Council of National Unity, or officials
of the Government Delegacy departments either in Krakow or in

small localities situated along the Electric Suburban Railway line, such as Otrebusy, Pruszkow, Komorow, Lesna Podkowa, Milanowek, and Grodzisk.

Some were missing. The Peasant Party representative on the Council of National Unity, Jozef Grudzinski, had been killed during the uprising. The director of the Department of Labor and Social Welfare, Judge Stefan Mateja, had been shot while fighting a fire on the roof of his apartment building. Gravely wounded were: Wincenty Bryja, head of the budget-finance section of the Delegacy, whose only son had been murdered by the Germans; Jozef Zajda, director of the Department of Finances; and Jerzy Lewandowicz, the Government Delegate for the district of Silesia, who was in Warsaw during the uprising. These three men were in the hospitals, a few of which had been evacuated from Warsaw. In addition, about 100 provisional hospitals were set up along the Electric Suburban Railway line due to the efforts of the Department of Social Welfare, the Central Welfare Council and the Polish Red Cross. They gave medical assistance to several thousand wounded and sick.

The most urgent task facing the civil authorities was to care for the several hundred thousand inhabitants of Warsaw, now dumped in the *General Gouvernement*, west of the Vistula. These people had nothing with them but a few articles of personal need, and—with very few exceptions—no money or means of livelihood. What they did have was an extremely high incidence of sickness. The relatively small area where the inhabitants of Warsaw were relocated (parts of the Warsaw, Lodz, Kielce and Krakow districts) became terribly overcrowded. The situation was alleviated in part by the uncommon generosity of the local people who opened their houses to the homeless and shared the little they had with them.

The critical situation of the expelled inhabitants of Warsaw caused the Home Cabinet and the Council of National Unity to issue on October 18, 1944, a joint appeal to the inhabitants of other districts of the *General Gouvernement* to come to the aid of the homeless. The proclamation stated that "the rescue of the people of Warsaw has now become a matter of honor for every Pole." It reminded that in the past Warsaw had provided shelter for thousands of Poles expelled from Pomerania, Silesia and the Poznan district, as well as those from Krakow, Kielce, Radom or Lodz who were pursued by the Germans, and that now was the time to repay the debt.

On the same day, Government Delegate Jankowski addressed the evacuated people of Warsaw, urging them not to give in to despair, but to persevere, to share the lives and problems of those who were sharing their homes with them, to join their hosts working in the fields or households, to help with the teaching of children, and to keep up the spirits of their fellow-sufferers.

A third appeal was issued jointly by the Home Cabinet and the Council of National Unity on October 18, addressed to the governments of allied and neutral countries, to the International Red Cross, and welfare organizations abroad. It stated that about one million people had been evacuated from Warsaw, that some of them had been taken to forced labor camps in Germany, but the rest—dispersed throughout the *General Gouvernement*—were left stranded and at the mercy of fate. It asked for food for children and for the sick, for medicines, and for warm clothing.

Apart from the three proclamations pertaining to Warsaw expellees, Government Delegate Jankowski issued—also on October 18—a proclamation announcing that "the Home Cabinet and the Council of National Unity have left Warsaw, following the cessation of the fighting, and continue to carry on their constitutional duties outside of the capital. All other political representation bodies, established outside of Warsaw during the duration of the Warsaw Rising, are hereby dissolved."

It was the purpose of the Government Delegate's proclamation to inform the people that the lawful authorities had not perished during the uprising and had not been captured by the Germans, but remained underground and continued to exercise their functions as heretofore. It also served to disavow the self-styled political leaders who had come to the fore outside of Warsaw, convinced that the underground leadership in Warsaw would either perish during the rising, or be taken captive by the Germans. Thus a quasi Government Delegacy, initiated by the Wolyn District Delegate Kazimierz Banach, had been established in the Grodzisk-Milanowek area for the territories west of the Vistula, still held by the Germans; for the territories east of the Vistula, already occupied by the Soviets, a similar quasi Government Delegacy was set up by an official of the Government Delegacy, Witold Bienkowski, joined later by Tadeusz Rek and Stanislaw Piotrowski of the Peasant Party. These substitute delegacies dissolved themselves when it became known that they were wrong in their assumptions regarding the underground leadership.

Simultaneously, the civil authorities addressed themselves to the task of salvaging from Warsaw whatever was of value to the nation. Article 10 of the capitulation agreement provided that: "The evacuation of all objects possessing artistic, cultural or religious value will be made possible. The German command will endeavor to safeguard both private and public property remaining in the city." The obligation explicit in Article 10 did nothing to stop the savage looting of

Warsaw. Plant equipment, machinery, tools, merchandise and com-
modities were taken to Germany, as was all private property such as
furniture, rugs, paintings, silver, china, furs, etc. Telephone and electric cables were ripped out of the ground, trolleycar lines were torn
down, whatever could not be carted away was either blown up or
burned down. A huge black cloud of smoke hung over Warsaw by
day, and half the sky was lit with fires by night.

Toward the end of the rising, Government Delegate Jankowski
recognized the necessity to find some ways to safeguard the city
after the evacuation. With this in view, he conferred a number of
times with the director of the Department of Internal Affairs Korbonski and with Stanislaw Wachowiak (minister for the formerly
Prussian territories after World War I), whom he thought best qualified to deal with the Germans. Numerous representations were
made to Fischer, the German governor of Warsaw, by Wachowiak,
by the deputy mayor of Warsaw Julian Kulski, and by the heads of
the Central Welfare Council and the Polish Red Cross, demanding
that the looting and burning of the capital be stopped and the terms
of the capitulation agreement observed. But all these efforts were in
vain. Two months after the capitulation, Warsaw became a desert
of burned-out rubble.

Meanwhile, Government Delegate Jankowski and his entourage
had left Krakow and moved to Piotrkow Trybunalski. In the monastery which had once sheltered members of the National Government
during the Insurrection of 1863, a joint conference was held by the
Home Cabinet and the National Council of Unity, attended also by
the directors of the Department of Press and Information (Kauzik),
the Department of Labor and Social Welfare (Bialas), the Department of Internal Affairs (Korbonski), and by the new Commander
of the Home Army, General Leopold Okulicki. The meeting was devoted to an analysis of the international situation, the Soviet occupation spreading gradually to the entire country, and the growing
rift within the Polish government in London between Premier
Mikolajczyk (pressing for concessions that might pave the way for a
Polish-Soviet understanding) and his opponents. As a result of
Churchill's mediation, Mikolajczyk went to Moscow again. On October 13, 1944, he attended a Kremlin conference with Stalin (accompanied by Molotov), Churchill (accompanied by Foreign Secretary
Eden) and the U. S. Ambassador Averell Harriman. Stalin rejected
Mikolajczyk's proposal to create—following the liberation of Warsaw—
a new Polish government with the participation of the Polish Workers
Party, and certain territorial concessions in the east, without, however, a specific recognition of the Curzon Line. He declared that the

Curzon Line was not open to discussion and reproved Mikolajczyk for ignoring the existence of the Polish Committee of National Liberation. Mikolajczyk returned to London empty-handed. In consequence, the underground leaders meeting in Piotrkow were pessimistic about the policies of their western allies, realistic about the future of Poland under Soviet occupation, and determined in principle to oppose the concessions advocated by Premier Mikolajczyk.

In the course of the conference, the three department directors reported on their operations. By that time, all three departments had managed to gather their workers together, to find new hideouts for their offices, and to resume their activities, disrupted by the capitulation and the evacuation of Warsaw. The Department of Press and Information took up again the publication of the Government Delegacy's organ *Rzeczpospolita* (The Republic) and organized anew the Press Agency. The Department of Labor and Social Welfare had already channeled through the Polish Red Cross and the Central Welfare Council funds needed for public assistance and for the maintenance of the provisional hospitals. The Department of Internal Affairs had reestablished radio contact with London, and was also in touch with all the district delegacies in German-occupied territories; two inspectors were making the rounds, acquainting the district delegates with current international and internal situations, as well as plans for future underground activities. For the time being, these plans were limited to preserving the existing organizational structure of the conspiracy, maintaining contact with the military authorities for self-defense purposes, and reporting regularly to the Department of Internal Affairs on the situation in the delegates' respective districts. In case their communication with the Department of Internal Affairs became disrupted, district delegates were given contact with radio stations maintaining liaison with London, either those that had already been operating in their respective districts, or those that were evacuated from Warsaw after the uprising. The radio communication center in London now had a two-fold function. Not only did it receive the proclamations and instructions transmitted from Poland to London by the underground military and civil authorities to be broadcast to Poland by the BBC and SWIT, but also it served as an intermediary in communication between the central and the local underground leadership. Thus, for instance, the Government Delegate for the Krakow district could communicate via London with the Chief Government Delegate in Piotrkow.

The meeting of the underground civil authorities in Piotrkow was the last to be held away from Warsaw and still under German occupation. The next meeting was held near Warsaw and under the Soviet occupation.

2. Military Authorities

On October 4, 1944, before going into German captivity, General Bor issued an order to all Home Army districts, informing them of General Okulicki's appointment as his successor and instructing them to limit Operation "Tempest" to a minimum and to concentrate instead on self-defense. General Okulicki had parachuted into Poland a short time before the uprising. Thus his presence in Poland was not known to the Germans and he was able to leave Warsaw on October 2 with the civilian population. He went to Czestochowa, assumed the command of the Home Army, and notified the government in London accordingly on October 7, 1944. Meanwhile in London, the outworn concept of commanding the Home Army from Great Britain came to the fore again, and General Stanislaw Tatar (pseudonym: Tabor) was chosen for the job. This undermined the position of General Okulicki, who had also run into some opposition in certain Home Army circles. The situation in London was clarified only when Government Delegate Jankowski sent a dispatch to the government in London demanding the official appointment of General Okulicki as the Commander of the Home Army. This was done by the decision of December 21, 1944.

The strength of the Home Army was still considerable after the Warsaw Rising. In the Radom district there were about 7,000 soldiers of the 2nd and the 7th Infantry Divisions under arms, and some 30,000 reserves in the underground. The Lodz district mobilized for Operation "Tempest" the 25th Infantry Regiment (1,200 men), and four special detachments on the county level of 80-100 men each. The Krakow district had units from the 6th and the 24th Infantry Divisions, and the Krakow Cavalry Brigade. In the territories incorporated into the Reich there were 27 battalions, although not at full strength. Finally, the Silesia district had several small partisan units, altogether about 900 men. All these forces, however, were poorly equipped with arms and ammunition.[1]

Despite the slowing down of Operation "Tempest" and the emphasis on self-defense, new fighting flared up in all districts when the Germans began the mop-up operations against the partisan units behind the front line, which stabilized for a few months on the Vistula and the three bridgeheads on its western bank. In the Radom district, three battalions of German gendarmerie attacked the 74th and the 2nd Infantry Regiments of the Home Army on October 27, 1944, in the Wloszczow county. The battle ended in a German defeat, and one battalion—together with its commanding officer, an SS major—surrendered to the Home Army. Large German units, several thousand strong, succeeded in surrounding several Home Army units on October 29 and 30, but the Poles managed to break through the encirclement, inflicting heavy losses on the Germans.

In the Lodz district the German mop-up operations began already in mid-September. But the 25th Infantry Regiment, surrounded by superior German forces, equipped with tanks, mortars and flame-throwers, succeeded in breaking through with only few casualties.

In the Krakow district, the local Home Army commander, Colonel Edward Godlewski (pseudonyms: Izabelka, Garda) had been arrested in late October, and was replaced by Lt. Col. Przemyslaw Nakoniecznikoff (pseudonym: Kruk II). Here, too, the Germans attempted to liquidate some units from the 16th Infantry Regiment and the 1st Mountaineer Rifles Regiment, which, however, escaped with few casualties and succeeded in inflicting heavy losses on the Germans and capturing substantial quantities of arms.

In Silesia, the Germans did not attempt to clear out the local partisan units, which limited their activities to diversionary operations, with losses on both sides.

Toward the end of December 1944, while this fighting was going on, a group of British military observers were parachuted into Poland. Led by Colonel Hudson, the British mission was composed of four British officers and one Polish officer in British uniform.* They were housed in the manor house of the Katarzyna estate, and were protected by a Home Army unit from the Czestochowa sector. Attacked by the Germans on January 1, 1945, this unit withdrew, together with the British mission, to the woods near Sznukry. On January 4, 1945, members of the mission met with General Okulicki in Zacisze near Odrowaz, Radom county. The British were outspoken in their admiration for what they had seen since their arrival in Poland. General Okulicki briefed them on the current military operations of the Home Army and their requirements for arms, ammunition, and other supplies. He also presented them with a detailed account of the disarmament of Home Army units by the Soviet army in the territories occupied by the Russians, and of deportations of Home Army soldiers to Russia.

The British mission did not remain long with the Home Army. In January 1945, the Soviet armies occupied the area where the British

---

* According to *Poland, SOE and the Allies* by Joseph Garlinski (p. 217), the Polish officer's name was Antoni Pospieszalski. In a book by the same author, *Politicians and Soldiers* (p. 285), the name is erroneously given as "Piespieszalski."

were staying. The British mission met with the Soviet command at the Zytno estate, and revealed their identity. They were treated with hostility, disarmed and imprisoned in the town of Czestochowa. Due to the intervention of the British government, however, they were shortly transferred to Moscow and, once there, allowed to take a plane for London.

The last act of Operation "Tempest" was played out west of the Vistula, when the Soviet offensive moved on in January 1945. In the Warsaw and Radom districts, the Home Army attacked and disarmed the retreating Germans, including the police and the functionaries, freed prisoners from German jails, blew up railway and highway bridges. In the Lodz district, too, the retreating German armies were attacked and their motorized columns ambushed, so that many cars and large quantities of arms were captured by the Home Army. In the Krakow district, the Home Army took part in the struggle for Krakow, their prime concern being to safeguard the national monuments in the ancient city from German destruction, and to secure the public utilities such as the waterworks or the power plant.

Special units from the troops commanded formerly by "Radoslaw" were stationed in Czestochowa to protect the Jasna Gora monastery against the possible depradations of the retreating German armies.

The Soviet NKVD and the Polish security police moved in everywhere in the wake of the retreating Germans. Immediately, there followed arrests and deportations of Home Army soldiers to the east. In this hopeless situation, General Okulicki saw no alternative but to issue on January 19, 1945, an order releasing the Home Army soldiers from their oath and dissolving the Home Army. The General's order was confirmed in the farewell address, broadcast by President Wladyslaw Raczkiewicz on February 8, 1945. It signaled the liquidation of the Home Army formations in districts, sectors and in the forests. About 50,000 soldiers laid down their arms and disclosed themselves to the Soviets; they were deported to the USSR.[2] Others refused to obey the order to disband and, together with their commanders, remained underground as Home Army units, dodging the pursuit of the NKVD and the security police. Among them was General Okulicki with his staff and those district commands that had not revealed themselves to the Soviets. This gave rise to the accusation that General Okulicki's order of January 19, 1945, had been fictitious and aimed at strengthening the conspiratorial cover of the Home Army. Many partisan detachments also remained in the forests and were shortly embroiled in battles with the security police and the NKVD forces. Finally, a few carefully selected men were recruit-ed for the ranks of NIE, an organization for which the groundwork had been prepared beforehand by General Bor, who—in his dispatch of November 26, 1943—reported his plans to the Supreme Com-mander, General Sosnkowski, in the following words:

"In the event of a second Soviet occupation, I am preparing in greatest secrecy a nuclear command network of a new underground organization to remain at your disposal. I shall report further details on completion of my decisions in this matter. In any event, this will be a separate network, unconnected with the general organization of the Home Army, which has been largely penetrated by Soviet agents."

The command of NIE was assumed by General Emil Fieldorf (pseudonym: Nil), withdrawn beforehand from the command of "Kedyw" (Diversion Command) and the Directorate of Under-ground Struggle. NIE was to be a mixed, political-military organiza-tion—a General Staff, rather than a mass organization—assembling together men of proven organizational and leadership abilities. Its structure could be likened to the ferroconcrete construction of a building that would have walls and interiors added at the proper mo-ment. It was assumed from the very beginning that a long time, per-haps many years, would elapse before such moment came.

XXV

THE BEGINNING OF SOVIET OCCUPATION

1. The Yalta Conference

In the course of the Soviet offensive of the winter of 1945, Soviet armies entered the ruins of Warsaw on January 17, 1945. Even before that, the Soviets had occupied the many suburban communities around Warsaw, and fast on their heels there also arrived the organs of the "Lublin Committee." The Home Cabinet, the Council of National Unity, and the High Command of the Home Army—which by the beginning of February had already reassembled in the suburban localities strung along the Electric Suburban Railway line—were now faced with an entirely new situation, worse in many respects than the German occupation, because the Polish arm of the Soviet NKVD, the Security Service—known generally as *bezpieka*—sprang into action instantly. Announcements were posted on the walls of buildings, ordering the registration of all members of the underground and the surrender of all weapons, and prohibiting listening to western broadcasts. Mass arrests of members of the underground and of the Home Army began immediately, greatly facilitated by previous infiltrating activities of the Polish Workers Party during the years of occupation. The rule of fear and terror began anew. This time around, the terror was more horrifying, because it was imposed not by the Germans, wearing their Gestapo or gendarmerie uniforms, but by the Poles, dressed in uniforms of the prewar Polish Army. Misery was compounded by poverty, caused by hasty economic reforms which relegated all commerce and exchange back to the black market. The most galling of all was the currency reform which required that all currency circulating during the German occupation be exchanged for new currency, but only up to 500 zlotys, the remainder to be left in the bank on deposit. This was tantamount to confiscation of all financial resources over and above 500 zlotys. Dollars, gold and rectified spirit became again the general means of exchange. The whole country felt despondent, helpless and hopeless.

At the same time a crisis was brewing within the underground leadership. It was caused by the resignation of Stanislaw Mikolajczyk (November 24, 1944), who was replaced as premier of the government-in-exile by Tomasz Arciszewski, a socialist, who had been brought to

London from occupied Poland during one of the "bridge" operations. Mikolajczyk's resignation caused great dissatisfaction among the underground leadership of the Peasant Party (the Premier's own party), which demanded Mikolajczyk's return to the government; if not, they threatened to withdraw all Peasant Party members from the Government Delegacy and the Council of National Unity. This demand was supported by the Home Cabinet, which warned Arciszewski's government in London against the dangerous consequences of the Peasant Party's withdrawal. In supporting Mikolajczyk, the Home Cabinet was guided by the same thought that had prompted disclosures to the Soviet authorities, i.e., that negation and protest alone would lead nowhere and that, under the circumstances of coercion, some practical alternatives of an arrangement with the Soviets must be explored. This was also Mikolajczyk's position. When these appeals to London went unheeded, the underground leadership of the Peasant Party resolved on January 12, 1945 that unless Arciszewski's government resigned by February 1 and Mikolajczyk were called back, the Peasant Party in Poland would join the opposition and Minister Bien, as well as those Department Directors who were members of the Peasant Party, would resign. Despite this, however, the Peasant Party leadership stressed their negative attitude toward the "Lublin Committee," declaring on that same day that the "Lublin Committee" was usurping the lawful authority and was backed by a foreign power.

Amid all this friction, news came from London regarding the decisions of the Yalta Conference of February 4-11, 1945. The message spoke only of the augmentation of the Polish Committee of National Liberation by inclusion of other Polish democratic leaders, both from within and without Poland, and of the change of the name of the Committee to "Provisional Government of National Unity." The Provisional Government of National Unity was to conduct, at the earliest time feasible, general, free, secret and unfettered elections. With regard to Poland's eastern frontier, the governments of Great Britain, the USA and the USSR decided that the border should follow the Curzon Line, with small deviations in favor of Poland in some places (5-8 km.) However, Poland was to receive territories in the north and in the west; the western frontier was to be determined at the peace conference.

On February 21, 1945, the Council of National Unity met in Podkowa Lesna near Warsaw for a two-day session devoted to the analysis of the decisions made at Yalta. Government Delegate Jankowski also took part in this meeting, which was conducted in a mood of utter despondency. The Yalta Conference was viewed as a complete victory for the Soviets who succeeded in obtaining British and American approval for their annexation of 48% of Poland's territory, situated east of the Curzon Line, as well as recognition for the Soviet puppet—the Polish Committee of National Liberation—as the nucleus of the future Polish government. However, the decision regarding the speediest conduct of democratic elections in Poland was viewed with great hope. No one among the members of the Council had any doubt that in such elections the Polish Workers Party and the pro-communist parties rallied around the Polish Committee of National Liberation would suffer a resounding defeat. Democratic elections were viewed as the last hope for salvation and their prospect had a decisive influence on the position of the Council of National Unity, when it passed the following resolutions:

The Council of National Unity declares that the decisions of the Crimean Conference, made without the participation and agreement of the Republic of Poland, impose on Poland the burden of new, extreme and inequitable sacrifices. The Council of National Unity protests in strongest terms the onesided decisions of the Conference, although it finds itself compelled to submit to these decisions, prompted by its desire to see in them the only avenue—under the present circumstances—of salvaging Poland's independence, of preventing further destruction of the nation, and of building the foundations permitting the mobilization of national strengths and the conduct of future independent Polish policies.

The Council of National Unity does so, confident that both the western allies of Poland and the USSR—mindful of the principles enunciated in the Atlantic Charter and the principles of democracy, which they endorse—will respect the quintessential independence of the Republic of Poland, and that the USSR will refrain from all interference in the internal affairs of Poland and will render it possible for the Government of National Unity to be the government of a truly independent Polish state, fully able to conduct elections and to function under the conditions of real freedom and democracy, without any pressure from a foreign power.

The Council of National Unity believes that the final determination of the frontier between Poland and the USSR will be made in direct negotiations between the two countries, or at a peace conference; on the other hand, Poland's frontier in the west will be moved to the Neisse River in Lusatia and to the Oder River, while in the north it will include East Prussia.

The Council of National Unity feels certain that the general formula of the Crimean Conference pertaining to the agreement between "democratic representatives from within Poland and from abroad" will acquire concrete meaning through consultations with the Council of National Unity in Poland and the government and the National Council in London, regarding the establishment of the Provisional Government of National Unity. In its capacity as the representation of Underground Poland, the Council of National Unity declares its readiness to undertake negotiations in this matter.

At the time of making the decision to begin the Warsaw Rising, no one had taken into account the possibility that the Soviet offensive might be halted intentionally. Similarly, no one at that meeting of the Council of National Unity admitted the possibility that a free general election could be turned into a farce. And yet, this was precisely what happened nearly two years later, on January 19, 1947.

Because of the new situation created by the Yalta Conference and the resolutions of the Council of National Unity of February 22, 1945, the Peasant Party did not withdraw from its participation in the underground leadership.

2. The Arrest of the Fifteen

There was a feeling of expectation, and even some small hope, in the air, when Government Delegate Jankowski and General Okulicki received two almost identical letters. (General Okulicki's letter arrived on March 6, at 11 p.m.) The letters were from a Russian Colonel of the Guards, Pimenov. They contained a proposal for a meeting with Colonel General Ivanov, representing the Soviet Command of the First Byelorussian Front. Pimenov's proposal was couched in general terms. It asserted only that such a meeting "may and certainly should resolve matters that cannot be readily resolved in any other way. Mutual understanding and trust will permit us to solve important problems and to prevent them from becoming acute." The letters ended with an assurance guaranteeing the safety of the Polish participants at the meeting.

Pimenov's letters reached the addressees through a number of intermediaries. On the one side, an anonymous officer of the Polish People's Army was involved (sought later by the NKVD), and on the other someone who had contacts with the Government Delegacy, possibly Tadeusz Wyrzykowski of the Peasant Party, who served as intermediary between Baginski and Colonel Pimenov.[1]

On receiving Pimenov's letter, Government Delegate Jankowski found himself in a quandary. On the one hand, he suspected a trap; on the other, he was reluctant to refuse Pimenov's offer for fear this would substantiate Soviet accusations before the western allies that the Polish underground leaders refuse even to meet with the Soviets. He decided therefore that Jozef Stemler (pseudonym: Dabski) should conduct exploratory talks to ascertain the true intent of the Soviet Command. Just in case, the Government Delegate suspended his daily meetings with Korbonski, the director of the Department of Internal Affairs, and instructed him to sever his contacts with everybody connected with the parleys and to stand by to alert the government in London should the proposal prove to be a trap. The government had been informed of Pimenov's proposal by a radio dispatch of March 11, 1945, and it expressed no objection to the meeting. As far as General Okulicki was concerned, he had no illusions; he thought the invitation was a subterfuge, and refused to take part in the meeting.

Stemler's interview with Colonel Pimenov and a man introduced to Stemler as Professor Chodkiewicz of Tashkent University (supposedly a descendant of a great Polish historical figure), resulted in a positive assessment of the Soviet proposal. Accordingly, in a series of meetings, Colonel Pimenov met with: Government Delegate Jankowski on March 17, 1945; representatives of the Polish Peasant Party on March 18, 1945; and representatives of the National Party, the Labor Party, and the Democratic Party—in separate meetings on March 20, 1945. Pimenov knew about the resolution of the Council of National Unity, pertaining to the Yalta Conference, and was aware of the parties' willingness to come out into the open, which was the main topic of discussion at the meetings. He gave each party delegation a form to fill out. Answers to this questionnaire were calculated to reveal not only the organizational structure and activities of each party, but also most sensitive information pertaining to the party-affiliated military units, merged into the Home Army. One of the questions focused on the manner of disclosure for each given party. The Polish Socialist Party was the only party that refrained from sending its representatives to a meeting with Col. Pimenov.

In the course of his meeting with Government Delegate Jankowskiski on March 17, Pimenov demanded the participation of General Okulicki in the meetings, as a condition for further negotiations, arguing that otherwise the General might not recognize as binding any agreement concluded with the Soviets. He also discussed the disclosure of the political parties and emphasized "the necessity of merging all democratic groupings in one mainstream." Government Delegate Jankowski requested, first of all, that transport be provided for representatives of the underground leadership to London and back, for the purpose of conferring with the government-in-exile. On March 20, Pimenov brought back the answer that the Soviet authorities had agreed to fly twelve underground representatives to London.

Prompted by Pimenov's statement on conditions for further parleys, Government Delegate Jankowski pressed General Okulicki to take part in the conferences. Although still unwilling, General Okulicki conceded and named Colonel Jan Rzepecki (who had escaped from German captivity and returned to Poland and the underground) as his successor in the event of a Soviet trap and his own arrest. On March 25, 1945, a joint meeting was held of the Home Cabinet and the Council of National Unity, with the participation of General Okulicki, and a formal resolution was passed to conduct negotiations with the Soviet Colonel General Ivanov. While the meeting was still in progress, the director of the Department of Internal Affairs Korbonski, brought to the vice chairman of the Council of National Unity, Kazimierz Baginski, a dispatch just received from Mikolajczyk, in which the former premier encouraged the Peasant Party to come out in the open and to engage in negotiations with the Soviet authorities. Baginski read the dispatch aloud to those present at the meeting. It confirmed the fact that both the current premier Arciszewski and the former premier Mikolajczyk favored the proposed conferences with Colonel General Ivanov.

On March 27, 1945, Government Delegate Jankowski, chairman of the Council of National Unity Puzak, and General Okulicki went to Pruszkow to meet General Ivanov. They did not return for the meeting of the Council of National Unity, scheduled for that same afternoon.

This did not seem alarming to other underground leaders, for on the following day, March 28, three members of the Council of National Unity and the delegates of the political parties, accompanied by interpreter Stemler, went to the same address in Pruszkow.

The underground intelligence service reported that on March 29 some cars, filled with people, had been seen leaving the villa in Pruszkow where the meeting was supposed to be held. When the Polish participants in the meeting failed to return by March 31, Korbonski alerted the government in London. On April 6, the Polish government in London issued a communique on the perfidious arrest of 15 leaders of the Polish Underground State. Arrested were the following: Government Delegate Vicepremier Jan Stanislaw Jankowski; chairman of the Council of National Unity Kazimierz Puzak; Commander of the Home Army General Leopold Okulicki; ministers: Adam Bien, Stanislaw Jasiukowicz and Antoni Pajdak; representatives of political parties: Kazimierz Baginski and Stanislaw Mierzwa (Peasant Party), Kazimierz Kobylanski and Zbigniew Stypulkowski (National Party), Jozef Chacinski and Franciszek Urbanski (Labor Party), and Eugeniusz Czarnowski and Stanislaw Michalowski (Democratic Party); also arrested was the interpreter, Jozef Stemler. This group of fifteen men was later augmented by Aleksander Zwierzynski (National Party), who had been arrested earlier. Air transport was, indeed, provided for the Polish leaders—not to London, but to to Moscow. They were placed in the famed Lubyanka prison. For General Okulicki this was a return engagement: as commander of the Union for Armed Struggle for the Soviet-occupied zone four years before, he had been arrested by the NKVD on January 21, 1941, and imprisoned at Lubyanka.

There followed allied interventions and inquiries, particularly with regard to Vicepremier Jankowski and the three ministers, whose names the western allies had given to the Soviets previously. All these queries were passed over in silence by the Soviets until May 4, 1945. On that day, in the course of the first UN conference in San Francisco, in reply to Foreign Secretary Eden's question, Molotov explained casually that the Polish underground leaders had been arrested because they were directing diversionary operations against the Soviet armies.

XXVI

FINAL MONTHS OF
THE POLISH UNDERGROUND STATE

1. Situation Within Poland

Meanwhile in Poland, an ever greater terror raged and anarchy reigned supreme. Thousands were swept into prisons—primarily, the soldiers of the Home Army. Mass arrests caused the young people to leave their homes again. Under the lash of terror, accompanied by the rise of anti-Soviet and anti-"Lublin Committee" sentiments, all those who were threatened with arrest or draft went into hiding, ran away to the "Wild West" of the Recovered Territories, or to the forests, which—in the districts of Lublin, Radom, Kielce, Rzeszow and Krakow—once again were filled with armed men. In the forest depths, the Poles often clashed with bands of deserters from the Soviet army, the so-called "vlasovites" and detachments of the Ukrainian Insurgent Army, also hiding there. The fever of flight to the forest also affected the army of General Berling (later, General Zymierski). Not only individual soldiers, but entire units would take to the woods. In Lublin, two-thirds of the cadet school went to the forest, as did a company from the cadet school in Chelm. Except for the Russian commanders and the few career-minded Polish opportunists, the army of General Zymierski—officers, noncoms and soldiers—was solidly anti-Soviet. The men feared that in the event of an outbreak of war between the USSR and Japan, they would be shipped to the Far Eastern front and liquidated there, because of their generally known anti-Soviet attitude.[1]

No one could stem this impetuous flight to the forests, especially since it was animated by an irrational conviction that this was but a transitory period, from which an independent Poland was about to emerge. Both the young people and the soldiers from the army of General Zymierski chose to bide their time in the forests, at least until winter.[2]

The "Lublin Committee" was fully aware of this state of affairs, and it announced a massive sweep-up operation conducted by the border NKVD forces and by two Polish divisions, trained specifically for partisan warfare and commanded by Russian officers.

Since villages and colonies on the edge of the forests supported the partisans and provided them with food, a ruthless pacification action was carried out. Entire villages were surrounded by the Soviet soldiers, all men (except the very young and the very old) were seized and deported to the east, all buildings were burned down. The pacification concentrated on the counties of Garwolin, Lukow, Lubartow, Zamosc and Wlodawa. During the pacification of Wlodawa county, fighting ensued with a few of the forest detachments, and tanks and Soviet planes were called in. On the other hand, a civic militia detachment on a pacification assignment near Myslenice, alongside a Soviet unit, turned on the Russians, killed them to a man, and fled to the forest.

The recovered territories became the scene of a different kind of violence. Local authorities, set up spontaneously by the Polish population in Kwidzyn (East Prussia), were arrested by the Soviets. In Pomerania, Soviet troops treated Poles who had been forcibly registered as Germans, as if they were German; they gang-raped their wives and their young daughters, and murdered the men who resisted their savagery. A few Kashubian villages were liquidated in this way, their wealth looted and taken to Russia.[3]

Existing prisons and the newly established concentration camps were promptly filled. About 8,000 people were held in the Zamek prison in Lublin, and 2,000 of these were later deported to Russia. In that same prison, 99 executions were carried out up to April 1945. In Lwow, about 7,000 people were arrested and deported to Russia. The main Russian distribution camp for Poles was located in Kaluga.

The concentration camp in Skrobow was established exclusively for soldiers of the Home Army. Another such camp was in Rembertow; it was seized by the partisans, and about 3,000 prisoners were set free.

Besides these mass arrests, there were also individual repressions. On Saturday before Easter, Wincenty Witos—the revered leader of the Peasant Party—was arrested in Wierzchoslawice and driven away for parts unknown. This aroused the suspicion that he might share the fate of Aleksander Zwierzynski, the prominent National Party leader, who had been added to the group of 15 Polish underground leaders abducted to Moscow. However, five days later, Witos was brought back to his village. He had been offered the task of forming the Provisional Government of National Unity, but made his agreement contingent on receiving the mandate to do so from the underground Peasant Party, and on the inclusion of Mikolajczyk in the government. These conditions were interpreted as a refusal.

Nothing was known of the fate of the 15 underground leaders except that they had been charged with conducting diversion behind the Soviet lines. Their arrest had greatly weakened the leadership of the underground political parties, which was broken up even further by successive arrests, but never completely liquidated, because the places of those who had been arrested were filled by others. The National Party suffered particularly heavy losses with the arrest of Mieczyslaw Jakubowski, Olgierd Pembowski, Roman Malecki, as well as the chairman and the members of the Warsaw leadership of the National Party—Tadeusz Macinski, Stanislaw Mrozinski, Zygmunt Domanski, Maria Triarska, Jadwiga Nieradzka—who were all locked up in the cellars of a provisional jail. From among the leaders of the Labor Party, or the Union, the following were arrested: the secretary of the Council of National Unity Boleslaw Biega, Jan Hoppe, Jan Chmielewski, and Wanda Maciejewska; they were taken first to the Rembertow camp, and later deported to Russia.

From among the leaders of the Polish Socialist Party, Stefan Rzeznik, Stefan Dressler and others were arrested in Krakow. Zygmunt Zulawski managed to escape minutes before his arrest by the NKVD. Also arrested in Krakow were several members of the district Government Delegacy and the former director of the Department of Internal Affairs, Leopold Rutkowski.

Among the prominent members of the Peasant Party arrested in Krakow were: Dr. Wladyslaw Kiernik, chairman for the Krakow county Jan Gajoch, and the district director of Civil Resistance Dr. Tadeusz Seweryn (pseudonym: Socha), and in Warsaw: Tadeusz Rek and Stanislaw Piotrowski. Narcyz Wiatr (pseudonym: Zawojna), commander of the Peasant Battalions in southeastern Poland, was simply shot by the Polish security police on April 25, 1945, in broad daylight, on a busy thoroughfare in Krakow. Finally, the wife of Premier Arciszewski, Melania, was arrested in Piotrkow.

The wave of arrests affected even those institutions, which the Germans had never dared to touch—the Polish Red Cross and the Central Welfare Council. Arrested were: Adam and Maria Tarnowski, Witold Wilkoszewski, Zbigniew Madejski and Mrs. Ziemska—all from the Polish Red Cross, and Janusz Machnicki from the Central Welfare Council. Members of the aristocratic families of Poland, always an easy target, were also arrested: Prince Janusz Radziwill (who had been arrested already once in 1939 and spent some time in a Soviet camp), Count Maurycy Potocki (jailed in the Pawiak prison by the Nazis), Count Jan Zamoyski, who was shortly set free by the Polish partisans, and former senator Eryk Kurnatowski.

Some of those who had been arrested—e.g., Adam and Maria Tarnowski and Wladyslaw Kiernik—were released after a few weeks, but most of them remained in prison (frequently, in Russia) a several months, and even years.

On the other hand, there were also an alarming number of killings of members of the Polish Workers Party and the functionaries of the hated *bezpieka*, which attracted to its ranks not only the communist fanatics of terror, but also the worst dregs of society.

2. Reorganization of the Government Delegacy

Details of the Soviet treacherous invitation and the subsequent arrest of the 15 underground leaders, were meanwhile transmitted to London. Broadcast by the BBC, they reached Poland at nearly the same time as the word-of-mouth news, which spread like wildfire throughout the country. The Soviet cynical and brutal subterfuge evoked bitter indignation in Poland. Even worse, the arrest of the underground leaders buried the last hope that some arrangement with the Soviets could be worked out to ensure an independent government and freedom for Poland. By the very nature of circumstances, the arrested men should have been considered as partners for negotiations and possible candidates for posts in such a government. Only now did people begin to realize that Teheran and Yalta meant not only the fourth partition of Poland, but also something infinitely worse, something that boggled the mind. The very worst suppositions were confirmed by the lack of any meaningful reaction on the part of the allies, although they were the ones who had given the Soviets the names of the Government Delegate and the three ministers. All at once, the country found itself without its underground leadership, once surrounded by an aura of secrecy and heroism, a leadership people trusted and whose instructions, although anonymous (or perhaps, because they were anonymous), they had learned to follow during the years of German occupation. Also, the underground leadership acted on behalf of the constitutional government of Poland. Now there was a void, and everybody asked himself: what next?

As during the Warsaw Rising, so now, too, various organizational centers sprang up, groping for the leadership of the underground. The National Armed Forces were in the forefront of these attempts, threatening to take over the agencies of the Government Delegacy, if need be, through a coup.

Under these circumstances, Korbonski—as chief of the most important of the Delegacy departments, that of Internal Affiars, and as

head of the Directorate of Civil Resistance—assumed the initiative.
Since the entire Home Cabinet had been arrested, as was the General
Commission of the Council of National Unity and since the Council
of National Unity itself was largely depleted, Korbonski called a
meeting in Warsaw, on April 7, 1945, to be attended by authorized
representatives of the same parties that had established the Council
of National Unity and had been represented in the Home Cabinet.
The meeting was called to chart the future course of action. In a
mood of grim determination, the delegates followed a path, trodden
in the rubble, to a half-burned house where the meeting was held.
Those present were: Professor Jozef Haydukiewicz (pseudonym:
Limanowski) for the National Party; Stanislaw Wojcik (pseudonym:
Kwasniak) for the Peasant Party; Zygmunt Kapitaniak for the Democratic Union; all members of the Council for National Unity; and,
substituting for Zygmunt Zaremba (Polish Socialist Party), who was
away from Warsaw at the time, his deputy for press affairs. Following Korbonski's report on the new situation created by the arrest of
the underground leadership, the parties' representatives, first of all,
decided unanimously to continue the underground resistance and to
charge Korbonski with the conduct of current business of the Government Delegacy.

In resolving to carry on the underground activities, the parties'
representatives were guided by their conviction that the maintenance of the Polish Underground State was the essential condition for
regaining Poland's independence; that the Polish Underground State
was the sole foundation on which the existence and the operation of
the Polish government in London was based; that the liquidation of
the underground would greatly facilitate the assumption of power
by the "Lublin Committee"; that the country expected the underground authorities to be reestablished, as witnessed by the many inquiries coming from all parts of Poland.

At the meeting on April 7, 1945, and in the course of the following meetings on April 16 and April 24, it was also resolved unanimously to reconstruct the General Commission of the Council of
National Unity, and the Council itself, but on a reduced basis and
with the proviso that members of both bodies would assume their
functions acting on behalf of the leaders detained by the Soviets;
it was felt that the detained leaders should retain the posts they held
before their arrest, because this might act as a restraint on the Soviet
authorities and facilitate the intervention of the government in London for their release.

On the other hand, the parties' representatives agreed unanimously not to reconstruct the Home Cabinet, since the departments of

the Government Delegacy constituted, in effect, underground ministries, and their supervision by the ministers was actually a formality. In practice, the Home Cabinet duplicated the work of the General Commission of the Council of National Unity, serving the Government Delegate in an advisory and consultative capacity.

Informed about the decisions of the parties' representatives, the government in London authorized Korbonski to substitute for the Government Delegate on a temporary basis (resolution of the Ministers' Committee for Homeland Affairs of April 10, 1945). As a consequence, the BBC and the Polish Radio broadcast repeatedly the news—circulated immediately by the underground press—that the underground authorities within Poland had been reestablished and continued their functions. This had a calming effect on the country and prevented the rise of other centers of authority and the coup contemplated by the National Armed Forces.

In accordance with the authorization received both from the government and from the party representatives, Korbonski proceeded immediately to reorganize the Government Delegacy, in line with the plans laid by Government Delegate Jankowski at the outset of the Soviet occupation of Poland. First of all, he liquidated all the departments whose work pertained to planning for the future. He retained only the Presidium Office, headed by Tadeusz Miklaszewski; the finance section, headed by Wincenty Bryja (who had meanwhile recovered from wounds, suffered during the Warsaw Rising); the Central Auditing Office, headed by former senator Waclaw Januszewski, following the arrest of its previous chief, Stanislaw Peszynski; the departments of Internal Affairs, Press and Information, Labor and Social Welfare; and the Bureau for the New Territories. The Department of Internal Affairs carried out a similar reorganization on the level of district delegacies, with whom regular contact was maintained. The Department of Press and Information continued to publish *Rzeczpospolita* (The Republic), as well as informational reports and bulletins; in addition, it increased the distribution of its monitoring service and of leaflets, denouncing the policies of the "Lublin Committee." The Department of Labor and Social Welfare continued its broadscale action of assistance to the sick, to children, and to the people of Warsaw, evacuated after the uprising. The financial resources of the Delegacy—very modest after the Warsaw Rising—were devoted largely to this program.

Meanwhile, new problems were piling up. In western Poland, communist authorities began to distribute for signature printed forms containing the so-called "assurance in lieu of oath." The form stated that the signer was in total accord with the July Manifesto, that he recognized the government created in Lublin as the only lawful government, and that he did not collaborate, either directly or indirectly, with any agency of the so-called emigré government in London. The Delegacy issued an instruction to boycott this action; it stated, however, that signing the form would not be considered as contrary to good citizenship, if done because of the threat of loss of job, loss of ration cards, or arrest.

From beyond the Curzon Line, word came that the Soviet authorities began to pressure Poles living east of the line to opt in favor of Poland and to move westward. The Delegacy instructed them not to move voluntarily, because Polish presence in these territories was crucial for their defense against the Soviet claims.

Finally, a courier from Hungary—Ludwik Angerer (pseudonym: Skalski)—came to Warsaw, requesting instructions for the Poles remaining in Hungary: should they return to Poland or wait for further developments? He was told that the Delegacy did not consider itself competent to issue instructions in this matter and that decision should be postponed until directives from the govenment in London were broadcast to Hungary.

In all the above circumstances, decisions of the Delegacy, or the government, were disseminated throughout Poland, or in Hungary by western radio stations, as well as by the underground press.

3. Delegate for the Armed Forces in Poland

Once the affairs of the Delegacy were put in order, it was the turn of the military. Korbonski met for a two-day session with Colonel Jan Rzepecki, the successor of General Okulicki. Colonel Rzepecki was not given the title of Commander of the Home Army. The government dispatch, received on May 13, 1945, appointed him as Delegate for the Armed Forces in Poland—an indirect confirmation of General Okulicki's order of January 19, 1945, dissolving the Home Army.

In the course of two days of deliberations, Rzepecki voiced his strong support for the continuation of the underground resistance, acknowledged the supremacy of the civil over the military underground authorities, and informed Korbonski that he had appointed Colonel Janusz Bokszczanin (pseudonym: Sek) as his successor in case of his arrest.

The matter of the NIE organization posed the immediate problem to be dealt with. Both Korbonski and Rzepecki were of the opinion that the secrecy of the organization had been destroyed by the Soviet intelligence, as proved by numerous arrests among its staff officers, whom Korbonski and Rzepecki knew personally, including its commander, Emil August Fieldorf (promoted meanwhile to the rank of general). For this reason, it was obvious that the organization would not be able to carry out the tasks for which it had been established. They decided therefore to recommend to the government and the Supreme Commander the dissolution of NIE, which followed within a short time.

Finally, they decided against retaliation for the arrest of the 15 underground leaders; although feasible, attempts on the life of key figures—either Soviet or from the "Lublin Committee"—could only worsen the position of the imprisoned leaders and bring about additional repressions in Poland.

Nonetheless, Korbonski and Rzepecki agreed that functionaries of the security police that were particularly cruel or overzealous should be liquidated in self-defense.

Subsequent meetings with Rzepecki were also attended by the commander of the Warsaw district, Lt. Col. Jan Mazurkiewicz (pseudonym: Radoslaw) and by the commander of the Bialystok district, Lt. Col. Wladyslaw Liniarski (pseudonym: Mscislaw), because—despite his "civilian" title of Delegate for the Armed Forces in Poland—Rzepecki maintained the command structure adopted previously by the Home Army.

4. The Council of National Unity

The first official outside act of the new civil authorities of the underground was the dispatch, sent jointly by the Council of National Unity and the Government Delegacy on April 13, 1945, expressing to the American people, on behalf of the Polish people, condolences on the death of President Roosevelt on April 12, 1945. Since the underground leaders had not been informed by the government in London about the negative role played by President Roosevelt in regard to Poland, they were totally unaware of it, which accounted for the following paragraph in the dispatch, totally at variance with reality:

"The Polish people feel a particularly keen sense of loss with the departure of a great statesman who would not be duped by sham trappings with which calamitous policies are attempting to cover up the real aims and the true face of Poland. He was the champion of our struggle to regain true freedom and democracy. All our hopes, connected with the person of the deceased president, are now turned to the American people and to his revered successor, Harry Truman."

The Council of National Unity ventured on the international scene again, when—following the resolution passed at the Council meeting on April 24, 1945—a dispatch was sent to the United Nations in San Francisco. Addressed to the chairman of the U.S. delegation, Secretary of State Stettinius, the message voiced the belief of the democratic parties, constituting the Polish Underground Parliament, that the United Nations would not ignore the tragedy of a people, embattled over the past six years, in the cause of freedom and independence of their country. "The Polish nation's right to sovereignty and freedom has been fully confirmed with the blood of its sons and the steadfastness of its devotion to the noblest of ideals."

At the next meeting, on May 3, 1945, the General Commission of the Council of National Unity was reestablished. It was composed of the following: Jan Matlachowski (pseudonym: Ozarowski) from the National Party, replacing Professor Haydukiewicz who had been arrested in the meanwhile; Stanislaw Wojcik from the Peasant Party; and Zygmunt Zaremba from the Polish Socialist Party, who had returned to Warsaw, or rather the vicinity of Warsaw. It was decided to augment the reduced membership of the Council of National Unity with one representative from each of the four parties; the fifth seat was to be rotated between the Democratic Union, "Fatherland," and "Raclawice." The chairmanship was to rotate each month.

At the same meeting, the text of the Council's message to the delegates assembled at the United Nations Conference in San Francisco was approved. The message described the course of negotiations between the underground leadership and Soviet Colonel Pimenov; it denounced the treacherous arrest of the 15 leaders; it gave an account of the situation in Poland, the activities of the Soviet authorities (or the Polish authorities acting on behalf of the Soviets), the mass arrests, particularly of the former soldiers of the Home Army, the pacification policies that turned entire villages to ashes. The conditions prevailing in Poland forced large numbers of Polish youth to flee to the forest. The country was threatened with anarchy, which the underground authorities were trying to prevent. The message reiterated conditions for the formation of a Provisional Government of National Unity: it must be based on the democratic parties, which had led the struggle of Underground Poland for over five years; it must be formed in consultation with the Polish Government in London and with the Council of National Unity in Poland; it must have a complete freedom of action and of command over the Polish armed forces. Foreign armies must leave Poland immediately upon the completion of war operations in the west. The message ended with the expression of regret that no Polish delegation was present at San Francisco; on the other hand, it welcomed the hope voiced at the conference that the Provisional Government of National Unity might be formed promptly enough for its representatives to attend the sessions in San Francisco.

Also at the same meeting, the representative of the Peasant Party, Stanislaw Wojcik, went beyond the resolutions that had been adopted by the Peasant Party on January 12, 1945, and made a motion calling for the liquidation of the hitherto acting underground authorities and their replacement by others, and for a vote of no confidence to be transmitted to the government in London.[4] These motions were rejected. Instead, it was voted (with Wojcik abstaining) to demand the government's reorganization and its adherence to the resolutions of the Council of National Unity of February 22, 1945. A motion calling for the resignation of President Raczkiewicz was passed, with a recommendation, however, that this be deferred until an agreement was reached between the government and Mikolajczyk.

At the subsequent meeting of the Council, on May 7, 1945, the representative of the Peasant Party, Wojcik, declared that his party would withdraw from participating in the work of the Council until the reorganization of the government in London was completed. For the time being, the Peasant Party did not wish to withdraw those of its members who were connected with the Government Delegacy, but reserved the right to do so if the government reorganization in London did not take place. In that event, the Peasant Party would proceed with the establishment of a new center of leadership. After delivering this declaration, Wojcik left the meeting.

Following this dramatic opening, Korbonski informed those present at the meeting about the reorganization of the Government Delegacy, which was approved "for financial and security reasons"; it was specified that "the conduct of current business by the present Acting Delegate of the Government Korbonski (Nowak) extends to all aspects of activities; it was determined that the government would be requested to name as Korbonski's deputies Bialas from the Polish Socialist Party and Kwasiborski from the Labor Party. Another deputy, representing the Square (National Party) was to be named later." Finally, it was requested that the government confirm Colonel Rzepecki as successor to General Okulicki; Korbonski suggested that, for prestige reasons, the government should promote Rzepecki to the rank of Major General.

At the time of their meeting on May 7, the Council members knew already that the war in Europe had ended. Yet they received the news without a feeling of relief. As for the reaction of the capital,

slowly filling up with people again, it was described in a dispatch to
the government on May 8: "The end of the war was received with indifference in Warsaw. It changes nothing here."

Amid the general feeling of uncertainty and foreboding, with the
grim shadow of the arrest of 15 underground leaders looming over
the country, in the face of a growing terror, on the one hand, and
chaos and anarchy on the other, the Council of National Unity and
Acting Delegate Korbonski determined that it was necessary to issue
a joint proclamation, informing the Polish people about the position
taken by the underground authorities with regard to the international and internal situation, and—above all—clarifying the goals and the
expectations of the underground leadership. The proclamation,
issued on May 17, 1945, stated that, in declaring on February 22,
1945 its readiness to accept the decisions of the Crimean Conference
as the basis for negotiations aimed at regulating the Polish-Soviet
relations, the Council of National Unity had made considerable concessions, despite which Russia kept on delaying the implementation
of the Yalta decisions. Notwithstanding this statement of principle,
the proclamation stressed the sincerity of the desire to establish
friendly relations with Russia, and expressed the belief that the Provisional Government of National Unity would be based on truly
democratic elements, and not on the usurpers and despots of the
Lublin Committee "who must bear the responsibility for the fact
that the same hand that has rejected our hand, outstretched in
friendship, is now killing and banishing into exile the best sons of
our country." It went on to say that the underground leaders,
treacherously arrested in Pruszkow, shoould take part in the formation of the government; freedom of speech, press and association
should be restored in the country, and the nazi-like ban on listening
to the western radio should be rescinded. Elections to the parliament
should be held under conditions of complete freedom, and after the
departure of Soviet armies from Poland. An equitable agrarian reform, socialization of the means of production, democratization of
the army, and other goals, listed in the proclamation of the Council
of National Unity of March 15, 1944, should be carried on until a
permanent reconstruction of the governmental structure in Poland
is achieved. Along with the friendly relations with the Soviet Union,
the closest possible relations should be maintained with the western
allies, who have rejected four times already the candidacy of the
"Lublin Committee" as the representative of Poland at the San Francisco Conference.

The proclamation appealed to the nation to persevere in its posture of resistance toward the usurpers from Lublin, and to oppose all attempts at depriving the Polish nation of its freedom and independence. However, the negative attitude toward the self-styled "Lublin Committee" should not hamper the work of reconstruction. The entire nation should rally spontaneously to lend their efforts in the work of reconstruction in all sectors—in industry, commerce, agriculture, communication, education, etc.—with the exception of the political administration, propaganda, and the security police, which should be boycotted.

Finally, the proclamation appealed to the people not to let themselves be provoked into armed struggle; and to the youth, who had escaped to the forests from mass arrests and persecutions, to try to go back to normal life and productive work, because to stay on in the forests would mean their ruin. If forcibly drafted into the army, the young men should not let themselves be used against their compatriots or in fighting for foreign causes away from Poland, in the east (i.e., in the event of a war between Russia and Japan).

The proclamation of the Council of National Unity and the Acting Delegate was complemented on May 27, 1945, by an appeal to the soldiers of the forest units, issued jointly by Acting Delegate Korbonski and the Delegate for Armed Forces in Poland, Colonel Rzepecki. Paying homage to the heroism of the Home Army over the five years of struggle, and denouncing disarmaments, arrests and killings of the Home Army soldiers by the Soviets and by the Polish security police, the two leaders also recalled the decree on the dissolution of the Home Army and called on the soldiers to forego fighting, to come out of the forests and to take part in the work of rebuilding the country; they reminded the soldiers of the necessity of taking precautions not to expose themselves to treachery and persecution.

Following the dissemination of the two proclamations through all means available to the underground, there was a mass influx of the intelligentsia to sectors named in the Council's proclamation of May 17, 1945. Until then, thousands of professionals refrained from applying for jobs in practically all the sectors of the economy, nationalized by the new regime, because they were unwilling to shirk their duty as Polish citizens and wanted to remain loyal to the constitutional government in London. The whole nation was waiting for guidance from the underground authorities in this matter. After the proclamation of May 17, there was a rush to join in the work of reconstruction, which the underground leadership declared to be the primary national goal, overriding the problem of proper attitude toward the "Lublin Committee," On instructions of Acting Delegate Korbonski, and with the approval of the Council of National Unity, the entire professional staff of the Bureau for the New Territories (about 2,000 specialists in each area) reported for work in the western territories. Within a short time, most of them were employed in the Ministry for the Recovered Territories, headed by Wladyslaw Gomulka, with Wladyslaw Czajkowski, former head of the Bureau for the New Territories, as vice minister.

Large numbers also left the forests, without, however, revealing themselves to the communist authorities or surrendering their arms, which was in line with the recommendations of the proclamation, advising utmost caution in order to escape treachery and persecution.

At the meeting of the Council of National Unity on May 29, 1945—which began as usual with Korbonski's report on the activities of the Government Delegacy—Korbonski announced his resignation, in accordance with the decision of the Peasant Party to withdraw its members from the Delegacy, which had been taken meanwhile. Since no answer from the government had come up to that time regarding the proposal to name Bialas and Kwasiborski as successive replacements for the Acting Delegate, Korbonski agreed to stay on until the next meeting of the Council, wich was scheduled for June 27, and was to be held in Krakow.

The decision of the Peasant Party heightened the crisis, because it was followed by the decision of the Labor Party to give the government in London four weeks in which to reorganize, i.e., to form a new government that would include Mikolajczyk; otherwise, the Labor Party threatened to leave the Council of National Unity and to withdraw its members from the Delegacy. If this came to pass, the Council of National Unity would cease to exist, because the Polish Socialist Party would not remain in the Council with the National Party only (for political reasons), and even if it did remain, this would not have been a Council of National Unity any longer, but merely a joint action by the two parties. If the Labor Party carried out its threat, the Delegacy would be paralyzed. It seemed that the political underground was about to break into two camps: the right and the left. The first would consist of the National Party, the National Armed Forces (NSZ), and segments of the National-Radical Camp (ONR). The second would comprise the Peasant Party, the Labor Party, the Democratic Union, the syndicalists, and the fraction of the Workers Party of Polish Socialists (RPPS). This second political center would no longer recognize the government in London as representing the homeland. As for the Polish Socialist Party, it found itself at the crossroads.

The thinking behind the creation of the left-oriented center of political leadership was that, following the unanimous acceptance— as a necessary evil—of the Yalta decisions by the Council of National Unity on February 22, 1945, the government in London had three options: to accept the Council's resolutions, to resign, or to dissolve the Council of National Unity. In not choosing either of these options, the government in London violated the principles that should have been binding for a constitutional and democratic government. This was viewed as a coup d'état of a sort. The Peasant Party felt that the passivity of the government in London could be justified only in the event of imminent hostilities between the USSR and the Allies. However, the policy of the western allies was to follow singlemindedly the course set at Yalta (even though the decisions of the Yalta Conference were being sabotaged by the Russians); under the circumstances, Mikolajczyk's policy appeared to offer the only practical chance in the peaceful contest over Poland between the Allies and the Soviets.[5] In preparing for the establishment of a new center of political leadership, the Peasant Party authorities demanded that Korbonski transfer the functions and offices of the Delegacy not to his successor—when appointed by the government in London—but to the new organization. Korbonski refused categorically to do so; he declared that he would transfer all the functions and offices of the Government Delegacy only to the appointee of the government in London, named as his successor. This refusal, in effect, buried the plans for a new leadership center.

5. Deliberations in Moscow on the Formation of the Provisional Government of National Unity

Meanwhile, on June 17, 1945, deliberations began in Moscow on the formation of the Provisional Government of National Unity. At the invitation of the U.S. Ambassador Averell Harriman, the British Ambassador Clark Kerr, and the Soviet Foreign Minister Vyacheslav Molotov, the following persons came to Moscow from Poland: Wladyslaw Kiernik (as a substitute for Wincenty Witos who excused himself because of real, or diplomatic, illness); Professor Stanislaw Kutrzeba; Zygmunt Zulawski (Polish Socialist Party). Professor Adam Krzyzanowski; and Henryk Kolodziejski, former Librarian of the Polish Parliament. Even today, no one knows who suggested these names to the ambassadors, but it was neither the underground, nor the government in London. Of the five representatives from Poland, only two were members of the underground: Zulawski and Kiernik. Kolodziejski had only limited contacts with the underground, and the two professors had none. Under the circumstances, only Zulawski and Kiernik were in some measure qualified to speak in the name of Poland, which in no way changed the fact that they had not been delegated either by the Polish underground authorities, i.e., by the Delegacy and the Council of Natonal Unity, or by official agencies, such as the Central Welfare Council or the Polish Red Cross.

From Great Britain, there arrived in Moscow: Stanislaw Mikolajczyk, Jan Stanczyk, and Antoni Kolodziej (who had already recognized the "Lublin Committee" a few months before).

The "Lublin Committee" was represented in Moscow by: Boleslaw Bierut, Edward Osobka (Morawski), Wladyslaw Kowalski, and Wladyslaw Gomulka.

After four days of deliberations, on June 21, 1945, the government was formed as follows: Premier—Osobka-Morawski; Vice Premiers—Mikolajczyk and Gomulka; National Defense—General Michal Rola-Zymierski; Foreign Affairs—Wincenty Rzymowski; Public Administration—Wladyslaw Kiernik; Security—Stanislaw Radkiewicz; Treasury—Kazimierz Dabrowski; Industry—Hilary Minc; Communications—Jan Rabanowski; Postal and Telegraph Service—Mieczyslaw Thugutt; Shipping and Foreign Trade—Stefan Jedrychowski; Health—Dr. Franciszek Litwin; Labor and Social Welfare—Jan Stanczyk; Culture and Arts—Wladyslaw Kowalski ; Reconstruction—Michal Kaczorowski; Information—Stefan Matuszewski; Justice—Henryk Swiatkowski; Education—Czeslaw Wycech (former director of the Department of Education of the Government Delegacy); Commerce and Provisioning—Jerzy Sztachelski; Forestry—Stanislaw Tkaczow. Out of the 21 members of the new government, only Czeslaw Wycech and Wladyslaw Kiernik had been active in the underground in Poland, and only Mikolajczyk and Mieczyslaw Thugutt (who declined the nomination, anyway) were affiliated with the government in London. Stanczyk, who did come from London, joined up with the "Lublin Committee" representatives immediately upon his arrival in Moscow. In the final reckoning, the "Lublin Committee" won 17 out of 21 ministerial portfolios, including the key ministries of Security, National Defense and Foreign Affairs. Mikolajczyk's group was given 4 portfolios.

The communist National Council of the Homeland, composed at the time of 444 members, was augmented by the addition of Witos, Mikolajczyk, Kiernik, Zulawski, Krzyzanowski, Kutrzeba, Kolodziejski, Stanczyk, Kolodziej, and Stanislaw Grabski, i.e., ten persons, of which only five could be considered as having any ties with the government in London or the underground in Poland. Soviet victory was complete.

6. The Trial of 16 Leaders of Underground Poland

On the day following the opening of the above deliberations, i.e., on June 18, 1945, the trial of the 16 Polish underground leaders began in Moscow. Instead of taking part in the deliberations on the formation of the Provisional Government of National Unity, the 16 members of the underground government and parliament were brought to court, charged with a number of crimes, all amounting to conducting activities hostile and detrimental to the Soviets and to the Red Army liberating Poland from under the Nazi yoke. This was the prosecution's way of summing up Operation "Tempest" and the disclosure to the Soviets of the Home Army commands and the civil underground authorities.

The entire trial, and the application of the Soviet Penal Code to the defendants, constituted a violation of the basic tenets of international law. According to international law, activities of a constitutional government, or its part (as was the case with the Home Cabinet), within its own country, cannot be considered as crimes, especially not on the basis of a Code in force in another country. In view of this, the arrest of the 16 underground leaders and their trial before a military Soviet court in Moscow, was an act of brutal lawlessness, whose impact, unfortunately, crushed most of the accused, who confessed to guilt, where there was no crime involved at all.

In the course of the trial, much was said about the NIE organization, which proved that it had been exposed, and confirmed that the decision made by Korbonski and Rzepecki to dissolve it had been correct.

Both the trial and the deliberations on the formation of the new government had been carefully staged and their time and place synchronized. The purpose of this was to exert psychological pressure on the recalcitrant members of the conference, and to browbeat them into amenity to Soviet demands. This was fully achieved. The knowledge that, while they deliberated, the elite of the Polish underground was on trial before a Soviet military tribunal—at the same time and in the very same city—hit the conferees like a bludgeon. Stunned, they did not raise their voices in protest against the drama enacted next door to their own conference rooms; instead of making their participation in the conference contingent on the release of the 16 undergroud leaders, they agreed to far-reaching concessions.

On the other hand, the news of the conference held in Moscow also reached the 16 arrested underground leaders. As a result, Baginski counseled his fellow-prisoners to "tone down the pronouncements to be made before the Soviets," in order not to hinder the progress of the conference.[6] In this instance, too, the Soviets achieved their purpose. The trial influenced the course of the conference, and the conference influenced the course of the trial—all according to Soviet intentions.

Profoundly shocked by the news from Moscow, the Council of National Unity issued a proclamation (undated) devoted to the trial. It protested against the lawlessness of the arrest and trial before a foreign court of 16 leaders of the Polish underground. It appealed to all Poles not to let this crime provoke them into armed action, but to react with solemn dignity. The proclamation ended with the words: "The entire nation stands united in the face of this tragedy."

The trial in Moscow lasted three days. On June 21, 1945, the sentences were pronounced: General Okulicki—10 years in prison; Government Delegate Jankowski—8 years; Bien and Jasiukowicz—5 years; Puzak—one year and a half; Baginski—one year; Zwierzynski—8 months; Czarnowski—6 months; Chacinski, Mierzwa, Stypulkowski and Urbanski—4 months. Michalowski, Kobylanski and Stemler were acquited. Pajdak was excluded from the trial because of illness. The curtain fell on the tragic spectacle, whose staging bore the imprint of Stalin's own perfidious hand.

7. The End of the Polish Underground State

The verdict in the trial of the 16 leaders and the creation of the Provisional Government of National Unity were already known to the Council of National Unity when it met in Krakow on June 27, 1945. Anyway, on that same day, the new government landed on the Okecie airfield in Warsaw. By rotation, the meeting was chaired by Jerzy Braun, brought into the Council by the Labor Party. The trial and the conference in Moscow dominated the meeting. The course and the outcome of the trial evoked deep indignation and despondency. But the new government inspired the hope that Mikolajczyk's group, with the powerful backing of the western allies, would be strong enough to ensure free elections, which would radically alter the situation. There was no other way, anyway, but to accept the existence of the Provisional Government of National Unity and to engage in an open political struggle, rather than in conspiracy, to obtain the goals of the Polish Underground State, which, in the new situation, should be liquidated. During the meeting, Korbonski announced his resignation as Acting Government Delegate. Since his successor had not been appointed by the government in London, Korbonski—with the approval of the Council—transferred his functions to the chairman of the Council of National Unity, Jerzy Braun.

Twenty-four hours later, on the night of June 28, Korbonski and his wife Zofia were arrested in their hideout in Krakow by the Soviet NKVD. They were placed at first in the security prison in Krakow, and later were transferred to the prison of the Ministry of Security in Warsaw.

On July 1, 1945, the Council of National Unity formulated its position in a proclamation, addressed to the Polish Nation and the United Nations. It reviewed the war aims of Fighting Poland, the Soviet policy in regard to Poland, and the program of Polish democracy. In a "Testament of Fighting Poland," it reiterated the previously stated political demands and the program of social, political and economic reforms. Then it set forth the reasons for its decision to discontinue further underground activities in the following words:

The end of the war against Germany left Poland in an extremely difficult, even tragic, situation. While other nations, particularly in the West, regained their freedom after throwing off the yoke of German occupation, and could resume their independent existence, Poland, in the wake of a war in which it had suffered the most, found itself under a new occupation, under the rule of a government imposed by a foreign power, and with no prospect of help from the western allies.

In these circumstances, the policy of intransigeance with regard to the Crimean decisions, pursued by the government in London, became incompatible with the faits accomplis, created in Poland by the Soviets. In particular, the conference in Moscow and the resulting compromise between, on the one hand, Mikolajczyk's group and a few Polish democratic representatives, and, on the other, the "Lublin Committee," created a situation that must be taken into account by Fighting Poland.

The establishment of the new government, and its recognition by the western powers, puts an end to the possibility of a lawful underground resistance, associated with the generally recognized government in London. The problem now arising is that of an open struggle of the democratic parties in Poland to achieve the national goals and the realization of their programs.

In this open struggle, the Underground Poland does not wish to create difficulties for men of good will who are associated with the Provisional Government of National Unity. Neither does it wish to restrict particular parties in their choice of ways and tactics which they may want to, or be forced to take.

At the session held on July 1, 1945, all the democratic parties of Underground Poland, represented in the Council of National Unity, unanimously resolved to dissolve the Council and to proclaim its dissolution at home and abroad.

With the proclamation of July 1, 1945, the Polish Underground State ceased to exist and passed into history.

XXVII

EPILOGUE

Upon the dissolution of the Government Delegacy and the Council of National Unity, a special commission was appointed to liquidate the activities of these bodies. It completed its task within a short time, but this did not put an end to underground political activity. A number of small, clandestine organizations—either new, or derived from the traditional political parties—appeared on the scene. Among the last were: the Independent Polish Socialist Party, the National Party, the Polish Democratic Party (headed by Henryk Jozewski), and the National Independence Party (formerly "Konwent"), led by Waclaw Lipinski. These four groups joined in establishing the Coordinating Committee of Polish Underground Organizations, known also as the Coordinating Commission of Political Parties or, briefly, "The Center." In addition, also active were the National Armed Forces (NSZ) and a number of smaller organizations, such as the Home Army Resistance Movement, the Directorate of Underground Struggle (not to be confused with the Directorate of Underground Struggle under German occupation), the Special Action Alert, the Polish Organization, the National Military Union, the National Military Association, the Polish Army of the Homeland, the Young Poland, the Youth of All Poland, the Secret Scouting Movement, the Lyceum, the Woods, the Forge, and many others.

These organizations concentrated on political activities, primarily on propaganda, directed against the new government, but with one exception: they supported Mikolajczyk and the Peasant Party, which had meanwhile changed its name to "Polish Peasant Party" at the Congress held on January 19-21, 1946. They also provided political backing for the partisans who, though greatly reduced in numbers, still remained in the forests, conducting two-way operations—making forays into the neighboring towns to release prisoners held in local jails or to liquidate functionaries of the security police and the Polish Workers Party, and defending themselves against the round-ups organized by the NKVD military forces and by the Internal Security Corps (*Korpus Bezpieczenstwa Wewnetrznego*—KBW), created by the decree of the "Lublin Committee" on May 23, 1945, specifically to combat the military underground.

In time, however, arrests, court trials (ending frequently in death sentences), and long jail terms destroyed these organizations, including "The Center," and put an end to their activities.

The dissolution of the Council of National Unity and the Government Delegacy necessarily affected also the Delegacy for Armed Forces. Colonel Rzepecki (who, despite Korbonski's recommendation had not been promoted to the rank of Major General) initially issued instructions to continue the struggle underground (April 11, 1945). However, three months later he changed his position and on July 24, 1945, called on his soldiers to go back to normal life. The arrest of Lt. Col. Mazurkiewicz (pseudonym: Radoslaw), the commander of the central region, toward the end of July, had an additional impact on Rzepecki. On August 6, 1945, he issued an order dissolving the Delegacy for Armed Forces in Poland. In its stead, he established on September 2, 1945, an organization differing from either the Home Army or the Government Delegacy and patterned more after the Service for Poland's Victory in that it was both political and military in character. It was called "Freedom and Independence" (*Wolnosc i Niezawislosc*—WIN) and adopted the conception and the structure of the dissolved NIE organization, modified to respond to the changed conditions of Soviet occupation. The political character of WIN became evident when the new organization joined "The Center," where it shortly began to play the major role. The political line followed by WIN was similar to that followed by "The Center": opposition to the new government, but support for the policies of Mikolajczyk and the Polish Peasant Party. WIN operated by means of whispered propaganda, infiltration of the Polish Peasant Party ranks (without revealing WIN affiliation), and clandestine press, remarkable for its variety, considering that it had to buck conditions even more difficult than under the German rule. Among these periodicals were: "Honor and Country," "The Polish Word," "Independent Poland" and "Echoes from the Forest."

WIN also took over those partisan detachments of either the Delegacy for Armed Forces or the Home Army, that remained in the forest.

As far as relations with the government in London were concerned, within a short time there was a WIN Delegacy established in the west, whose task it was—besides representing WIN—to collect funds for its operations in Poland. But the relationship between the government and WIN and "The Center" could not be likened to the ties that bound the government in London with the Delegacy, the Home Cabinet or the Council of National Unity, because these bodies—

established or recognized by the government on the basis of the Constitution of 1935—had acted in an official capacity. WIN and "The Center" did not possess a similar standing, and their relationship with the government was limited to contacts only.

It was not for long that Colonel Rzepecki remained free. Arrested on November 5, 1945, he was pressured (similarly to Lt. Col. Mazurkiewicz) into issuing an order commanding his men to come out into the open, and was brought before a military court in Warsaw on January 4, 1947, together with other members of the WIN General Staff: Colonel Antoni Sanojca (pseudonym: Kortum), the commander of the southern region of WIN, and former officer on the High Command of the Service for Poland's Victory, the Union for Armed Struggle and the Home Army; Colonel Jan Szczurek (pseudonym: Slawbor), the commander of the western region of WIN; Ludwik Muzyczka (pseudonym: Benedykt), the former chief of "Briefcase"; and Emilia Malessa (pseudonym: Marcysia), a functionary of the WIN High Command. Rzepecki based his defense on contrition. He stated that it was a grave error on his part to remain underground; he promised to redeem himself and to liquidate WIN; he disclosed the names of all his associates, under the condition they would not be arrested (a promise which the Security did keep); he surrendered all funds, amounting to about one million dollars; he criticized the policies of the government in London and the underground leadership, sparing only Korbonski, and citing for his defense the proclamation of May 27, 1945 (which he and Korbonski had issued jointly), calling for the cessation of fighting and the return of the partisans to normal life. Other defendants refused to follow the same line; they testified to facts, without condemning the past. On February 3, 1947, the following sentences were announced: Rzepecki—8 years in prison; Szczurek—7 years; Sanojca—5 years; Muzyczka—10 years; Malessa—2 years. With the exception of Muzyczka and Malessa, they were released because of the amnesty proclaimed by Bierut to commemorate the opening of the *Sejm* on February 4, 1947.

Despite Rzepecki's promise, WIN was not liquidated. Rzepecki's place was taken by Colonel Franciszek Niepokolczycki (pseudonyms: Franek, Saper), who continued the political-military activities of the organization. He, too, was shortly arrested, together with seven members of his staff, and was brought before a military court in Krakow on August 11, 1947. Members of this second High Command of WIN were joined on defendants' benches by Stanislaw Mierzwa of the Polish Peasant Party (one of the 16 underground leaders abducted to Moscow in 1945), released from the Soviet prison, and Karol

Buczek, the editor of *Piast*, the organ of the Polish Peasant Party. The purpose of the maneuver was to incriminate the Polish Peasant Party by linking it with the illegal WIN, which did support the policy of the Peasant Party and Mikolajczyk, as the only appropriate policy under the circumstances.

In the course of the trial, Niepokolczycki admitted that in the area of Bialystok alone, WIN had three battalions under arms. The trial also revealed that Colonel Wladyslaw Liniarski (pseudonym: Mscislaw), WIN commander in the Bialystok district, had been previously arrested. By a court decision of September 11, 1947, based on the decree of June 13, 1946, pertaining to "crimes especially dangerous during the period of the reconstruction of the state" (grimly reminiscent of the Nazi decree on "threatening the work of reconstruction in the *General Gouvernement*"), the defendants received the following sentences: Niepokolczycki and the seven members of his staff—sentence of death, changed later to long-term imprisonment; Mierzwa—10 years in prison; Buczek—15 years in prison.

Despite these heavy blows, the remnants of WIN survived until 1954, when Adam Boryczko, possibly the last emissary from the WIN Delegacy in the west, crossed the Polish frontier on June 13, 1954, on his way to the still existing WIN cells in Poland. Arrested within three days, he never fulfilled his mission.

Simultaneously with the rise of the new conspiracy, the recently established Provisional Government of National Unity also attempted to liquidate the remnants of the old underground by means other than arrests, prisons, executions, round-ups and pacification actions, the most drastic of which was the burning of the small town of Wawolnica on May 2, 1946. To commemorate the establishment of the Provisional Government, an amnesty was announced on August 2, 1945, for those members of the underground who would come out in the open. While the amnesty law was still being debated, Korbonski and his wife Zofia were released from jail. On his return to his old hideout, Korbonski found a dispatch from the government in London, thanking him for fulfilling the duties of the Government Delegate during such a perilous period.

The second amnesty law was passed by the *Sejm* on February 22, 1947. At that time, Korbonski was already a member of the *Sejm*, as representative of the Polish Peasant Party for the city of Warsaw, and member of the *Sejm* Amnesty Commission. At the plenary session of the *Sejm*, on February 21, 1947, Korbonski demanded in his speech that full "amnesty" be granted to all members of the underground, following their disclosure, and that all those who had been arrested previously be released, regardless of the length of sentence imposed. Of the amendments proposed by Korbonski, the commission approved changing the death penalty to 15 years of imprisonment, and extending the amnesty to all cases, including deserters from Zymierski's army. However, the demand for the release of all those who had been sentenced to prison was rejected; instead, prison terms were reduced, proportionately to their length.

According to the official communiqué, issued by the Ministry of Public Security on May 7, 1947, as a result of the two amnesties 55,277 persons have come out in the open, including 22,887 members of WIN, 4,892 members of the National Armed Forces, 8,432 members of the "forest bands," and 7,448 deserters from Zymierski's army. In the process, 14,151 items of armament were surrendered, including: 10 light cannon, 12 mortars, 72 heavy machine guns, 832 light machine guns, 2,752 submachine guns, 2,740 hand guns, and 6,830 rifles.

The government action described above did not bring an end to arrests and persecutions. From among the 16 underground leaders abducted to Moscow, Delegate Jankowski, General Okulicki and Minister Jasiukowicz died in Soviet prisons, but others, like Puzak and Baginski, were arrested again in Poland, and it was in prison that Puzak died on April 30, 1950. Within a few years after the war, nearly every one of the civil and military underground leaders, who did not escape abroad, served a term in prison. Some were not released until after October 1956.

The attempt to win back Poland's independence by means of free elections—on which the Council of National Unity had relied so heavily in passing its resolutions of February 22, 1945, and in terminating its own existence on July 1, 1945—ended in 1947 in a national catastrophe. The election was held on January 19, 1947, preceded by a wave of unspeakable terror, such as the murders by the *bezpieka* of 118 regional leaders of the Polish Peasant Party, whose names were listed in the memoranda presented by the Polish Peasant Party on December 18, 1946 and January 18, 1947 to the Ambassadors of Great Britain, the United States and the USSR in Warsaw.[1] During the electoral campaign about 100,000 Polish Peasant Party members were subject to arrests and interrogations that lasted from a few days to several weeks. Also imprisoned were 162 Peasant Party candidates for representatives in the *Sejm*, 1,962 regional organizers, and all those who represented the Polish Peasant Party on the electoral commissions—5,227 persons in all. The security police conducted 327 searches in the offices of the Polish Peasant Party; in 48 instances they planted arms there. The Polish Peasant Party was banned in 29 counties, and in 10 electoral districts (which were to elect 76 representatives), lists of candidates for the Peasant Party representatives were invalidated.

In the course of the elections, there occurred about 50 kinds of forgery or falsification. These were itemized in 52 protests, pertaining to each of the electoral districts, and in one general protest for the whole country, brought by the Polish Peasant Party before the Supreme Court, which never bothered to consider any of them. Although the Polish Peasant Party actually received 68% of the votes, it was given only 28 seats out of a total of 444 seats. It was truly a drop in the ocean.

The finale of this utter defeat came in October 1947, with the flight of Mikolajczyk and Baginski, who escaped before their imminent arrest. Korbonski and his wife fled in November 1947. The Polish Peasant Party was taken over by the pro-communist elements and shifted to a policy of support for the government. The last legitimate opposition disappeared from the political scene in Poland.

SOURCES

CHAPTER I

1. *Studia z dziejów ruchu ludowego* (Historical Studies of the Peasant Movement), Ludowa Spółdzielnia Wydawnicza, Warsaw, 1971. Tadeusz Nowak's report on territories incorporated into the Reich, pp. 278-281.

2. Wladyslaw Bartoszewski, *Warszawski pierścień śmierci* (The Warsaw Ring of Death), Interpress, Warsaw, 1970, p. 421.

3. *The Service: Memoirs of General Reinhard Gehlen*, Popular Library, New York, 1971, p. 111.

CHAPTER II

1. *Polskie Sily Zbrojne w Drugiej Wojnie Światowej* (Polish Armed Forces in WWII), vol. III, *Armia Krajowa* (The Home Army), Instytut Historyczny im Gen. Sikorskiego, London. 1950. pp. 517 and 518.

Armia Krajowa w dokumentach, Studium Polski Podziemnej, London, 1970, pp. 211, 341, 342.

2. Interesting comments regarding the role played by Major Galinat were published in the weekly *Stolica*, November 15, 1970 and February 28, 1971.

3. *Wielka Encyklopedia Powszechna*, Państwowe Wydawnictwo Naukowe, Warszawa, vol. X, p. 804.

4. *Strajk chlopski w 1937 roku*, Ksiazka i Wiedza, Warszawa, 1960, pp. 196-199.

5. Ibid, p. 379.

6. Michal Tokarzewski-Karaszewicz, "U podstaw tworzenia Armii Krajowej," *Zeszyty Historyczne*, Instytut Literacki, Paris, 1964, No. 6, p. 27.

7. Janina Karas, *Pierwsze polrocze armii podziemnej*, Instytut Jozefa Pilsudskiego, London, 1948.

8. Michal Tokarzewski-Karaszewicz, "U podstaw tworzenia Armii Krajowej," *Zeszyty Historyczne*, Instytut Literacki, Paris, 1964, No. 6, p. 27.

9. *Armia Krajowa w dokumentach*, Studium Polski Podziemnej, London, 1970, pp. 4, 31.

10. The exact date of delivery could not be established.

CHAPTER III

1. Ibid., p. 73.

2. Ibid., pp. 85-87.

3. Ibid., pp. 167, 168.

4. Ibid., p. 185.

5. Jan Karski's letter in *Kultura*, no. 9/83, Instytut Literacki, Paris, September 1954.

Studia z dziejów ruchu ludowego, Ludowa Spółdzielnia Wydawnicza, Warsaw, 1971, pp. 223, 232.

6. Zygmunt Zaremba, *Wojna i konspiracja* (War and Conspiracy), B. Swiderski, London, 1957, pp. 178, 179, 183, 184.

7. Kazimierz Iranek-Osmecki, "Sprawozdanie i dziennik podróży emisariusza Antoniego," *Zeszyty Historyczne*, no. 21, pp. 122, 125, Instytut Literacki, Paris, 1972.

8. *Studia z dziejów ruchu ludowego*, Ludowa Spółdzielnia Wydawnicza, Warsaw, 1971, Korbonski's report, accepted by the Central Leadership of the Peasant Party, pp. 223, 225.

CHAPTER IV

1. *Armia Krajowa w dokumentach*, Studium Polski Podziemnej, London, 1970, p. 260.

2. Ibid., pp. 271-273, 277, 278, 296, 305.

CHAPTER V

1. Ibid., pp. 332, 368, 383, 384, 422.

2. Ibid., pp. 402, 404, 405.

3. Ibid., pp. 402, 436, 446, 447.

CHAPTER VI

1. Ibid., pp. 190, 191, 350, 359, 393.
   Studia z dziejow ruchu ludowego, Ludowa Spółdzielnia Wydawnicza, Warsaw, 1971, p. 231.

2. *Armia Krajowa w dokumentach*, Studium Polski Podziemnej, London, 1970, pp. 274-277, 294.

CHAPTER VII

1. Ibid., pp. 219, 221, 508.

2. Stanislaw Dolega-Modrzewski, *Polskie panstwo podziemne* (The Polish Underground State), London, 1959, pp. 81, 82. *Katalog polskiej prasy podziemnej 1939-1945*, Wydawnictwo Ministerstwa Obrony Narodowej, Warsaw, 1962, p. 198.

3. *Generalna Gubernia w planach hitlerowskich*, Państwowe Wydawnictwo Naukowe, Warsaw, 1961, p. 49.

4. *Wielka Encyklopedia Powszechna*, Państwowe Wydawnictwo Naukowe, Warsaw, vol. IX, pp. 41, 79. Czeslaw Wycech, *Z dziejów tajnej oświaty w latach okupacji 1939-1944* (History of Clandestine Teaching during the Occupation Years 1939-1944), Warsaw, 1964, p. 142. Jerzy Michalewski, "Relacja", *Zeszyty Historyczne*, no. 26, Instytut Literacki, Paris, 1973, pp. 80-83.

5. *Armia Krajowa w dokumentach*, Studium Polski Podziemnej, London, 1970, p. 220.

CHAPTER VIII

1. Full texts may be found at the Studium Polski Podziemnej in London.

CHAPTER IX

1. *Polskie Siły Zbrojne w drugiej wojnie światowej* (Polish Armed Forces in WWII), vol. III, *Armia Krajowa*, Instytut Historyczny im. Gen. Sikorskiego, London, 1950, p. 124.

2. Jozef Garlinski, *Politycy i żołnierze* (Politicians and Soldiers), Polska Fundacja Kulturalna, London, 1968, pp. 286, 287.

3. *Polskie Siły Zbrojne w drugiej wojnie światowej*, vol. III, *Armia Krajowa*, pp. 305-307.

4. Kazimierz Iranek-Osmecki, "Meldunek Specjalny 1/R. No. 242. Pociski rakietowe", *Zeszyty Historyczne*, No. 22, Instytut Literacki, Paris, p. 65.

Polskie Siły Zbrojne w drugiej wojnie światowej, vol. III, *Armia Krakowa*, p. 309.

5. Ibid., pp. 922, 923.

Garlinski, *op. cit.*, pp. 232, 233, 252.

6. Ibid., p. 252. According to *Polskie Siły Zbrojne w drugiej wojnie światowej*, vol. III, p. 346 "in the years 1939-1944, the homeland (i.e., more precisely, the Home Army—*Author's note*) received in various ways: about $27 million in paper currency, about $350,000 in gold, about 2,000 pounds sterling in gold, about 4,000 marks in gold, about 1,500 rubles in gold, about 4 million German marks (paper), about 90 million "mlynarki" (occupation currency), and small sums in pesetas, leus, korunas, lats, pengös and francs."

7. *Armia Krajowa w dokumentach*, Studium Polski Podziemnej, London, 1970, p. 11.

8. *Polskie Siły Zbrojne w drugiej wojnie światowej*, vol. III, *Armia Krajowa*, p. 361.

CHAPTER X

1. Ibid., p. 455.

Report of emissary Jan Karski, Studium Polski Podziemnej, London.

2. Underground *Biuletyn Informacyjny*, no. 47, December 3, 1942.

3. *Armia Krajowa w dokumentach*, Studium Polski Podziemnej, London, 1970, p. 220.

4. Ibid., p. 229.

Polskie Siły Zbrojne w drugiej wojnie światowej, vol. III, *Armia Krajowa*, Instytut Historyczny im. Gen. Sikorskiego, London, 1950, p. 460.

5. *Biuletyn Informacyjny Koła Byłych Żołnierzy AK, Oddział Montreal*, no. 4/55, December 1972, pp. 5, 6.

6. Stefan Korbonski, *W imieniu Rzeczypospolitej*, Instytut Literacki, Paris, 1954, pp. 109-111.

7. *Polskie Siły Zbrojne w drugiej wojnie światowej*, vol. III, *Armia Krajowa*, p. 475.

8. Dispatches of the Directorate of Civil Resistance of May 21, June 10, and July 16, 1943, cited in Korbonski, *op. cit.*, pp. 221, 222.

9. *The Strategy of Civilian Defense*, Adam Roberts, ed. See article by Juliusz Mieroszewski, *Kultura*, no. 10/240, October 1967, p. 49.

10. Dispatch of the Directorate of Civil Resistance of August 4, 1943, Studium Polski Podziemnej, London.

11. Dispatches of the Directorate of Civil Resistance of July 9, August 14, and October 7, 1943, Studium Polski Podziemnej, London.

CHAPTER XI

1. *Polskie Siły Zbrojne w drugiej wojnie światowei*, vol. III, *Armia Krajowa*, Instytut Historyczny im. Gen. Sikorskiego, London, 1950, p. 464.

2. Ibid., p. 473.

3. Ibid., p. 453.

4. Kazimierz Banach, *Z dziejów BCH* (History of the Peasant Battalions), Ludowa Spółdzielnia Wydawnicza, Warsaw, pp. 181-185.

CHAPTER XII

1. Full texts of declarations, proclamations and statements may be found at the Studium Polski Podziemnej in London.

CHAPTER XIII

1. Full texts of declarations, proclamations and statements may be found at the Studium Polski Podziemnej in London.

CHAPTER XIV

1. *Polskie Siły Zbrojne w drugiej wojnie światowej*, vol III, *Armia Krajowa*, Instytut Historyczny im. Gen. Sikorskiego, London, 1950, p. 62.

Władysław Pobog-Malinowski, *Najnowsza Historia Polityczna Polski*, vol. III, London, 1960, pp. 341, 342, 347.

Jan Rzepecki, *Wspomnienia i przyczynki historyczne*, Czytelnik, Warsaw, 1956, p. 203.

CHAPTER XV

1. Ibid., pp. 278-280.

Z. S. Siemaszko, "The Rampart Group and the National Armed Forces," *Zeszyty Historyczne*, no. 21, Instytut Literacki, Paris, 1972, p. 20.

2. Ibid., p. 25.

Polskie Siły Zbrojne w drugiej wojnie światowej, vol. III, *Armia Krajowa*, Instytut Historyczny im. Gen. Sikorskiego, London, 1950, pp. 62, 149-158.

3. Ibid., pp. 62, 520.

Władysław Pobóg-Malinowski, *Najnowsza historia polityczna Polski*, vol. III, London, 1960, pp. 342, 373.

"Prawda o Paxie i Piaseckim", Rozglosnia Polska Radia Wolna Europa ("Truth About PAX and Piasecki", Radio Free Europe), London, 1968.

CHAPTER XVI

1. *Wielka Encyklopedia Powszechna*, Panstwowe Wydawnictwo Naukowe, Warszawa, vol. IX, p. 53.

Władysław Pobóg-Malinowski, *Najnowsza historia polityczna Polski*, vol. III, London, 1960, , pp. 399-410.

Tadeusz Bór-Komorowski, *Armia podziemna*, 3rd ed., Veritas, London, 1966, pp. 119, 120, 168-170.

2. *Polskie Siły Zbrojne w drugiej wojnie światowej*, vol. III, *Armia Krajowa*, Instytut Historyczny im. Gen. Sikorskiego, London, 1950, pp. 62, 63.
Pobóg-Malinowski, *op. cit.*, pp. 361, 362.
Wielka Encyklopedia Powszechna, vol. II, p. 344.
"Meldunek specjalny Komendanta Armii Krajowej", *Zeszyty Historyczne*, no. 24., Instytut Literacki, Paris, 1973, p. 195.

3. Pobóg-Malinowski, *op. cit.*, pp. 411-413.
Jan Rzepecki, *Wspomnienia i przyczynki historyczne*, Czytelnik, Warsaw, 1956, p. 262.
Stefan Korbonski, *W imieniu Rzeczypospolitej*, Instytut Literacki, Paris, 1954, pp. 273, 274.

CHAPTER XVII

1. Lucjan Dobroszycki, *Centralny katalog polskiej prasy konspiracyjnej 1939-1945*, Wydawnictwo Ministerstwa Obrony Narodowej, Warsaw, 1962, pp. 5-18.

2. Wladyslaw Chojnacki, *Bibliografia zwartych druków konspiracyjnych*, Państwowe Wydawnictwo Naukowe, Warsaw, 1970, pp. 12, 13.

CHAPTER XVIII

1. Philip Friedman, *Their Brothers' Keepers*, Crown Publishers, Inc., New York, 1957, p. 13.
Wladyslaw Bartoszewski and Zofia Lewin, *Ten jest z ojczyzny mojej*, Znak, Krakow, 1966, pp. 7-17.
Kazimeriz Iranek-Osmecki, *Kto ratuje jedno zycie . . . Polacy i Zydzi 1939-1945*, Orbis, London, 1968, pp. 23-32.

2. Bartoszewski and Lewin, *op. cit.*, pp. 7-69.

3. Jan Karski, *Story of a Secret State*, Houghton Mifflin, Boston, 1944.

4. Bartoszewski and Lewin, *op. cit.*, pp. 49, 141-146, 506-510.

5. Yuri Suhl, *They Fought Back*, Crown Publishers, Inc., New York, 1967, p. 109.

6. Raul Hilberg, *The Destruction of European Jews*, Quadrangle Paperbacks, Chicago, 1967, p. 720.

CHAPTER XIX

1. Stanislaw Piotrowski, *Dziennik Hansa Franka* (The Diary of Hans Frank), Wydawnictwo Prawnicze, Warsaw, 1956, pp. 87, 156, 504.

2. *Roczniki dziejów ruchu ludowego*, Zaklad Historii Ruchu Ludowego, Warsaw, 1963, no. 5, p. 210.

3. Jan Weinstein, "Wladyslaw Studnicki w świetle dokumentów hitlerowskich II wojny", *Zeszyty Historyczne*, no. 11, Instytut Literacki, Paris, 1967, pp. 3-41.

4. *Armia Krajowa w dokumentach*, Studium Polski Podziemnej, London, 1970, p. 498.

5. *Pod pregierzem*, Zarzad Glowny Kola Zolnierzy AK, London, 1971. Statement by Adam Galinski, Government Delegate for the Wilno District. Also, a denial of charges by Jozef Mackiewicz.

CHAPTER XX

1. Kazimierz Skarżynski, "Katyn i Polski Czerwony Krzyż", *Kultura*, no. 5/91, Instytut Literacki, Paris, 1955, pp. 127-141.
The Katyn Forest Massacre, Hearings before the Select Committee, U. S. Congress, part 4, pp. 712-718.
J. K. Zawodny, *Death in the Forest: The Story of the Katyn Forest Massacre*, University of Notre Dame Press, Notre Dame, Indiana, 1962.

2. Ibid., pp. 65-70.
Stefan Korbonski, *W imieniu Polski Walczacej*, B. Swiderski, London, 1963, pp. 172, 173.

3. Tadeusz Cyprian and Jerzy Sawicki, *Sprawy polskie w procesie norymberskim*, Instytut Zachodni, Poznan, 1956, pp. 254, 255.

CHAPTER XXI

1. *Polskie Siły Zbrojne w drugiej wojnie światowej*, vol. III, *Armia Krajowa*, Instytut Historyczny im. Gen. Sikorskiego, London, 1950, pp. 562, 580.

CHAPTER XXII

1. *Polskie Siły Zbrojne w drugiej wojnie światowej*, vol. III, *Armia Krajowa*, Instytut Historyczny im. Gen. Sikorskiego, London, 1950, pp. 580-648.
Tadeusz Bor-Komorowski, *Armia podziemna*, 3rd ed., Veritas, London, 1966, pp. 181-195.
Witold Babinski, "Wymiana depesz między Naczelnym Wodzem i Dowòdcą Armii Krajowej, 1943-1944", *Zeszyty Historyczne*, No. 24, Instytut Literacki, Paris, 1973, pp. 159-211.

CHAPTER XXIII

1. *Armia Krajowa w dokumentach*, Studium Polski Podziemnej, London, 1970, pp. 2, 11, 302.

2. Col. Gen. S. Sztiemienko, "Na drodze do zwyciestwa", *Zeszyty Historyczne*, no. 19, Instytut Literacki, Paris, 1971, p. 39.
Stanislaw Mikolajczyk, *The Rape of Poland*, McGraw-Hill Book Co., New York and Toronto, 1948, p. 74.

3. *Na Antenie*, Rozglosnia polska Radia Wolna Europa (Radio Free Europe), London, August 16-September 6, 1964, interview with Captain Jan Nowak, p. III.

4. Zygmunt Zaremba, *Wojna i konspiracja*, B. Swiderski, London, 1957, p. 238.
Polskie Sily Zbrojne w drugiej wojnie światowej, vol. III, *Armia Krajowa*, Instytut im. Gen. Sikorskiego, London, 1950, p. 658.

5. T. Rawski, Z. Stapor and J. Zamojski, *Wojna wyzwolencza narodu polskiego w latach 1939-1945*, Warsaw.
Antoni Przygonski, *Z problematyki Powstania Warszawskiego*, Warsaw, 1964.

6. Leon Mitkiewicz, "Powstanie Warszawskie", *Zeszyty Historyczne*, no. 1, Instytut Literacki, Paris, 1962, pp. 130-143.

7. Zaremba, *op. cit.*, p. 238.

8. "Dziennik Dzialan Nr 11 Dowodztwa 9 Armii", *Zeszyty Historyczne*, no. 15, Instytut Literacki, Paris, 1969, pp. 79-82.

9. Mikolajczyk, *op. cit.*, p. 66 and ff.

10. "Dziennik Dzialan Nr 11 Dowodztwa 9 Armii", pp. 79, 112, 126, 127, 129.

11. J. Niemczynskij, "Warszawa w ogniu", *Zeszyty Historyczne*, no. 18, Instytut Literacki, Paris, 1970, p. 148.

12. "Dziennik Dzialan Nr 11 Dowodztwa 9 Armii", pp. 81, 82.

13. Marshal Konstantin Rokossovsky. "Obowiazek zolnierski", *Zeszyty Historyczne*, no. 15, Instytut Literacki, Paris, 1969, "Marszalek Rokossowskij o Powstaniu Warszawskim", p. 136.

Marshall Konstantin Rokossovsky, "Warszawa", *Zeszyty Historyczne*, no. 18, Instytut Literacki, Paris, 1970, p. 143.

14. Ibid., pp. 142, 143, 145.
Sztiemienko, *op. cit.*, p. 54.

15. "Dziennik Dzialan Nr 11 Dowodztwa 9 Armii", p. 128.

16. *Polskie Siły Zbrojne w Drugiej wojnie światowej*, vol. III, *Armia Krajowa*, p. 823.

17. Ibid., pp. 819, 824.

18. "Dziennik Dzialan Nr 11 Dowodztwa 9 Armii", p. 97.

19. Sztiemienko, *op. cit.*, p. 49.

20. Andrzej Pomian, ed., *The Warsaw Rising, A Selection of Documents*, London, 1945.

CHAPTER XXIV

1. *Polskie Siły Zbrojne w drugiej wojnie swiatowej*, vol. III, Instytut Historyczny im Gen. Sikorskiego, London, 1950, pp. 906, 921.

2. Ibid., p. 926.

CHAPTER XXV

1. Kazimierz Baginski, "Proces Szesnastu w Moskwie", *Zeszyty Historyczne*, no. 4, Instytut Literacki, Paris, 1963, pp. 89-90.

CHAPTER XXVI

1. Korbonski's dispatch to the government in London of April 27, 1945, Studium Polski Podziemnej, London. (Twenty-eight years later the same fears, and for the same reasons, were rife in the Polish Army in connection with the threat of a Sino-Soviet war. See "List do emigranta", Instytut Literacki, Paris, 1970, pp. 13-16).

2. Korbonski's dispatches to the government in London, dated April 27 and May 26, 1945, Studium Polski Podziemnej, London.

3. Korbonski's dispatches to the government in London, dated April 13, 18, 24, 26 (two), 27, and May 7, 1945, Studium Polski Podziemnej, London.

4. Wladyslaw Pobóg-Malinowski (*Najnowsza historia polityczna Polski*, vol. III, p. 876) mistakenly ascribed to Korbonski "resistance" against the reconstitution of the Council of National Unity. Minutes of the meeting, held on May 3, 1945, indicate it was Stanislaw Wojcik (pseudonym: Kwasniak) of the Peasant Party, who opposed it.

5. Korbonski's dispatch to the government in London, dated June 5, 1945, reporting on the state of underground leadership, Studium Polski Podziemnej, London.

6. Kazimierz Baginski, "Proces Szesnastu w Moskwie", *Zeszyty Historyczne*, no. 4, Instytut Literacki, Paris, 1963, p. 105.

CHAPTER XXVII

1. Stefan Korbonski, *W imieniu Kremla*, Instytut Literacki, Paris, 1956, pp. 374-376, list of the 118 murdered Polish Peasant Party leaders.

"Slownik biograficzny ofiar terroru PRL," *Zeszyty Historyczne*, no. 6, Instytut Literacki, Paris, 1964, pp. 7-15, presents a list of 128 names of Peasant Party leaders murdered, or who died in prison; in addition, 4 members of the Polish Socialist Party perished similarly.

APPENDIX

POLISH MEN AND WOMEN RECOGNIZED BY YAD VASHEM AS "RIGHTEOUS AMONG THE NATIONS"*
(up to May 31, 1974)

Abramowicz, Natalia (USA)
Adamkowska, Maria
Arczynski, Marek
Arvanitti, Helena
Babilinska, Gertruda (Israel)

Barancewicz, Larisa
Bartoszewski, Wladyslaw
Bazyli, Bogdan
Bereska, Helena
Bieganski, Piotr
Blam, Sara
Boczkowski, Stanislaw
    and Zofia
Bogucki, Karol
Bonkowski, Wladyslaw
Buchholz, Janina
Budnik, Piotr
Bukowinski, Leon
Bussold, Stanislawa

Celka, Szymon
Chacze, Edward
Charmuszko, Pawel
Chelpa, Anna
Chodon Gertner, Marysia

Choms, Wladyslawa
Chmilel, Aniela
Cieply, Jan
Cimek, Jadwiga
Ciemiega, Stefania
Cywinski, Feliks
Czajkowski, Szymon and
    Bronislawa
Czezowski, Tadeusz,
    Antonina and Teresa

Deba, Magdalena and son Jan
Demel, Jozefa
Demska, Stanislawa (Israel)
Duda Family
Dudziak, Zofia
Duracz, Jerzy
Dyrdal-Kielbasa, Maria
Dziedzic-Skrzypiec, Wiktoria

Egermaier, Waclaw and Leonia
Eliasz, Jan

Fakler, Jan and Maria
Filipowicz, Wanda
Fink, Jozef and wife

---

* "We should like to make it clear that this list is not in any way a complete one. There are, of course, many other Polish people that are worthy of honor but have not been brought to our attention, or have been put aside owing to lack of first-hand testimonies and evidence which because of the break-off of diplomatic relations are unobtainable. The prevailing diplomatic situation has closed off many avenues of research, and we should like to request that if this list is published, it should be made quite clear that it is incomplete and incidental, in order to be fair to those who remain unknown and anonymous."

—*Excerpt* from letter from Donia Rosen, Head of the Department for the Righteous of the Yad Vashem, Martyrs' and Heroes' Remembrance Authority, Jerusalem, to Mr. Stefan Korbonski, June 5, 1974.

Fomienko, Witold
Franio, Dr. Zofia
Fularski, Antoni
Gaworska, Janina
Gawelczyk, Julian and
  Bronislawa
Gidzinska, Maria
Gill, Jozef and Janina
Glinka, Stefan
Golowacz, Waclaw
Gorecki, Dr. Zbigniew
Gosk, Mieczyslaw,
  Helena and Stanislaw
Gregorczyk, Wladyslaw
Grudzinska, Dr. Hanna Jozefa
Gut, Marianna
Haifter, Magdalena
Hencel, Ludwik
Hessen, Bronislawa
Horbaczewski, Dr. Pawel
Hrekow, Andrzej and Wiera
Hupalo, Franciszka
Iwanski, Henryk and Wiktoria
Jackow, Staszek (USA)
Jacyna, Waclaw and
  Marcelina
Jamiolkowski, Jan and
  Janina
Janc, Boleslaw and Helena
Janicki, Dr. and wife
Jankiewicz, Tadeusz
Jaromirska, Leokadia
Jaskolka, Wladyslaw, Maria
  and Stanislaw
Jeziorski, Wladyslaw and
  Anna
Kabaczynski Family
Kakol, Jan and Magda
Kalwinski Family
Kanabus, Dr. Feliks
Kann, Maria
Karsov, Szymaniewska,
  Stanislawa
Klemens, Zofia

Klepacka, Maria
Kmita, Katarzyna
Kmita, Mikolaj i Karolina
Kobylec Family
Koczerkiewicz, Mieczyslaw
Kodasinski, Jozef
Korczeniewska, Helena (Israel)
Korkuc, Kazimierz
Korniecka, Jozefa
Kostrz, Andrzej
Kozminska, Teresa
Kozminski, Henryk
Kowalski, Wladyslaw
Kowalski, Witold and Maria
Krawiec, Maria
Krzemienski, Stanislaw
Krzysztonek, Aniela (Israel)
Kucharzek, Irena
Kuriata, Mikolaj
Kurjanowicz, Ignacy
Kuropieska, Leopolda
Kurowiec, Dymitr and Boguslaw
Kurylowicz, Boguslaw, Jan and
  Zofia (Switzerland)
Kuzin, Maria
Lintner, Stefan (Israel)
Lipczynska, Ewa
Lipke Janis, Joanna
Lisikiewicz, Dr. Miron
Lubczynski, Ignacy (USA)
Lubicz-Nycz, Bronislawa and
  Izabela
Lasica, Tadeusz
Lozinska, Pelagia
Lozinska, Zuzanna
Maciejko, Wojciech
Majewska, Bronislawa (Canada)
Makara, Rozalia
Malkiewicz, Aniela
Marchwinski, Jozef (Denmark)
Marcinkiewicz, Aleksandra
Markiewicz, Szymon and Anna
Matysiak, Wladyslaw

Miazio, Emilia

Migden (Rzepecka), Apolonia (Israel)

Mikolajkow, Aleksander and Leokadia

Miluski, Jan

Miller, Stefa and Marcelina

Mikuski, Jan

Miller, Stefa and Marcelina

Mirek, Jan and Aniela

Misiuna, Wladyslaw

Moycho, Anna

Muzolf, Stanislawa and husband

Myrta, Jozef and Katarzyna

Naruszko, Ignacy and Genowefa

Nazarewicz Gruszko, Kazimiera

Niewiadomski Family

Nowak, Franciszek

Nowinski, Waclaw and wife

Ogonowski Family

Oldak, Aleksander and Apolonia

Olszanska, Janina

Osiewicz, Jan

Onowska, Jadwiga

Paszkiewicz, Rozalia

Pastuszynski, Zygmunt

Pawlicka, Janina (Israel)

Pawlicki, Jan

Pawlowska, Kleopatra

Persiak, Zofia

Peska, Wladyslawa (Australia)

Pekalski, Franciszek

Pierzycki, Franciszek and Stanislawa

Pietkun, Jan

Pikulski, Jan and Waclaw

Pilat, Piotr and Matylda

Piotrowska, Dr. Alicija

Piotrowski, Jozef and Zofia

Plaskacz, Bronislawa

Podworski, Wladyslaw

Pogorzalski, Julian and Stanislaw

Polewka, Franciszek and Barbara

Prask, Karol

Procailo (Procajlo) Family

Przewalski, Jan and Jozefa

Puc, Stanislaw

Pukaite, Genia

Raczynski, Stefan (Israel)

Reicher Galikowska, Lucia

Renska, Barbara (England)

Rolirad, Henryk (Israel)

Roslan, Aleksander (USA)

Roslaniec, Julian (Sweden)

Rozen, Zofia and Katarzyna (Israel)

Rozwadowski, Dionizy

Rykowska, Jadwiga and son Janusz and his wife

Rytel, Zygmunt

Rzeczycka, Sylwia

Sadzikowska, Kazimiera

Sawicka, Maria

Schutz, Irena

Schussel, Dr. Alfred

Sendler, Irena

Siewierska, Stefa

Slebocki, Stanislaw and Halina

Sloboda, Julia

Sobala, Stefan

Sobczak, Stanislaw

Sobecka, Maria

Socha, Jozef

Sokolowska, Zofia (USA)

Spasinski, Stanislaw

Stakowska, Jozefa

Stawski, Stanislaw Kazimierz and Wanda Antonina

Strzelecka, Maria

Strojwas, Franciszek and Anna

Strusinski, Dr. Zygmunt and Wiktoria

Strzalecka, Jadwiga

Strzelec, Stanislawa

Swierczynski, Bernard-Konrad
Swietochowski, Wladyslaw
Szczypiorski, Aleksander and
Antonina
Szelagowski, Kazimierz
Szemet, Helena
Szepelowski, Wladyslaw
Szlichta, Teodor
Szostak, Stanislaw and Zofia
Szymczukiewicz, Witold

Tarasiewicz, Hieronim and
Bronislawa
Tarasowa-Cajtag, Aleksandra
Tomczak, Natalia
Tomczyk, Jozef and Genowefa
Trojanowski, Prof. Andrzej
Twornicki, Janusz
Tymoficzuk, Stanislaw

Ustianowski, Ignacy
Uszczanowski, Antoni

Wachalska, Anna
Wasilkowski, Jozef and
Vasilena (Germany)
Werstler, Antoni
Wiater, Adam and Helena
Wiatr, Tadeusz
Wieth, Imgard (USA)
Wiszniewski Family
Wajcik, Waclaw (USA)
Wolfinger, Marcus and
Julia (USA)
Wolosianski, Izydor and
Jaroslawa
Woloszyn, Stanislaw
Wozniak, Stanislaw
Wunsche, Jerzy

Zadarnowska, Irena (Switzerland)
Zagorski, Waclaw (England)
Zajac, Ewa
Zawadzki, Boleslaw
Ziental, Bronislawa Irena (Israel)
Zwolakowski, Dr. Janusz

Zwonarz, Jozef and Franka
Zabinski, Jan and Antonina
Zukowski, Dr. Grzegorz and
Wanda (Germany)

INDEX OF NAMES

Ahrens, Friedrich, Col., 149

Ajzenman-Kaniewski, Julian, 136

Albrecht, Janusz, Col., 57

Ancerowicz, Czeslaw, 143

Anders, Wladyslaw, Gen., 56, 61, 100, 107, 170

Andress, 77

Andrzejczak, Wladyslaw, 131

Angerer, Ludwik, 226

Anielewicz, Mordecai, 123, 133, 135

Antczak, Antoni, 46

Antonov-Markov, Marko, Prof., 148,149

Apfelbaum, Dawid Moryc, 132

Araszkiewicz, Stanislaw, 53

Arciszewska, Melania, 222

Arciszewski, Tomasz, 33, 60, 213, 214, 218

Arnes, Col., 148

Bach-Zelewski, Erich von, Gen., 182, 186, 187, 202

Baginski, Kazimierz, 47, 196, 216, 218, 235, 236, 242, 243

Banach, Kazimierz, 46, 206

Banach, Roman, 145

Barcikowski, Waclaw, 114

Barski, Jozef, 46

Bartoszek, Franciszek, 131

Bartoszewski, Hieronim, Dr., 145

Bartoszewski, Wladyslaw, 124

Barzminski, Jozef, Dr., 137

Basilevsky, Boris, Prof., 148

Beck, Jozef, 140

Berezowski, Zygmunt, 59

Berle, Adolf, 129

Berling, Zygmunt, Col., later Gen., 112, 154, 156, 157, 159, 160, 161, 163, 166, 172, 188, 190, 220

Berka, Waclaw, Mjr., 20

Berman, Adolf, Dr., 123, 125, 128, 130, 138, 167

Berman, Jakub, 167

Bialas, Franciszek, 52, 116, 196, 207, 229, 232

Biddle, Anthony Drexel, Amb., 129

Biddle, Attorney General, 129

Biega, Boleslaw, 222

Bien, Adam, 39, 192, 193, 194, 214, 218, 236

Bienkowski, Witold, 124, 206

Bierut, Boleslaw, 23, 112, 234, 240

Bittner, Ludwik, Gen., 160

Bninski, Adolf, 30, 37, 38, 45

Bochenski, Aleksander, 108

Bokszczanin, Janusz, Col., 226

Bor, Gen., see Komorowski, Tadeusz

Borowy, Waclaw, Prof., 48

Boryczko, Adam, 241

Borzecki, Marian, 40

Braun, Jerzy, 39, 236

Braun, director, Warsaw Housing Office, 86

Briesemeister, Stanislaw, 108

Broniewski, Mjr., 107

Bryja, Wincenty, 45, 205, 225

Bryla, Stefan, Prof., 53

Brzeski, Leon, 48

Buczek, Karol, 241

Buerckel, 86

Bujak, Franciszek, Prof., 45

Burdecki, Feliks, 142

Byelfyev, Gen., 160

Chacinski, Jozef, 218, 236

Cheshire, Leonard, Cpt., 130

Chmielewski, Jan, Peasant Party, 45

Chmielewski, Jan, Labor Party, 222

Chmielewski, Jerzy, Cpt., 60, 62

Chodakowska, 75

Chodkiewicz, Prof., 217

Cholewa, Wladyslaw, 45, 160

Choltitz, Dietrich von, Gen., 179

Chromecki, Tadeusz, 45

Chrusciel, Antoni, Col., later Gen., 131, 171, 179, 181, 187, 196, 197

Churchill, Winston, 93, 129, 173, 174, 190, 192, 207

Cranborne, 129

Cukierman, Icek, 133, 135

Cyrankiewicz, Jozef, 29, 38, 39

Czajkowski, Wladyslaw, 47, 232

Czapski, 54

Czarnomski, 105

Czarnowski, Eugeniusz, 111, 218, 236

Czechon, Zofia, 2

Chernyakhovsky, Gen., 157

Dalton, Dr., 129

Dabrowski, Kazimierz, 234

Debski, Aleksander, 26, 31, 34, 35, 37

Didur, Kazimierz, 144

Dietz, Hugo, 86

Dobrzanski, Henryk, Mjr., 14, 89

Dobrzanski, Jerzy, Dr., 30, 46, 143

Dolanowski, Mikolaj, 101

Dolina, Jozef, 160

Dolzycki, 75

Domanski, Jan, 43, 60

Domanski, Zygmunt, 222

Domoslawski, Bronislaw, 53

Draza, Mjr., 159

Dressler, Stefan, 222

Drewnowski, Kazimierz, Prof., 40, 51

Dubois, Stanislaw, 19, 25, 113

Dymsza, Adolf, 75

Dziekan, 54

Eden, Anthony, 59, 129, 139, 207, 219

Eichborn, Reinhard von, Lt., 149

Eichmann, Adolf, 120, 137, 138

Federowicz, Zygmunt, Dr., 46

Feiner, Leon, Dr., 123, 124, 125, 128, 130

Felczak, Zygmunt, 35, 73

Fieldorf, Emil, Col., later Gen., 84, 212, 227

Filipkowski, Wladyslaw, Col., 159

Finder, Pawel, 110

Fischer, Ludwik, Dr., 68, 207

Fiszer, 45

Flaschke, 86

Fleming, 86

Frank, Hans, 8, 26, 121, 142, 149, 178

Frankfurter, Felix, 129

Frenkel, Pawel, 124

Fuchs, Paul, 107

Fuldner, Martin, 77

Gaik, Wladyslaw, Lt., 135

Gajoch, Jan, 222

Galinat, Edmund, Mjr., 15, 16

Galinski, Adam, 30, 46, 73, 143

Gaulle, Charles de, Gen., 195

Geist, 91

Gelb, 137

Gering, August, 86

Gerstein, Kurt, 130

Gieysztor, Marian, Prof., 73

Glowinski, Franciszek, 48

Godlewski, Edward, Col., 163, 210

Goebbels, Paul Joseph, 94, 141, 144

Goetel, Ferdynand, 142, 144

Goldman, Nachum, 128, 129

Gomulka, Wladyslaw, 47, 111, 232, 234

Göring, Herman, 148

Grabiec, Jan, 126

Grabner, 128

Grabski, Stanislaw, 234

Grasberg, Jerzy, 122

Greenwood, Arthur, 129

Grzegorczyk, Marian, 48

Greim, Ritter von, Gen., 182

Grobelny, Julian, Dr., 125
Grodzicki, Edward, 144
Gruber, Mieczyslaw, 136
Grudzinski, Jozef, 26, 35, 205
Grushko, Gen., 159
Grynszpan, Chil, 135
Gubbins, Colin, Gen., 174

Handelsman, Marceli, Prof., 105
Harriman, Averell, Amb., 172, 207, 233
Harris, Arthur, 130
Hausner, Gideon, 138
Haydukiewicz, Jozef, Prof., 224, 228
Heinrich, Dr., 146
Hempel, Zygmunt, 101, 103
Hess, Rudolf, 93
Heydrich, Reinhard, 120, 141
Himmler, Heinrich, 49, 178
Hitler, Adolf, 1, 7, 16, 17, 93, 94, 139, 178
Hoess, 128
Hoffman, Gestapo, 86
Hoffman, Director, Labor Office, 86
Holeksa, Karol, 29
Holze, Willi, 86
Hoppe, Jan, 222
Horodynski Family, 77
Hott, Lt., 148
Hubicki, Stefan, Dr. Gen., 102
Hudson, D. T., Col., 65, 210
Hurst, Cecil, 129

Iłłakowicz, Jerzy Olgierd, 104
Iranek-Osmecki, Kazimierz, Col., 59
Ivanov, Gen., 159
Ivanov, Gen. Col., 216, 218
Iwańska, Wiktoria, 132
Iwanski, Henryk, Cpt., 132
Iwanski, Roman, 132
Iwanski, Waclaw, 132
Iwanski, Zbigniew, 132

Jalbrzykowski, Archbishop, 143

Jagiello, Stanislaw, 73
Jakobiec, Jan, Prof., 29, 45
Jakubowski, Mieczyslaw, 222
Jankowski, Jan Stanislaw, 39, 44, 45, 51, 54, 56, 78, 81, 100, 113, 135, 136, 147, 150, 151, 154, 155, 156, 169, 171, 175, 177, 192, 193, 194, 197, 204, 205, 206, 207, 209, 214, 216, 217, 218, 219, 225, 236, 242
Januszewski, Waclaw, 45, 225
Jarnuszkiewicz, 64
Jasinski, Stanislaw, 145
Jasinski, Wladyslaw, 14, 89
Jasiukowicz, Stanislaw, 39, 192, 194, 218, 236, 242
Jaworski, Wladyslaw, 35
Jegier, Samuel, 135
Jeschonek, Hans, Gen., 61
Jezioranski, Zdzislaw, 59, 170, 177
Jedrowski, Leon, 45
Jedrychowski, Stefan, 234
Jedrychowski-Kern, Tadeusz, 131
Joselewicz, Berek, Col., 136
Jozewski, Henryk, 98, 102, 103, 238
Jozwiak, Franciszek, 111
Jung, 86

Kaczanowski, Wlodzimierz, 73, 132
Kaczorowski, Michal, 234
Kalenkiewicz, Maciej, Lt. Col., 158
Kaminski, 185
Kaminski, Aleksander, 68
Kaminski, Wladyslaw, 30
Kammertenz, 86
Kann, Maria, 136
Kapitaniak, Zygmunt, 224
Karas, Janina, Mjr., 20
Karcz, Tadeusz Stefan, 126
Kasznica, Stanislaw, 107
Kauzik, Stanislaw, 49, 196, 207
Kawecki, Wladyslaw, 144
Kern-Jedrychowski, Tadeusz, 131
Kerr, Clark, 233

Ketrzynski, Wojciech, 108

Kharitonov, Col., 156

Kiernik, Wladyslaw, 30, 222, 223, 233, 234

Kiwerski, Jan Wojciech, Mjr., 155, 156

Klapert, Stanislaw, 145

Klarner, Czeslaw, 54

Kleeberg, Franciszek, Gen., 14

Kmicic, 91

Knoll, Roman, 45

Kobylanski, Kazimierz, 218, 236

Koc, Adam, Col., 101

Kolski, Tadeusz, 48

Kolodziej, Antoni, 234

Kolodziejski, Henryk, 233, 234

Kolodziejski, Stefan, 145

Kolpachev, Gen., 160

Komorowski, Tadeusz, Col., later Gen., 21, 29, 57, 58, 70, 84, 105, 106, 151, 152, 168, 169, 170, 171, 174, 175, 177, 179, 180, 186, 187, 188, 189, 192, 193, 194, 197, 212

Kondrat, 75

Kopanski, Stanislaw, Gen., 170

Koppe, Gen., 95

Korbonska, Zofia, 39, 78, 237, 241, 243

Korbonski, Stefan, 18, 19, 20, 26, 27, 29, 30, 31, 34-37, 39, 40, 44, 47, 54, 73, 76-80, 84, 109, 116, 127, 130, 134, 137, 145, 149, 167, 196, 201, 207, 216, 218, 223-227, 229-233, 235-237, 239-243

Korfanty, Wojciech, 46

Kosciuszko, Tadeusz, 112, 172

Kossak-Szczucka, Zofia, 73

Kossakowski, Tadeusz, Gen., 60

Kot, Stanislaw, Prof., 33, 40, 41

Kotowicz, Jan, Col., 160

Kotowski, Alfons, Mjr., 186, 187

Kowalski, Wladyslaw, 234

Kozielewski, Jan, Prof., 31, 59, 128, 129

Kozietulski, Jan, Col., 135

Krahelska, Janina, 105

Krajewski, Henryk, Col., 161

Kretschman, 86

Kruk-Strzelecki, Tadeusz, 20, 26, 27, 33

Krüger, Gen., 86

Krystek, Janusz, 126

Krzeptowski, Waclaw, 142

Krzywoszewski, Stefan, 48

Krzyżanowski, Adam, Prof., 233, 234

Krzyżanowski, Aleksander, Col., 143, 157, 158

Kulczynski, 45

Kulski, Julian, 140, 207

Kukiel, Marian, Gen., 22

Kumor, Emil, Cpt., 20

Kunat, Richard, 3

Kurnatowski, Eryk, 222

Kurt, Bruno, 86

Kutschera, Franz, Gen., 63, 85, 86

Kutrzeba, Stanislaw, Prof., 233, 234

Kutrzeba, Tadeusz, Gen., 15

Kwasiborski, Jozef, 35, 45, 196, 229, 232

Kwiecinski, Franciszek, 32, 35, 37, 40

Lachert, Wladyslaw, 140

Lados, Aleksander, 22

Lakinski, Jan, 126

Landycz, Zdzislaw, 77

Lange, 86

Lasocki, Zygmunt, 29

Laszkiewicz, Kazimierz, 46

Latishonek, Mjr., 188

Law, Richard, 129

Lechner, 86

Leist, Ludvig, 140

Leitgeber, 86

Lerski, Jerzy, Prof., 59

Lewandowicz, Jerzy, 46, 205

Lewandowski, Zbigniew, Cpt., 124

Lieberman, Herman, 30

Liniarski, Wladyslaw, Col., 161, 227, 241

Lipinski, Waclaw, 101, 102, 238

Litwin, Franciszek, Dr., 234
Lorentz, Stanislaw, 50
Lorkiewicz, Teofil, 52

Machnicki, Janusz, 222
Maciejewska, Wanda, 222
Macinski, Tadeusz, 222
Mackiewicz, Jozef, 143, 146
Madejski, Zbigniew, 222
Magalas, Eugeniusz, 77
Majski, Ivan, 31
Makowiecki, Jerzy, 105, 137
Maksymowicz-Raczynski, Gen., 102
Malessa, Emilia, 240
Malicka, Maria, 75
Malinov, see Serov, Ivan
Malecki, Roman, 222
Marcinkowski, Wladyslaw, 104, 106, 107
Marczak, Ludomir, 137
Maringe, Witold, 52
Markowski, Wincenty, 31
Marszalek, Jozef, 40, 73
Martens, Marian, 145
Masaryk, Tomasz, 68
Mateja, Stefan, 51, 196, 205
Matlachowski, Jan, 228
Matuszewski, Stefan, 234
Mazurkiewicz, Jan, Lt. Col., 133, 183
    190, 211, 227, 239, 240
Michalewski, Jerzy, 25, 33, 41, 43, 54
Michalowicz, Mieczyslaw, Prof., 17, 18,
    19, 25
Michalowski, Stanislaw, 218, 236
Mierzwa, Stanislaw, 29, 218, 236, 240,
    241
Miklaszewski, Boleslaw, Prof., 51
Miklaszewski, Tadeusz, 44, 225
Mikolajczyk, Stanislaw, 153, 169, 170,
    176, 190, 194, 195, 207, 208, 213,
    214, 218, 221, 229, 232, 233, 234,
    236, 237, 238, 239, 241, 243
Miller, Romuald, 114
Minc, Hilary, 234

Mitkiewicz, Leon, Col., 174
Mlynarski, Feliks, 140
Moder, von, Gen., 94
Moltke, Hans von, 140
Molojec, Edward, 110
Molotov, Vyacheslav, 172, 207, 219, 233
Mooney, Archbishop, 129
Morawski, Eugeniusz, 131
Mosdorf, Jan, 137, 138
Mosinski, Jan, 48
Mrozek, Jozef, Col., 167
Mrozinski, Stanislaw, 222
Muzyczka, Ludwik, 70, 240

Nakoniecznikoff, Przemyslaw, Lt. Col.,
    210
Nakoniecznikoff-Klukowski, Stanislaw,
    Col., 75, 106, 107
Naville, François, Prof. Dr., 148
Neyman, Lech, 107
Niecko, Jozef, 18
Niedzialkowski, Mieczyslaw, 18, 19, 25,
    32, 41
Niedzielski, Mieczyslaw, Lt. Col., 186
Niepokolczycki, Franciszek, Mjr., later
    Col., 20, 240, 241
Nieradzka, Jadwiga, 222
Nowaczynski, Adolf, 138
Nowodworski, Leon, 17, 18, 19, 25, 26,
    29, 32, 53
Noworol, Waclaw, 126
Nowotko, Marceli, 110

Oberhäuser, Eugen, Gen., 149
Odorkiewicz, Cyprian, Cpt., 186
Ohlenbusch, 94
Okulicki, Leopold, Col., later Gen., 20,
    54, 169, 171, 179, 180, 187, 207,
    209, 210, 211, 216, 217, 218, 219,
    226, 229, 236, 242
Olszewski, Antoni, 53
Oltarzewski, Stanislaw, 59
O'Malley, Amb., 129

Orzechowski, Konrad, Dr., 144

Osobka, Edward. 112. 114. 234

Ossowski, Izydor, 75

Ostrowski, Adam, 45, 73, 159

Otter, von, 130

Pacholczyk, Wladyslaw, 107

Pajdak, Antoni, 39, 192, 194, 218, 236

Pajor, Antoni, 126

Pawlowski, Stefan, 44, 111

Pelczynski, Tadeusz, Gen., 57, 84, 169,
   171, 179, 180, 187

Pembowski, Olgierd, 222

Peschel, 86

Perzanowska, Stanislawa, 75

Peszynski, Stanislaw, 45, 225

Pfeiffer, Edward, Col., 186

Piasecki, Boleslaw, 108, 109

Piasecki, Julian, 102, 103

Piasecki, Stanislaw, 137, 138

Piekalkiewicz, Jan, Prof., 38, 39, 43, 73,
   105, 125

Pienkowski, Stanislaw, Prof., 51

Pietrzak, Antoni, 126

Pilnik, Bogumil vel Borys, 126

Pilsudski, Jozef, 17, 23, 32, 41, 46, 58,
   101, 102

Pimenov, Col., 216, 217, 228

Piotrowski, Stanislaw, 206, 222

Plater, Emilia, 135

Plucinski, 75

Pohorski, Zygmunt, 145

Ponury, 91

Pokrovsky, J. V., Col., 148

Poplavsky, S., Gen., 191

Poprawa, Marcin, 45

Porowski, Marceli, 45, 196

Pospieszalski, Antoni, Cpt., 210

Potocki, Maurycy, 222

Pottebaum, 86

Praglowski, Dr., 145

Pradzynski, Jozef, Monsignor, 30

Prochownik, Kazimierz, 144

Prozorovsky, Victor, Prof. Dr., 148

Prochnik, Adam, 31, 113, 114

Przybyszewski, Jozef, 46

Pszenny, Jozef, Cpt., 130, 131

Putek, Kazimierz, Col. 164

Puzak, Kazimierz, 18, 25, 26, 27, 30, 31,
   32, 34, 35, 36, 98, 113, 175, 192,
   193, 195, 197, 218, 236, 242

Quisling, Vidkun, 143

Raabe, Leszek, 73, 132

Rabanowski, Jan, 234

Raczkiewicz, Wladyslaw, 135, 211, 229

Raczkowski, Czeslaw, 59

Radkiewicz, Stanislaw, 167, 234

Radziwill, Janusz, 222

Radziwill, Stanislaw, 147

Rak, Albin, Col., 106

Rapacki, Marian, 140

Rataj, Maciej, 17, 18, 19, 20, 25, 26, 32,
   41, 186

Ratajski, Cyryl, 36, 37, 38, 39, 40, 41,
   43, 44, 47, 76

Reis, 79

Rek, Tadeusz, 206, 222

Rekst, Lt., 148

Renner, Kurt, Gen., 86

Retinger, Jozef, Dr., 60

Rhode, Maksymilian, Prof., 50

Ribbentrop, Joachim von, 141

Ringelblum, Emanuel, Dr., 137

Rogowski, Bazyli, 102

Rojkiewicz, Ludwik, Cpt., 145

Rokicki, Jozef, Lt. Col., 186

Rokossovsky, Konstantin, Marshal, 180,
   188, 190

Ronikier, Adam, 51, 140

Roosevelt, Franklin Delano, 59, 129,
   139, 174, 190, 192, 227

Rosciszewski, Witold, 73

Rostworowski, Stanislaw, Gen., 163

Rowecki, Stefan, Col., later Gen., 18, 20, 24, 25, 26, 28, 29, 30, 32, 33, 34, 37, 40, 43, 54, 57, 63, 69, 70, 77, 78, 84, 102, 105, 151

Rozmus, Antoni, 126

Rommel, Juliusz, Gen., 15, 16, 168

Rudnicki, Klemens, Col., later Gen., 21, 58

Rudnicki, Witold, 126

Rutkowski, Boleslaw, 52

Rutkowski, Jerzy, 108

Rutkowski, Leopold, 47, 222

Rychlik, Piotr, 46

Rydz-Smigly, Edward, Marshal, 15, 21, 22, 23, 102, 168

Rymar, Stanislaw, 29

Rzepccki, Jan., Col., 54, 69, 84, 217, 227, 229, 231, 235, 239, 240

Rzeznik, Stefan, 222

Rzymowski, Wincenty, 234

Sacha, Stefan, 35

Salski, Tadeusz, 104

Samborski, 75

Sammern, von, Dr., 134

Sanojca, Mjr., later Col., 20, 240

Sapieha, Adam, Cardinal, 21, 145

Satoath, Dov, Amb., 133

Schön, Dr., 80

Schultz, 86

Schwartzbart, Ignacy, Dr., 128

Sciborek, Boleslaw, 73

Selborn, member of Government, 165

Selbourne, Lord, 129

Seweryn Tadeusz, Prof. Dr., 73, 222

Seyda, Marian, 22

Seyfryd, Edmund, 144

Sergeyev, Gen., 156

Serov, Ivan/Malinov/, Gen., 109, 167

Shtemenko, Gen., 180, 188, 190

Sikora, Ignacy, 46

Sikorski, Wladyslaw, Gen., 21, 22, 23, 24, 28, 31, 32, 36, 37, 38, 40, 41, 56, 78, 81, 82, 101, 102, 128

Sikorski, (cont.), 135, 136, 151, 153, 168

Skarzynski, Kazimierz, Jerzy, 145, 146

Skiwski, Jan Emil, 142, 144

Skokowski, Julian, Gen., 114

Skorobohaty-Jakubowski, Jan., Col., 34, 35, 36, 37, 41

Skotnicki, Mieczyslaw, Dr., 136

Skroczynski, Albin, Gen., 162

Skupienski, Jerzy, Lt., 131

Slawek, Walery, Col., 101

Sobolta, Franciszek, Col., 107

Sokolowski, Franciszek, 126

Sosnkowski, Kazimierz, Gen., 22, 24, 25, 29, 69, 78, 151, 152, 153, 165, 166, 169, 170, 174, 176, 177, 187, 212

Spychalski, Jozef, Mjr., later Col., 20, 163

Spychalski, Marian, 20, 111, 163

Stalin, Jozef, 93, 110, 169, 170, 172, 173, 174, 176, 188, 189, 190, 191, 207, 236

Stalkowski, Zbigniew, 131

Stankiewicz, Jozef, 78

Stanczyk, Jan, 22, 23, 234

Starzynski, Stefan, 15, 16

Stemler, Jozef, 216, 217, 218, 236

Stettinius, Edward, 228

Stritch, Archbishop, 129

Stroop, Jürgen, Gen., 133

Strowski, Jerzy, 70

Strychanski, Lt. Col., 158

Strzeszewski, Jan, 111

Studnicki, Wladyslaw, 141, 142

Stypulkowski, Zbigniew, 104, 106, 218, 236

Sulik, Nikodem, Col., later Gen., 30

Suzycki, Tadeusz, 29

Susczynski, Hieronim, Lt. Col., 162

Susz, Tadeusz, Dr., 145

Swiatlo, Jozef, 110

Swiatkowski, Henryk, 234

Swierczewski, Eugeniusz, 63

Swierkowski, Romuald, 30, 143

Swietlicki, Andrzej, 108
Swiecicki, Roman Leon, 75
Swietochowski, Ryszard, 40, 41
Switalski, Adam, Col., 160
Sym, Igo, 142
Szafer, Wladyslaw, Prof., 51
Szatkowski, 142
Szczurek, Jan, Col., 240
Szebesta, Adam, Dr., 145
Szlaski-Prawdzic, Janusz, Lt. Col., 158
Szostak, Boleslaw, 126
Szpotanski, Tadeusz, 40
Sztachelski, Jerzy, 234
Sztumberg-Rychter, Tadeusz, Mjr., 156
Szwedowski, Stefan, 73, 114
Szymanski, Jerzy, Mjr., 22, 28
Szymek, 136

Tarnowska, Maria, 222, 223
Tarnowski, Adam, 222, 223
Tatar, Stanislaw, Gen., 174, 209
Tempka, Wladyslaw, 29
Thugutt, Mieczyslaw, 234
Thumann, 77
Thun, Stanislaw, Lt. Col., 20
Tkaczow, Stanislaw, 234
Tokarzewski-Karaszewicz, Michal, Gen.,
     15, 16, 17, 18, 19, 20, 21, 22, 23, 24,
     25, 26, 27, 28, 32, 57, 58, 168
Traugutt, Romuald, 186
Trajdos, Mieczyslaw, 35
Tretiak, Andrzej, Prof., 48
Triarska, Maria, 222
Truman, Harry, 227
Trzeciak, Jan, 46
Tudrej, Mieczyslaw, 73
Tumidajski, Kazimierz, Col., 160
Tyczynski, Romuald, 40, 73

Urbanski, Franciszek, 35, 218, 236

Vorman, von, Gen., 179

Wachowiak, Stanislaw, 207
Waldman, 129
Ward, John, 181
Wawrzkowicz, Otmar, 104, 107
Weber, Stanislaw, Mjr., 124
Wefels, Ernest, 86
Wiatr, Narcyz, 222
Wiacek, Jozef, 14, 89
Widerszal, Ludwik, 105, 137
Widy-Wirski, Feliks, Dr., 73
Wiechcinski, Czeslaw, 77
Wiernik, Jankiel, 136
Wieckowski, 131
Wilk, Jozef, 131
Wilkinson, Ellen, 129
Wilkoszewski, Witold, 222
Wilner, Arie, 123
Winkler, Wojciech, 73
Wise, Stephen, 128, 129
Witos, Wincenty, 21, 30, 141, 221, 233,
     234
Wodzinowski, Jerzy, 145
Wojciechowski, Zygmunt, Prof., 48
Wojkiewicz, Jan, 30, 45
Wolinski, Henryk, 123
Wojcik, Stanislaw, 224, 228, 229
Wycech, Czeslaw, 51, 234
Wyrzykowski, Tadeusz, 216

Yevtimov, Col., 159

Zadrowski, Feliks, 53
Zajda, Jozef, 54, 205
Zakharov, Gen., 161
Zakrzewski, Kazimierz, Prof., 73, 114
Zaleski, Zygmunt, 52
Zamoyski, Jan, 222
Zapora, 91
Zaremba, Zygmunt, 18, 224, 228
Zarski, Witold, 48
Zenczykowski, Tadeusz, 95
Zhukov, Gen., 161

Zhukov, Gregory, Marshal, 188

Ziemiecki, Bronislaw, 53

Ziemska, 222

Ziemski, Karol, Col., 185

Zietarski-Lizinski, Mieczyslaw, Col.,
    162, 163

Zulawski, Zygmunt, 29, 222, 233, 234

Zwierzynski, Aleksander, 218, 221, 236

Zygielbojm, Szmul, 128, 135

Zymierski, Michal, Gen., 112, 159, 220,
    234, 242

LIST OF UNDERGROUND ORGANIZATIONS AND INSTITUTIONS

Armed Confederacy
Assembly of Organizations for Independence
Association of the Reserve Noncommissioned Officers
"Bory"
Camp of Fighting Poland
Central Committee of Organizations for Freedom (CCOF)
Centralization of Democratic, Socialist and Syndicalists Parties
Central Political Committee
Civic Anticommunist Committee (ANTYK)
Civic Self-Defense Organization
Collective Delegacy
Coordinating Commission
Coordinating Commission of Political Parties [The Center]
Coordinating Committee of Polish Underground Organizations [The Center]
Corps of Security
Council for National Defense
Council of Assistance to Jews — "Zegota"
Council of National Unity
Delegate for the Armed Forces in Poland
Democratic Alliance
Democratic Party
Directorate of Civil Resistance
Directorate of Underground Struggle
"Fatherland"
Freedom and Independence
Freedom and People Union
Front Odrodzenia Polski
Government Delegacy
Hashomer Hacair
Holy Cross Brigade
Home Army
Home Army Resistance Movement
Independent Polish Socialist Party
Jewish Fighting Organization
Jewish Military Union
Jewish National Committee
Jewish Socialist Organization "Bund"
"Kuznia"

Labor Party
"Liceum"
"Musketeers"
National Armed Forces
National Confederation
Narional Council of the Homeland
National Independence Party
National Military Association
National Military Organization
National Military Union
National Party
National Political Representation
National Radical Camp
National Radical Organization — "ABC"
"Nie"
Organization for Independent Poland
Party for Polish Democracy
Peasant Party
Peasant Battalions
People's Army
People's Central Committee
People's Guard
"Pobudka"
Polish Army of the Homeland
Polish Boy Schouts — "The Grey Ranks"
Polish Democratic Party
Polish Military Organization
Polish Organization
Polish Peasant Party
Polish People's Army
Polish Socialists
Polish Socialist Party — "Liberty, Equality and Independence"
Polish Workers Party
Pilsudskite Group of Olgierd
Political Bureau
Political Coordinating Committee
Provisional Polish Government
"Rampart Group"
Secret Military Organization
Secret Polish Army (SPA)
Secret Scouting Movement
Service for Poland's Victory — [SPV]

Socialist Fighting Organization
"Spartakus"
Special Action Alert
Ukrainian Insurgent Army
"Unia"
Union for Armed Struggle — [UAS]
Union for Military Action
Union for the Republic's Reconstruction
Union of Polish Syndicalists
Union of Reserve Officers
Union of Salamander
Union of Struggle for Liberation
"Uprawa"
Workers Party of Polish Socialists
Young Poland
Youth of All Poland
"Zryw"

EAST EUROPEAN MONOGRAPHS

1. *Political Ideas and the Enlightenment in the Romanian Principalities, 1750-1831.* By Vlad Georgescu. 1971.
2. *America, Italy and the Birth of Yugoslavia, 1917-1919.* By Dragan R. Zivojinovic. 1972.
3. *Jewish Nobles and Geniuses in Modern Hungary.* By William O. McCagg, Jr. 1972.
4. *Mixail Soloxov in Yugoslavia: Reception and Literary Impact.* By Robert F. Price. 1973.
5. *The Historical and Nationalist Thought of Nicolae Iorga.* By William O. Oldson. 1973.
6. *Guide to Polish Libraries and Archives.* By Richard C. Lewandski. 1974.
7. *Vienna Broadcasts to Slovakia, 1938-1939: A Case Study in Subversion.* By Henry Delfiner. 1974.
8. *The 1917 Revolution in Latvia.* By Andrew Ezergailis. 1974.
9. *The Ukraine in the United Nations Organization: A Study in Soviet Foreign Policy, 1944-1950.* By Konstantin Sawczuk. 1975.
10. *The Bosnian Church: A New Interpretation.* By John V.A. Fine, Jr. 1975.
11. *Intellectual and Social Developments in the Habsburg Empire from Maria Theresa to World War I.* Edited by Stanley B. Winters and Joseph Held. 1975.
12. *Ljudevit Gaj and the Illyrian Movement.* By Elinor Murray Despalatovic. 1975.
13. *Tolerance and Movements of Religious Dissent in Eastern Europe.* Edited by Bela K. Kiraly. 1975.
14. *The Parish Republic: Hlinka's Slovak People's Party, 1939-1945.* By Yeshayahu Jelinek. 1976.
15. *The Russian Annexation of Bessarabia, 1774-1828.* By George F. Jewsbury. 1976.
16. *Modern Hungarian Historiography.* By Steven Bela Vardy. 1976.
17. *Values and Community in Multi-National Yugoslavia.* By Gary K. Bertsch. 1976.
18. *The Greek Socialist Movement and the First World War: The Road to Unity.* By George B. Leon. 1976.
19. *The Radical Left in the Hungarian Revolution of 1848.* By Laszlo Deme. 1976.
20. *Hungary between Wilson and Lenin: The Hungarian Revolution of 1918-1919 and the Big Three.* By Peter Pastor. 1976.
21. *The Crises of France's East Central European Diplomacy, 1933-1938.* By Anthony J. Komjathy. 1976.
22. *Polish Politics and National Reform, 1775-1788.* By Daniel Stone. 1976.
23. *The Habsburg Empire in World War I.* Robert A. Kann, Bela K. Kiraly, and Paula S. Fichtner, eds. 1977.
24. *The Slovenes and Yugoslavism, 1890-1914.* By Carole Rogel. 1977.
25. *German-Hungarian Relations and the Swabian Problem.* By Thomas Spira. 1977.
26. *The Metamorphosis of a Social Class in Hungary During the Reign of Young Franz Joseph.* By Peter I. Hidas. 1977.
27. *Tax Reform in Eighteenth Century Lombardy.* By Daniel M. Klang. 1977.
28. *Tradition versus Revolution: Russia and the Balkans in 1917.* By Robert H. Johnston. 1977.
29. *Winter Into Spring: The Czechoslovak Press and the Reform Movement 1963-1968.* By Frank L. Kaplan. 1977.
30. *The Catholic Church and the Soviet Government, 1939-1949.* By Denis J. Dunn, 1977.
31. *The Hungarian Labor Service System, 1939-1945.* By Randolph L. Braham. 1977.
32. *Consciousness and History: Nationalist Critics of Greek Society 1897-1914.* By Gerasimos Augustinos. 1977.
33. *Emigration in Polish Social and Political Thought, 1870-1914.* By Benjamin P. Murdzek. 1977.
34. *Serbian Poetry and Milutin Bojic.* By Mihailo Dordevic. 1977.
35. *The Baranya Dispute: Diplomacy in the Vortex of Ideologies, 1919-1921.* By Leslie C. Tihany. 1978.
36. *The United States in Prague, 1945-1948.* By Walter Ullmann. 1978.
37. *Rush to the Alps: The Evolution of Vacationing in Switzerland.* By Paul P. Bernard. 1978.
38. *Transportation in Eastern Europe: Empirical Findings.* By Bogdan Mieczkowski. 1978.
39. *The Polish Underground State: A Guide to the Underground, 1939-1945.* By Stefan Korbonski. 1978.
40. *The Hungarian Revolution of 1956 in Retrospect.* Edited by Bela K. Kiraly and Paul Jonas. 1978.